To my mother and father

*without whose support and encouragement
this book would never have been written*

contents

contents

This book is a work of non-fiction. However, the names of all the Chinese appearing in its pages have been altered, and certain persons appear in different places from those where I met them in reality. Any resemblance to a real name is purely coincidental. I hope the reader will overlook this small manipulation of facts, understanding that, under a totalitarian regime, the Chinese are directly responsible for their words and thoughts, and I think it right to protect their privacy.

When writing Chinese names and words, I have used the *pinyin* transliteration system favoured by the Chinese government and largely accepted in the international media. This system renders Peking as *Beijing* and Mao Tse-tung as *Mao Zedong*. In a very few cases I have retained traditional English spellings or names, since the *pinyin* versions are sufficiently different as to confuse anyone unfamiliar with the Chinese language. Canton, for example, would be rendered *Guangzhou*, and Tibet is known to the Chinese as *Xizang*.

The Chinese monetary unit, the *yuan*, is made up of ten *jiao*, or one hundred *fen*. To convert Chinese *yuan* to Australian dollars the reader may divide by five, the approximate exchange rate during the time of my stay in China. Thus one Chinese *yuan* is about twenty cents, one dollar is about five *yuan*.

The names of Chinese dynasties and periods are often used when referring to historical time. A chronological table, giving the dates of these dynasties, appears at the end of the book.

I would like to thank Brett Laidlaw, American author and fellow China survivor, for his pertinent advice on an initial draft of this book, as well as his encouragement of my literary efforts; Åse-Marie Nilsson for her friendship in China and her continued insights into that country which have contributed to my ideas and inspiration; and the many members of my family for reading and commenting on my manuscript as it progressed.

Here in Australia, Trevor Hay supplied very constructive criticism of, and encouraging comments on, the completed manuscript, while Adrienne de Kretser did an invaluable editing job and also pointed out areas for further clarification. The book is the better for them both. I also wish to thank Teresa Pitt, commissioning editor at Melbourne University Press, for her support of my book and the professionalism and friendliness with which she has guided me through the publication process.

Most importantly, to all the Chinese who unwittingly supplied me with material and insights for *Boxing with Shadows*, and who made my stay in China so enjoyable, I offer my greatest appreciation and thanks. I wish I could have identified them all and given them the recognition they deserve, for without these many friends and casual encounters this book would not have been possible.

Without leaving his door
He knows everything under heaven.
Without looking out of his window
He knows all the ways of heaven.
For the further one travels
The less one knows.

Tao Te Ching

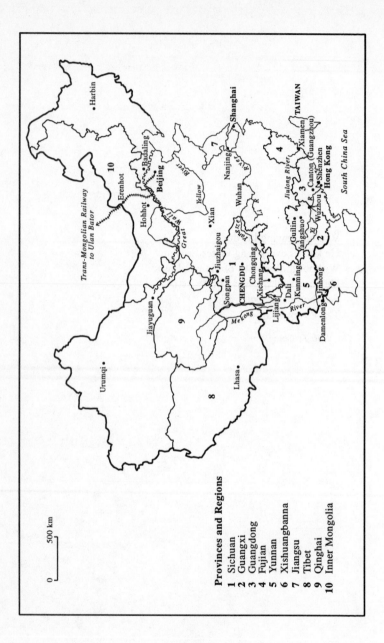

Provinces and Regions
1 Sichuan
2 Guangxi
3 Guangdong
4 Fujian
5 Yunnan
6 Xishuangbanna
7 Jiangsu
8 Tibet
9 Qinghai
10 Inner Mongolia

prologue: arrival

The chartered plane from Hong Kong came down in darkness: no lights, just the black emptiness of a terrible void over China. Then suddenly, without warning, we hit a runway, and soon I was stumbling across the tarmac of Chengdu airport into a cavernous hall, as poorly lit as the set of some disaster movie. Customs officers sat in little wooden boxes with counters so low I had to crouch awkwardly for a glimpse of a hand, a green uniformed sleeve and a sullen face; a stamp in my passport and I was officially in the People's Republic.

Outside, a motley assortment of ill-dressed passengers was engaged in an unholy scrimmage for baggage, like a horde of rapacious scavengers squabbling over spoils on battlefields. I extracted my suitcase from the tumbled mound deposited unceremoniously in the middle of the hall, and shoved through the crowds to the exit. There were large numbers of expectant, welcoming hosts, grinning affably out of the gloom and holding aloft pieces of paper, jagged along the edges as if torn hurriedly from notebooks: *Mr Roderick, Mr Wang Tao (Taiwan), Golden Dragon Electric Company*, they read in wavering script. Yet despite having sent a telegram from Hong Kong, there was no one to meet me, no scrawled sign that acknowledged my existence. I felt as if I had arrived at the ends of the earth: this cavernous and dusty, echoing airport perched in a black void was an antechamber to purgatory. I could have burst into tears.

The taxi I took from the airport was incredibly dusty, and dust hung in thick clouds along the roadside, where villagers

1

coughed and spluttered out of the darkness like disembodied souls. 'Jinjiang Hotel,' I had said to the taxi driver, a shifty-looking character with a scar on his chin and a cigarette hanging limply from his lips. 'Jinjiang, Jinjiang,' I repeated, dropping the English word and resisting the impulse to speak loudly, as if to an idiot child. It was the name of the only hotel for foreigners in Chengdu, according to my outdated guide-book, and the taxi driver seemed to understand me. Once into the city, we sped along wide, empty boulevards lined with dim streetlamps that glowed as orange as the tip of the driver's cig-arette. We stopped in the centre of the city: I was indeed at the Jinjiang Hotel. Entering its lobby was like stepping into the middle of a glass ornament, glittering and shiny, marble floors glowing yellow with the light from the chandeliers that lent the place a cheap and garish elegance. At the reception desk a harassed clerk juggled with the keys of a dozen rooms for a group of French businessmen, who nursed their briefcases with the same smug satisfaction as young mothers cradle their babies. Tibetans in red and gold coats and multicoloured sashes congregated in the lobby, heaving suitcases across the marble floor. I filled in a registration form with slow concentration, but the receptionist took it from me carelessly, pushing a key across the counter.

When I emerged from the lift a floor attendant trailed towards me and showed me to my room grudgingly, managing to suggest by her behaviour that she did not think this was a normal part of her duties. She banged the door behind her con-temptuously. The hotel room was dark, with heavy bottle-green carpets and uninspiring brown bedspreads, the furniture ponderous and shabby, as if sprung from the pages of a le Carré novel. I expected to find a corpse in the bathroom, but there was nothing but a puddle of rusty water, a discarded shower cap and a packet containing needles and thread. Beside the bed there was a flask of boiled water, and I poured some into a glass. It tasted dusty, the same as the smell on the road from the airport. I tweaked back the brocade curtains and peered down onto the street, where bicycles glided up and down in the orange gloom. Then I lay down on my bed, feeling lost and abandoned, and fell asleep.

'Put your heart in your chest. Do not raise it up to your throat,' said Xiao Han to me the next day as we sat in a car heading through the city. I contemplated this instruction with alarm. 'In a word, do not worry. You will enjoy living in Chengdu, and are very welcome.'

Xiao Han had met me in the lobby of the Jinjiang Hotel, a small woman fussy as a mother hen, with permed hair and a sensible skirt, who worked for the Foreign Affairs Office at Sichuan University, where I was destined to work and which I had phoned early that morning. She had laughed with relief when we finally made contact.

'I saw you before!' she chirped. 'But I did not know if you were the right person. I called to you in a low voice, "Johnston!" but without a glance at you. From the angle of my eye I saw you hurrying away across the lobby without any response. I decided it wasn't you! Now indeed I see you are the very one.'

'I'm sorry, I didn't hear you.'

But I had studied her, baffled. I had not known why this little woman was lurking in the glass and chrome of the hotel entrance, whispering 'Johnston' from the corner of her mouth as if she were a contact in a mediocre spy novel. She scuttled off to the reception desk, where she paid my bill with a fistful of battered Chinese *yuan*. Then I was bundled into a fusty university car with white antimacassars on the back seats, embroidered with pandas so fat they looked like piebald snowmen. I sat and stared blankly at the city, trying to follow her erratic and highly personalised English. Bicycles wobbled past on both sides of the car. They were all black, embossed on the crossbars with gold phoenixes, pheasants and seagulls, and were pedalled by people in black slippers. The river was brown, dull as cold coffee, moving sluggishly in the same direction as our car—I hadn't had any coffee that morning, and my head was aching slightly. The rest of the city was grey: grey buildings like slabs of featureless plasticine, dusty grey roads, ugly grey bridges and sagging unhappy grey trees, and most of all a grey sky that hung low, threatening as the lid of a lead coffin.

'As you can see, Chengdu is a beautiful city,' continued Xiao Han from the front passenger seat. She tapped the window and gestured vaguely towards the far side of the river. 'Famous for its silk and other things. A centre for south-west China in culture, industrious and transport.'

I looked again through the car windows, momentarily amused by Xiao Han's English. I did not see any of the silk for which Chengdu was apparently renowned. The bicycle riders were bundled up against the February cold in blue padded cotton jackets that made them appear as bloated and asexual as beached whales, and had woollen scarves up around their mouths. They wore cotton trousers that ended halfway down their shins, exposing pink long-johns in a splash of colour that seemed violent and gratuitous in this otherwise monochromatic city. I did not know what 'other things' made Chengdu famous. In fact I knew nothing about this place, except that it was the capital of Sichuan, a province in south-west China twice the size of Britain, the exact location of which I had been obliged to look up in an atlas after being offered a job here.

'The food here is very delicious,' observed Xiao Han. 'Not only delicious, but also very good-looking, and famous all over the world. Every vegetable and poultry is good to eat, and you will hardly look at them in the market without thinking of a square meal. I hope you will be happy here.'

I did not feel happy, though I did not say so to Xiao Han, who had twisted around in her seat and was beaming at me. I felt a vast emptiness inside my stomach at this vision of thousands cycling through this cold wilderness of depressing concrete buildings. It was the sort of thing one saw on television, these monotonous scenes of China, with all the people looking incredibly small, as if one were peering at them down the wrong end of a telescope. Here in real life they were not small. They seemed large and, in their sheer numbers, threatening. I slouched low in the car seat, sagging down in sympathy with its springs, intimidated.

The car ploughed through the thronging bicycles, the driver blaring his horn and sometimes shouting irascibly through the window. Finally we crossed the river, turning down along its banks through a small fruit market. Tangerines gleamed with bright promise from the roadside, and dumpy old women with straw baskets haggled over apples and bananas, tipping their buys into metal pans to be weighed, scrutinising the scales with canny interest. At the edge of the footpath a man squatted among pieces of shrivelled leather and shoe heels, tapping distractedly at a black boot as he stared up at the passing car. We passed a row of shuttered cafés (*Bamboo Bar* said one crooked sign in English, painted with what was clearly meant to represent shoots of bamboo but which looked more like boiled asparagus) before turning through a large grey gateway enlivened with four huge red Chinese characters. A guard in a baggy hand-me-down uniform raised a barrier, red and white like a barber's pole, to let us through.

'Welcome to Sichuan University,' said Xiao Han encouragingly. 'It was founded in 1905 and is one of the oldest universities in China. Ba Jin, one famous Chinese writer, was a student here!'

We soon stopped, outside another pair of gates. They led into a courtyard surrounded by low blocks of flats, the whole enclosed by a high wall. It was the Foreigners' Compound, which I was soon to learn the Chinese referred to irreverently as the Panda Park, owing to the fact that Westerners had white skin and big eyes and lived in this zoo-like enclosure. I had been warned before coming to China that I, as a barbarian, would be living behind such a Great Wall; keeping foreigners and Chinese separate was a centuries-old custom.

'This is where you will live. I will show you your accommodation, then leave you to have a rest.'

I answered helpfully, 'I'm really not tired.'

'You will have a rest,' said Xiao Han firmly. 'You are tired.' It was a common Chinese pronouncement, I was soon to realise—Westerners were frequently imagined to be delicate, perhaps because of the Chinese liking for Victorian novels with their consumptive heroines. 'At eleven o'clock students will come to show you around the university campus.'

'Yes,' I said meekly.

Xiao Han bustled away. After she had gone I realised how quiet the room was, as echoing and hollow as the feeling in my stomach. I sat in my empty flat in a grey town feeling very small and lost and out of place, stunned by the enormity of the impulsive decision that had brought me to this country. Here I was. China. I had arrived.

Had I been in a film, I thought to myself, the camera would have been hovering somewhere just above my head, before drawing backwards, backwards, to reveal my empty room, the campus, backwards, backwards, until I was a tiny speck in the city, in the wide immensity of all China.

the one *chinese kaleidoscope*

Around the edge of the university playing field old men in blue Mao tunics waited silently among dusty bushes, motionless as lamp-posts, their faces drained of all expression. I thought they might, with Taoist intensity, be contemplating the pond, fringed with willow trees and loud with the groaning of frogs, that lay at the heart of the university campus. But after some time they slowly moved, twitching from the hands upwards through the arms to the shoulders and head, like Frankenstein creations coming to life. Then they waggled their arms in the air and lifted up a leg, turning their bodies sideways with elegant slowness, as if impelled by a heavenly puppeteer. I looked around, startled, but the Chinese were strolling by, oblivious to this display.

Two students, third-year undergraduates who I was soon to teach, were guiding me around the campus. They had called at my flat and introduced themselves in a quick flurry of Chinese names I immediately failed to remember. Secretly, for want of something better, I named them Ping and Pong. Ping hung on to Pong's arm, giggling nervously, displaying a row of white teeth, and had her hair tied back with a yellow ribbon. Pong was slightly taller and thinner, with a scattering of faint freckles across her nose. They had both studied me carefully, with inoffensive solemnity, before taking me out for a walk.

'What are those men doing?' I hissed, as if afraid they would hear me and take flight.

'That is the movement of white cranes holding up their wings,' said Ping carelessly, as one of the men bent his knees slightly, flapping his arms in front of him.

6

'Oh.'

'And that other one is parting the wild horse's . . . how do you say . . . neck hair on both sides.' The old man swept smoothly at the air in front of him with outstretched palms as if wading through deep water, jiggling a foot and waggling his head mournfully. Ping fiddled with her own long hair, black and lustrous, as if in demonstration.

'They are some of the movements of *taiji*,' interjected Pong more helpfully. 'It is a kind of martial art called in Chinese *qigong*, which consists of hard *qigong*, or *wushu*, and soft *qigong* or *taiji*, which you foreigners sometimes call shadow boxing.'

'It looks rather slow and genteel for a martial art.'

'Yes, *taiji* is very slow and is made up of movements such as ball-holding, movement of crab-like walking, floating like a cloud and other essential movements. In fact one can conquer strength through gentleness,' added the student with what I thought was true Chinese cunning. 'With such concentration one can harness the earth's energy. It can arouse your peculiar ability!'

'Er . . . what peculiar ability might that be?'

'Like your sixth sense, yes? During practice I met many interesting phenomena,' claimed my earnest guide.

'For example,' broke in Ping, 'the ability to break a pencil without touching it!'

'Ah. I see.' I was not entirely clear about the uses of this ability.

'By practising *taiji* you can live to a ripe old age and be in harmony with nature. Even turn your white hair to black when you are an old man! You know, the Yellow Emperor practised *taiji* movements, enabling him to enjoy the company of more than one thousand concubines without damage to his health!' Pong laughed nervously at the daring of her announcement.

'Mm,' I grunted, impressed.

'Certainly *qigong* can expand people's velocity, stamina, agility, and many other physical accomplishments. It can comprehensively exercise the nervous system, digestive system, muscles and skeleton. It has a miraculous effect in the field of medicine,' said Ping with the peculiar formality of Chinese English, squinting sideways at me with great seriousness.

'Most probably, you will be a great giant if you try to learn *qigong* for only two years. A good example is Wang Jie of the Tang Dynasty. Passing by Wei Bridge one day he saw two stone lions by the side of the road weighing a thousand *ji* each. For fun, Wang Jie told people he could raise up the stone lions and throw them into the field. Naturally they did not believe him, so Wang Jie lifted one of the stones and threw it several metres. All the folks around were dumbfounded! Three young men from a nearby village did not want to be outdone. But even with the efforts of all three they did not succeed in raising the stone lion!'

There were other people lurking in the bushes by the pond. Students lounged under bedraggled willows which seemed to retain a tattered aura of dignity and elegance under their limp, dust-covered branches. These students had black-framed glasses, often with cracked lenses, and they thumbed through hefty dog-eared textbooks with the earnestness of caricatured academics, their hands mottled with cold, muttering to themselves. A few couples sat on benches behind a discreet screen of foliage, bashfully holding hands and gazing shyly in opposite directions, as if overcome by their forwardness.

'I have passed twenty springs and autumns,' said Ping, giving a little hop. 'The age of twenty means youth, energy, imaginations. Do you agree? Now I am in the golden time.' She skipped lightly along in order to keep up with my long stride, and did not seem to expect an answer. Across the pond, in front of a huge building with rows of grimy windows that made it look like a train station, towered a grey concrete colossus of Chairman Mao, his right hand raised in cheery acknowledgment of my arrival. A lone student wobbled on rollerskates around its base, frantically gyrating his arms.

'That is the Physics and Engineering Department,' said the Pong girl, whose real name I still could not remember. I gazed at its massive 1950s Soviet-style bulk. It was a ponderous building of unadorned granite.

'Sichuan University has twenty other departments, not to talk about four colleges, twenty-two research institutes, twelve research sections, and fourteen centres for other teaching and research.'

'Do you like it here?'

'Of course! There are forty-four specialities and thirteen hundred courses for undergraduates, and fifty-two specialities and six hundred courses for graduates!'

'But you are only doing one course, surely,' I pointed out.

We were passing a row of notice boards, posted with announcements and black-and-white photos of the latest model workers, staring out at the world in their tightly buttoned Mao tunics, as fiercely and righteously as statesmen in frock coats stared out of Victorian portraits. They were surrounded by murals of vigorous soldiers and peasant girls, dresses whipped tight against them by revolutionary winds, holding up red flags and clenched fists. I glanced back at my two companions, fresh-faced as fifteen-year-olds, with their innocent patter and shy friendliness. If you continue to dole out statistics like that, I thought to myself, you will look as grim as these model workers one day. Perhaps you will even *be* model workers.

'. . . There is a faculty of seventeen hundred, including six hundred professors and eight hundred lecturers,' Pong was saying in a breathless gasp, rounding off her statistics with satisfaction.

'But do you *like* it?' I persisted with Western indelicacy.

The student suddenly capitulated. 'No! In fact I think university is rather boring—so many classes and lessons! Really some of them are quite useless.'

'Which class do you find the most boring?'

'Political Studies, without a doubt! It is held in the big lecture hall every Tuesday afternoon, for all the students of our year in the department. Often we girls sit in the back rows and make our knitting! We hope the speaker will be finished as possible as quick,' answered Pong in engagingly confused English.

'I learned knitting from my classmates in middle school, as my mother was always too busy to teach me,' interrupted Ping. 'I think it is one of the ways of relaxing. Once I earned some money and bought ten *liang* of wool and knitted a jacket for my mother. She felt so happy she did not know what to say when I gave it to her. She was lucky as a dog to get such a gift!'

'So you see Political Studies is not so bad!' chimed in Pong. 'For in it I too have managed to knit a beautiful sweater for my boyfriend, so I cannot say it is a waste of time!'

I said nothing, somewhat shocked. I had always thought the Chinese were diligent in their study of the socialist way, assiduous in memorising long pages of Mao Zedong thought and studying the party political line. Now I laughed in spite of myself at the idea of rows of girls furiously knitting socks and sweaters for their boyfriends, hearing but not listening to the theories of Marx. Behind glass the photos of the model workers seemed to frown in disapproval; their stern rectitude seemed a sham. It was only much later that I came to realise nothing was simple; these models of virtuous socialism were as real as bored university students, and much more powerful, and the real China was not pictured in black-and-white. I was to learn how misleading hasty generalisations were, and I came to accept that, as Thomas Hardy said of his novels, I should record impressions, not conclusions, about this land that resisted summary.

Ping and Pong propelled me onwards around the campus, along its straight, wide boulevards lined by gnarled plane trees, their bases painted white against the encroachment of insects and to mark the road edge in the dark nights of Chinese cities. The trees had been cut back for the winter, standing knobby and bare as broccoli stalks. In the narrower lanes, among the student dormitories and teachers' accommodation, washing hung banner-like from balconies. Pots and pans clattered cheerfully from behind open windows as food was prepared, and bedraggled, clucking hens, soon for the pot, ran hysterically around the shrubbery like animated feather-dusters. Under a tree nearby sat a bicycle repair man, his bolts, inner tubes and pumps spread out on a cloth, his bicycles upended and partially dismantled like the mechanism for some incredible new invention. Here you can stop and have your tyre pumped up for the princely sum of one *fen*, a hundredth of a Chinese *yuan*, Pong told me. Down another street stood a campus shop in a ramshackle shed that looked as if it had been transplanted from a Caribbean beach, stacked with tins and bottles, then the baker's, piled high with bursting sacks of flour, where a middle-aged man in a blue Mao cap rolled dough and produced rounds of flat bread over a charcoal fire. Next was the biscuit lady with her yellow cart, then the cobbler sitting on the ground amid his scraps of leather and shoe-laces. Beside him under a tree was the cart of the honey seller, where I became a regular customer, buying ladles of oozing golden honey thick with the essence of summer.

Sichuan University was a pleasant and well-regulated place. All ten thousand students lived on the campus, as did the teachers, professors and support staff, in a tightly knit community behind high walls punctured by a few gates guarded by uniformed men. It was a mere gesture—the guards dozed in the sun or swung on their chairs, spitting and indolently watching the stream of people passing in and out, rousing themselves to strangled shouts if someone did not maintain the proprieties by dismounting from their bicycle to pass through the gates. In fact one need never have left the sprawling sixty-five acre campus. There were dining halls for the students: cavernous places like the inside of a factory workshop, where giant cauldrons of noodles were stirred by paddles the size of oars, and other vats held rice, steamed bread rolls and dumplings. At midday and in the evenings students came here for food, dumped into their bowls without ceremony by cooks wielding large ladles, and then filed back towards their rooms, flicking food into their mouths with their chopsticks and blowing on their steaming rice. There were more expensive restaurants on the campus too, shops and markets and much more besides—repair men, a nursery for staff children, a swimming pool, a theatre that doubled as a cinema, an excellent museum concerned with the culture of south-west China's ethnic minorities, dilapidated tennis and badminton courts with nets as tattered as cinematographic cobwebs, a printing house, a huge library containing more than two million volumes, a post office, a medical centre, even a radio and television station.

In this respect Sichuan University was no different from any other large work unit in China, whether a college or factory or government department. It was the basic social cell of all urban Chinese, an enclosed world in which one worked and through which one's life was mapped, from permission to marry through to birth control and salary rises and leave to travel. Many foreigners balked at the idea of such constriction and Orwellian watchfulness, but these work units were also the source of life-long job security (the famous 'iron rice-bowl' of communist China), virtually rent-free accommodation, pensions, low-cost health care and a wide range of other social benefits. Work units could make it easier to obtain scarce sleeper spaces on the railways, gave out free cinema tickets, supplied banquets on special occasions, and arranged sight-seeing trips and other entertainments. They offered the supportive care of a parent as well as exercising the control of a Big Brother. Many Chinese, though often resenting undue interference in their lives, were nevertheless reassured by feeling part of a group, and work units gave them an enormous sense of security, I realised. There was little graffiti, vandalism or alcoholism in China; these and other minor social ills stemmed from a feeling of social dislocation and uselessness that seemed alien to the young Chinese living under strong government paternalism. Many were dissatisfied, but few placed themselves outside the bounds of conventional society. The work unit was their extended family, and like a family they treated it with a mixture of annoyance, resentment, respect and familiarity, and ultimately did not see how they could live without it.

A few days after my guided tour of the enclosed world of the university I started teaching. Lists of Chinese names swam in front of my eyes in baffling monosyllables. But after some weeks they fell into place, and I began remembering them. Suddenly the Chinese did not look alike any more, and it became increasingly easy to distinguish one from another and put names to faces. Some were tall and pale-skinned northerners, others short and stocky, with the darker skin of the hot and humid south; some had freckles, some brown eyes and some black. I began to learn that the men of Shandong Province, on the coast south of Beijing, were renowned for their strength, their heroism and their ability to drink vast quantities of alcohol—but a friend from Shandong I was to make was short and slight and grew fuddled on two glasses of beer. The Cantonese were hot-tempered and energetic and spoke in the fast southern staccato that was a different language, the people of Beijing were reputed to be cold and arrogant and rolled their Rs like the Parisians, and everyone made jokes about the Hunanese of central China and their slow, peasant stupidity, despite (or because of?) the fact that Mao Zedong was a native of the province. I remembered these anecdotes, placing them carefully in my mind like rare treasures, delighting that this vast country with its vast population was not the homogeneous mass it had often appeared to be on television at home. Slowly it began to take on form and diversity, and thirty faces in a classroom gradually became thirty individuals.

The weather became warmer and the Chinese reduced their bulky layers, emerging like colourful butterflies from their winter cocoons of clothes. On the campus, the magnolia trees burst out in improbable blossoms, waxy as artificial flowers, and opposite the History Department peach saplings took on a blushing suggestion of pink. It was suddenly the glorious, transient Chinese spring, a passing phase between the cold of winter and the stifling humidity of the long summer, in which the blue skies sometimes broke through the pollution of the city and crickets scraped among the bamboo of Chengdu's parks. As February passed into March and April, Chengdu did not look as grey and indifferent as my first impressions had suggested. It was the season for cycling into the surrounding countryside to view the peach blossoms, and for kite-flying. Chinese thronged the bridges, using the clear space over the river to launch their paper kites—invented by their ancestors centuries ago—which floated erratically in the shapes of goldfish and birds in the sky above. In the centre of town hawkers roamed with coloured city maps and bangles to attract the first trickle of overseas tourists, and markets swelled with fat cabbages, pineapples from Yunnan Province, spring rolls and strawberries.

Once a week, down by the river not far from the Jinjiang Hotel, the warm weather brought out groups of aspiring foreign language students, who came from all over the city to congregate under the trees and practise their English, chatting to each other solemnly in this alien tongue, rarely resorting to Chinese despite frequent misunderstandings. Known as English Corners, these gatherings were viewed with suspicion by the government and had recently been banned on university campuses. But they were tolerated in public areas, and common in cities all over China.

In those early months I visited Chengdu's English Corner several times, which offered the opportunity to meet Chinese who were not students or professors but often ordinary workers. Such encounters were often tedious, as the standard questions and answers swirled back and forwards with monotonous predictability, largely because the majority of Chinese did not speak good enough English to venture any further.

'How old are you, sir?'

'Are you married?'

'What do you think of our China?'

'How old are you?'

'Where do you come from?'

'Excuse me, are you married?'

At other times, however, a small group of people would gather round and a genuine conversation would begin with Chinese whose English was sometimes extraordinarily fluent.

'There is a Chinese saying: "Life is short, Art is long." Do you agree?' I was asked at one gathering, by a short woman in a blue Mao tunic, her hair in pigtails.

'Er . . . well, yes, yes. I suppose I do.' I was a little taken aback by this abrupt opening sally.

'All art is created to give enjoyment to other human beings,' chimed in another figure standing close by, a good-looking young woman with a daring dash of lipstick to match her pink coat. 'Imagine a dark world without a spark of light, and then you can think of the misery of the lives of people who spend their time with no art to encourage them!'

She put a wealth of drama into her comment, pulling her coat around her and shrinking into it theatrically as if threatened by an evil wind from a world without art. There was a sudden stir of interest in the people around us, and they shifted closer into a tightly knit group.

'Yes,' said Pigtails. 'Like the Chinese saying: If you have two pennies left in the world, buy a loaf of bread with one, and a lily with the other.'

'I don't think so,' said a middle-aged man with greying hair and a slight stoop. 'In the 1950s we could see paintings such as a peasant carrying in his arms a sweet potato weighing fifty kilograms. We could easily find a poem such as: "When an oil worker shouts / The earth will shake three times / And the oil worker is so energetic / He can conquer anything." Do you think these give enjoyment?' His voice was dry and sarcastic.

'That kind of art,' I said, 'is a social ideology which demonstrates ideas by means of striking images, such as that huge potato. It's supposed to educate and inspire people. Mao Zedong himself said that art and literature should be used to serve the people and could only be created by the people. In that sense propaganda is still art. Isn't great art supposed to teach you something?'

The man with the grey hair sniffed doubtfully. 'When I was a middle school student my physics teacher always told us that art could teach us nothing and could do no good for people,' he replied. 'Even collecting all the famous artists of the world together, they could not build one bridge. But his physics students could. One of his students designed and built a walking-bridge after having left school. He was a hero in the hearts of the villagers. The teacher hoped his students would reject art, and he was sure the world would be improved much more quickly if all the students studied physics.'

'Albert Einstein studied physics, and yet he held in esteem the happiness brought to him by art,' retorted Pink Coat. 'Beethoven said that music makes people's spirits spark. He said that music was a greater and higher inspiration than all wisdom and science and philosophy.'

'Exciting music can encourage pessimistic people, while melodious light music can console those who are unhappy!' chimed in the woman with the pigtails who had initiated the conversation and had since then been standing on the sidelines, as if taken aback by the debate she had unleashed.

'Take sculptors,' said Grey Hair after a moment's deliberation, passing indifferently over the meaning of music and sweeping onwards with his own argument. Some of the audience did not know the word, and there were hurried consultations on its meaning.

'These sculptors claim to create beauty. But the real beauty is in man himself, which makes quite awkward the sculpted wood, metal or stone. It is very loathsome to look at a carved frozen countenance, whether it appears good-looking or not. If one wants to enjoy real beauty, one should get in contact with an animate person, rather than stand in front of a motionless and dull model. Sculptors only do something useless. They should spare such efforts to make a good meal for themselves! Sculptors only make a false beauty, which is stale and flat and unprofitable.'

I looked sharply at him as he uttered these final words. I found it peculiar that this man was paraphrasing Hamlet in English while denouncing art as useless.

'That brings us around to the original point, that art is long and life is short,' I interjected. 'I'm sure that a human figure is more beautiful than a statue, but we may admire the statue for ever, a human's beauty only transiently.'

'If there were no art to accompany me on my journey through life, to finish the journey would be impossible,' said Pink Coat. 'Around a track you run and run, aimless, lonely, tired, distressed, and at last die of disappointment. It is the fate of all those who regard art as useless. Art is an everlasting flower whose fragrance will never diminish with the passing of time, and whose beauty always evokes hope and fine feelings and encourages people to live by them!'

There was a sudden silence after this poetic outburst. We all stared at the woman in the pink coat, who lowered her eyes, suddenly abashed. During the lull the little knot of people shifted and dispersed as quickly as it had formed, the brief ideas and scattered conversation unresolved. I wondered about the woman in pink and her evocative words, and whether she were an artist or a student.

I asked lamely, feeling stupid and clumsy, 'Where do you work?'

The woman drew back into her coat, one hand clutching it closed in front of her, the other sweeping her hair behind her ears with nervous motions. She looked suddenly older, worn out. There were flecks of grey in her hair, at the sides, which I hadn't noticed before, and delicate lines fanned out from the corners of her eyes. I thought they made her more handsome.

'I'm a factory worker,' she said quietly. 'I operate machinery cutting leather for a shoe company.'

Moments later she had vanished into the night, and was gone.

At Sichuan University the campus was now suffused in green, and the spring sun lent a honeyed softness to the grey concrete buildings. Just beside the Foreign Languages Building, in front of the university theatre, rows of stone ping-pong tables began to resound with the patter of balls, and students lounged in the steadily warming sun, giving cries of encouragement to the players. They built nets of broken bricks and dodged slow-drying puddles by the tables, but when they played on their makeshift equipment they smashed and sliced with violent expertise.

Inside the classroom I began to feel restless with the warmer weather, and gazed out of the windows over the sports field, where joggers swerved to avoid bevies of girls wielding metre-long batons, practising martial arts. But my students were as attentive as ever, well drilled in discipline and eager to take advantage of their foreign teacher. These youngsters were the elite of China, the lucky few who had the chance of a higher education. They had studied long and hard at school in order to pass the tough university entrance examination that failed all but a fraction of those who sat it, and at college they continued to work diligently, sitting in classes for most of the day, six days a week, and often studying or doing homework long into the evening. 'They surpass other nations in the excellence of their manners and their knowledge of many subjects, since they devote much time to their study and to the acquisition of knowledge,' Marco Polo had written seven hundred years ago.

As far as academic work was concerned their studies seemed little more than an extension of their secondary school life: they sat in class with little active participation, listening to teachers and rarely disputing their words, speaking—and often standing up—only when asked a direct question, and studying intensively from textbooks for all-important examinations. Not surprisingly, the greatest impression recorded by Chinese about their foreign teachers was their casualness. 'You, my foreign teacher,' confided a student to me once, 'are unlike any of those Chinese teachers who might stand stationed in one place when lecturing for fear of any break in formality. You seem to be always free, sometimes sitting on the back of the chair, sometimes on the edge of the desk, which might be regarded as out of place in China. No wonder our China lags behind in the world—there may be something lacking in our spirit!'

In reality it was the utilitarian education system that often lacked in spirit, for I was to find these students who seemed so regimented in class were rarely as spiritless, unthinking and docile as they appeared. But Chinese university education dis-approved of outspokenness, and discouraged dissidence. The purpose of education was not so much to produce top-quality thinkers as to produce citizens who would fit into society's mould and be of service to others, performing a well-defined role to the satisfaction of the community as a whole and the government in particular, and thus maintaining the status quo. Convention was encouraged and liberal thoughts were frowned upon. The greatest values in teaching were still the good Confucian qualities of order, harmony, stability and the cultivation of social virtue: in this respect Chinese univer-sity students were rather like British public schoolboys at the turn of the century, when education was subservient to a good upbringing and an awareness of one's place in society.

Increasingly, however, the Chinese students' idea of their social position no longer corresponded with that of Confucius or their government, and I was to find many Chinese caught by their education in a mentality that was no longer appropriate to the present realities of China. These young Chinese, puzzled and wary of the world about them, were to prove among the most interesting and friendly people I would meet, providing me with views of China I had never imagined.

It sometimes still astonished me that I was here in China, in a country that had started as a joke, an elaborate pantomime for my entertainment. As a small boy I had pulled the corners of my eyes upwards with my thumbs, and shouted 'Wing wong ding dong' at my friends before dissolving into helpless laugh-ter. The Chinese had always been an alien race, and everywhere were examples of their cunning: they had invented the wheel-barrow a thousand years before Western people, as well as the umbrella, the parachute, the stink bomb (an achievement I had then particularly admired) and the sulphur match. As if this were not enough, the Chinese had also dreamed up dominoes, Chinese chequers and playing cards.

Here in Chengdu, years later, the real Chinese still seemed quaint and slightly amusing people: men danced in slow motion in the shrubbery, and university students stood stiffly to attention in the classroom, aghast at being asked a question.

They were funny: the young women wore stockings that ended just below the hemlines of their outmoded skirts, and had trendy silver glitter in their hair; the men slouched around in black canvas shoes and baggy pea-green trousers held up by imitation leather belts wrapped twice around their skinny waists.

I was beginning to realise with humility, however, that their culture was not a farce: these people had fought and suffered more than any other on earth, had lived through famine and invasion and foreign interference and political campaigns and social disruption. This sea of humanity jammed into buses, jostling in shops, regimented in classrooms like photocopied reproductions, was revealing itself as a collection of individuals, with their own emotions and thoughts, happiness and tragedy. Some of them, like Pink Coat, impressed me fleetingly, nameless; some of them were to become my friends, and a few would influence me greatly. The Chinese were indeed a funny people, all eyes and black hair like the caricature I had imagined. But as they began to reveal themselves as individuals it became a humbling and inspiring experience. Sometimes, irrationally, during the two and a half years I spent in China, I hated the Chinese for not being what I would have liked them to be—more like *me*, more attuned to my Western attitudes to the world—but I grew to admire and appreciate them for what they were.

Then, too, this was not the country of industrial outputs—nineteen thousand bicycles a day produced in Shanghai—and soaring rice yields and political machinations and turmoil that I had once read about in the dry journals of the West: it was much more immediate and human than that. Not one of the books I had read had told me that China was an omnipresent smell: the acrid tang of heated rapeseed oil stinging the back of my nose, the choking dust, the ammonia of stale urine, the fusty smell of burning coal like the back parlour of a Victorian terrace house. No one had told me China was endless noise: dinging bicycle bells, the sizzle of vegetables thrown into a wok behind an open window, the terrible spitting that began as a long *uggaaarrrgh* in the back of the throat, the high-pitched semi-shout in which all Chinese seemed to conduct their conversations. Nor was it as grey and ugly as I had seen it on my first day, for China was a visual display of new patterns and pictures: bamboo as delicate as a Japanese painting, dark against the sky; bunches of dangling hens on a passing bicycle's handle-bars; weaving groups of blue Mao tunics in a market street; flickering pools of light thrown out by guttering kerosene lamps.

At night I slept restlessly and uneasily, slotting these new sensations into a meaningful collection. Old childhood fantasies, stale recollected excerpts from explanatory books on China, and fresh new scenes settled in my mind like the glass pieces in a kaleidoscope. Only minutes later the pattern was upset by some remembered detail into a swirling confusion of sparkling fragments, resisting conformity, until I agreed on a new form, the old colours and shapes subtly rearranged. The kaleidoscope of China, I thought. I twisted my impressions slowly, marvelling.

As the spring drifted away the hot summer bore down with a steamrolling wave of humidity. And as the term drew to a close, I planned a holiday into my past, into my early odd, randomly acquired facts and fantasies of China, but also into a future as yet little understood, of the Chinese and their real lives, and into ideas as yet unformed.

into the hanging mountains

two

A dilapidated and suspiciously rusty Russian turbo-prop plane, swaying tipsily, propelled me over an undulating mosaic of flooded rice fields, bald mountaintops and mop-headed trees towards the town of Guilin in north-eastern Guangxi Autonomous Region. Oxen below moved infinitely slowly, small as ants in handkerchief fields. Farms, scattered and insignificant, formed villages huddled against the mountainsides. Safely on the ground things took on a more normal perspective: the oxen great, shaggy prehistoric creatures armoured in dried mud, the farms grey-slated and ramshackle. Against the sky loomed mountains, domed as camels' humps, like the irrational drawings of children on a pantomime backdrop. These mountains have made Guilin and the surrounding countryside one of China's oldest and most renowned tourist sites, and for more than a millennium the region has been a source of inspiration not only for travellers but for Chinese writers, poets and painters. I had been determined to make my first destination these strange hills that had coloured my early imagined landscape of this country. Mountains like these appeared improbably in ancient Chinese watercolours, and now I had stepped through the picture frame and was here among them, on a shabby road from the airport. Beside me on the bus a high-ranking army officer lay asleep with his head tipped back against the seat, his hard green cap askew, mouth gaping open in a parody of theatrical amazement.

Once into the city of Guilin the extraordinary mountains receded like a mirage. The streets were hot, dusty and built from the usual grey concrete often associated with hurried post-war reconstruction. The newness of Guilin might seem surprising, for the thirty-four kilometre Ling Canal, linking the Pearl and Yangtze river systems, had made Guilin an important focus of river transport as long as two thousand years ago. Guilin, the region's local administrative headquarters for centuries, is said to have been a city of beautiful palaces and colourful temples, but these were razed by the Japanese when they captured the town in 1944. Guilin is now a completely reconstructed industrial city, very small by Chinese standards. I trudged through the streets, skirting piles of rubble and planks of wood that made the city seem more one of destruction than of construction, as if these bits had been pulled off buildings and left carelessly lying, abandoned to a meaningless future. Guilin's greyness was the greyness of ghosts, a colourless shadow lingering in sad reflection of its days of greatness. It was a place not built to last and holding out little hope for the future, crowded with reactionary buildings of breeze-blocks and disillusionment already crumbling into shabbiness, betraying its modernity.

Having found a hotel subsiding into seedy indifference off the main street, where a mummified staff hid behind tortured potted plants in fake Ming vases, I set forth to obtain a boat ticket for the trip I wished to make next day down the river to Yangshuo. My first step was the bus station. Are boat tickets sold here? I wondered. A grudging admission from a woman lurking goblin-like behind a grimy window that they were.

'Could I have a ticket for tomorrow morning?'

'No.'

'Why not? Are there none left for tomorrow?'

'Many are left.'

'Then could I buy one please?'

'We don't sell tickets to foreigners.'

'But you just said I could buy a ticket here!'

'Only if you're Chinese.'

'Why did you say I could buy one if I can't?'

'You asked if boat tickets were sold here, saying nothing of foreigners.'

'Do I look Chinese? Do I speak like a Chinese?' I asked crossly.

'Foreigners cannot buy tickets here.' Then she added the fateful words that ring like a death knell across the hopes of travellers in China: 'There is a regulation.'

'Sorry to trouble you,' I smiled sweetly, gritting my teeth. 'I'm not a foreigner. I mean, I am a foreigner, of course'—a theatrical laugh—'but not a *tourist*. Surely one who is working in China might buy a ticket here?' I plucked my residence and worker's cards from my wallet, waving them like a magic charm before her indifferent eyes. I was particularly proud of my worker's card with its plastic cover of bright communist red, embossed with the name of my university in gold characters.

'No.'

'Well, where can I buy a ticket then?'

'I don't know.' After some prodding, 'Well, maybe over there on the other side of the street.'

'Can foreigners buy tickets over there?'

'Maybe. All I know is, foreigners cannot buy tickets *here*.'

Nor could foreigners buy tickets across the road. At the reception desk of a nearby hotel there were tickets, but another mysterious regulation prevented me from obtaining one. I knew these regulations: they had been invented long ago by the Taoist philosophers and were exacerbated under communism, where no reward was given for effort made. It is the tall pine that gets struck by lightning, goes a Chinese proverb: that was regulation number one. No need to stand out in a crowd or to resist the forces beyond you. If a foreigner asks you for a ticket and you are unsure of the regulations, then do not challenge destiny. If you sell him one and discover you made a mistake all sorts of complications and trouble may fall upon your unsuspecting head. If on the other hand you do nothing, the foreigner may never get his ticket but at least you cannot be blamed for whatever happens. This was a very Chinese attitude, and it probably gave rise to the cliché of the inscrutable Oriental, who puts on a bland and indifferent face, practising the non-resistance of Taoist sages and giving nothing away. It was an appealing attitude to hold but an intensely frustrating one to face, and at that moment it was making me very cross.

Finally, I tracked a ticket down in an office off the lobby of another hotel, and proffered my RMB (*renminbi* or People's Money, the ordinary currency of China).

'No! Only FEC!' These were Foreign Exchange Certificates, available only with foreign currency, used by tourists and much in demand on the black market.

'I don't have any. I'm a teacher,' I replied, again fishing out my cards to prove this. They were scrutinised and flung back across the table. I had by this time already laboriously negotiated a ten percent reduction on the cost of the return ticket, as I would not be coming back to Guilin.

'No reduction if you pay in RMB.'

'But I'm a *teacher*,' I moaned. 'Look!' I waved my Purchasing Certificate at her, stamped by the Bank of China, permitting me to pay in RMB. 'I shouldn't have to pay extra!'

'No reduction. You are a foreigner!'

'No, I'm a *teacher*. Teacher, teacher, teacher,' I repeated hysterically, like an incantation. 'Look!' I jabbed a finger down on rule two of my card. '"*The certificate is effective when paying accommodation expenses and transportation expenses inside China*",' I read out in a loud voice, enunciating every word as if addressing a recalcitrant child.

'No reduction. You can buy your ticket somewhere else,' responded the saleswoman pitilessly.

'But I can't! This is the only place that sells tickets to foreigners!'

She said nothing: no doubt she knew it. Her eyes flickered blankly and with complete basilisk indifference across my face, my cards and the wall behind me, the way a tyrant might fleetingly glance at a prisoner before indicating, with a twitch of the finger, that he was to be executed.

'I'll take it then,' I gave in with bad grace. Three hours after I began the search I had the ticket in my hand, though I had no feeling of triumph. Conversations in textbooks for beginner's Chinese, I thought irritably, always seemed so polite and reasonable. In those books, young ladies with the name of Miss Zhang or Miss Wang asked what the weather was like in your country, and smiled and nodded, and sold tickets with generous affability, mentioning numerous delightful tourist sites in the vicinity.

It was exceedingly hot. The humidity curled in big oily waves through the streets, and I was exhausted with the effort of trying to converse in Chinese and ready to weep with frustration that my language was as yet too limited to give anyone a piece of my mind. Sometimes I felt sure that the Chinese had joined in some vast conspiracy of harassment in a modern version of their water torture, in which water dripped onto the forehead of an immobilised victim until he was driven insane. So too was one worn away by constant unhelpfulness, and only ended up feeling foolish at eventually shouting in the face of this Eastern indifference.

I went back to my room and, in a rage, ate chocolate.

A while later I emerged from my hotel, having regained some of my equilibrium. *Laser and demonstration butterfly shadow* a neon sign proclaimed in bold pink and scarlet English across the hotel facade, topped by a bright neon butterfly, the lights around the edges of its wings flashing on and off cryptically. 'Laser and demonstration butterfly shadow,' I muttered to myself, grinning, trying to guess its meaning. 'Laser and demonstration butterfly shadow.' Shoals of bicycles drifted lazily through the half-demolished streets. The main boulevard was lined with restaurants, their menus on display in cramped wire cages: snake, quail, civet cat, turtle, toad. Once they had served owl and lynx, but these had been eaten to the verge of extinction and were now protected species. Restaurant owners lounged indifferently against the cages, smoking Great Wall cigarettes and picking their teeth. Sometimes they called 'Hello, hello, have a meal?' in the desultory fashion of a much-repeated ritual, as if they had already made up their minds that I wouldn't eat there.

I wandered into the state department store which, despite the town's smallness, had a better range of goods than in Chengdu. Salesgirls, lifeless as the mannequins in the shop windows, lolled against the counters, lips rouged into scarlet wounds. Sometimes they spat idly into plastic spittoons. There was an escalator (upward only), a mechanism I had never seen in Chengdu and which, like a peasant in from the countryside, I felt obliged to ride in amazement. Its metal panels groaned and protested.

Outside the department store, walking beside the river, I fell in with two hotel workers. Despite being on their honeymoon,

Zhou Yong and Li Xiaohong were anxious to make my acquaintance, for both were taking evening courses in English. Zhou Yong was tall and solemn, rather silent behind gold-rimmed glasses, with a shadow on his upper lip that had long ago given up trying to become a moustache. His wife was pretty, her hair very long and gathered in a coil on top of her head. She was voluble, obviously eager to show off her excellent English. They took me up Fubo Hill to see the view over the town and the surrounding peaks that have made the area famous: they mushroomed against the horizon like the fantasies of opium addicts. Fubo Hill, like many in the area, was riddled with caves, prompting the poet Luo Dajing in 1784 to a rather bizarre metaphor:

> Seeing the blue hills from the outside
> Is like touching the exterior of a person;
> Seeing the hills from inside the caverns
> Is like plucking his internal organs.

Such violent metaphors seemed appropriate. Peace had always rested uneasily here: Chinese power had frequently been disputed in this remote mountainous region. Some of the hills around Guilin, such as the quaintly named Elephant Trunk Hill, had been used for gun emplacements during major uprisings that had plagued the central government well into the last century.

More romantically, Zhou Yong told me, one of the hills is said to be an old man, turned into stone while waiting for his irresponsible son to return from pearl fishing; another is said to have been created by a beam falling from the roof of heaven. For myself, a prosaic geography enthusiast, the countryside around Guilin was a textbook example of tropical karst landscape, the extraordinary domed hills, rising out of the sugar cane and grain fields, the result of solution weathering of the limestone from which the entire area was made about three hundred million years ago. Huge subterranean caverns formed by erosion eventually collapsed, leaving these flat-bottomed valley and steep mountains. I had studied such landscapes at school, and now these hills loomed in front of me like a fragment of my past made real, dragging back lost memories of geography lessons.

I had a long dinner with my new-found acquaintances, though I eschewed the culinary exotica in the cages, and we dined off fresh river fish topped with onions, ginger, sliced mushrooms, bamboo shoots and orange peel in a rich sweet-and-sour sauce. By that time I had decided that Li Xiaohong was not just pretty, she was beautiful. Her mouth was perhaps a shade too full, without being sensuous, yet she had high, well-defined cheekbones that gave her a slightly Mongolian look that was not without attraction. But it was her eyes that were her most striking feature; they were perhaps the most beautiful I had seen. They were large and oval and a very unusual dark grey colour.

'Maybe you are wondering how we met?' asked the talkative Li Xiaohong, pulling out hairclips and loosening her long hair down her back. I hadn't actually been wondering any such thing, but I nodded politely.

'Well, prior to working in the hotel, Zhou Yong was a student at college. One evening, he left the classroom and started for home. He cycled slowly in the crowding traffic and was rather impatient—the traffic was heavy because of the rush hour.'

'Crowded,' said her husband.

'What?'

'*Crowded* traffic, not *crowding*.'

'Busy,' I arbitrated pedantically. 'Congested. I'm not sure that traffic can be crowded. Or crowding.' I couldn't call her eyes grey, I decided. Grey gave the impression of something dull, like slate; these eyes were the grey of . . . of clouds across the moon.

'Well,' continued Li Xiaohong a little crossly, 'At the corner of Fuxingmenwai Street, he saw a large crowd of people gathered near a bus, and there was a lot of noise. Great curiosity rose in him. He got off his bike and went over. When he got there, he saw a young lady and a middle-aged woman quarrelling.

'"Why didn't you buy a ticket?" the elder woman, a conductor, was saying curtly.

'"I've told you, I forgot to bring my money," replied the young lady, rather embarrassed.

'"Then why did you get on the bus?"

'"I didn't *realise* until I had got on the bus."

'"But you must pay the fare," shouted the woman. "You can leave only after you give me five *jiao*!"

'"I'll pay it tomorrow."

'"Tomorrow? When and where? Heaven knows where you'll be tomorrow!" retorted the conductor acidly. She was planted squarely on her feet, with one hand on her hip, the other pointing at the young lady, whose face was red with indignation. The young woman didn't utter a word now. She stared at the conductor with both anger and tears in her eyes. Zhou Yong was stirred. The conductor's harsh words also angered him. Is it worth bickering over a five *jiao* bus ticket? he thought. He squeezed his way through the crowd and went up to the older woman.

'"Don't be so mean and hard on people," he said to her. "Here is five *jiao*. Let the lady leave!" Then he threw the money at her, quickly turned around and went away. People burst into roars of laughter. He didn't look back. He went directly to his bike, got on it and rode away.'

Li Xiaohong sat amid the debris of a finished meal—fish bones and greasy chopsticks and flecks of rice in the bottom of chipped bowls—animated by her recollections, her eyes glittering. *Occhi parlanti*, talking eyes, the Italians called them; smiling eyes the Irish. Outside in the street a bicycle bell rang as urgently as a fire alarm, making me look up. A young man wobbled past, swerving to avoid collision with a woman carrying panniers on a shoulder pole. Zhou Yong did not even look around. He picked indolently at the fish bones with his chopsticks, his cheeks flushed with beer. I was sure he had heard this story many times before.

'A couple of weeks later, on a Saturday afternoon, Zhou Yong was riding home,' continued Li Xiaohong, drawing me back to her story. 'Near the corner of Fuxingmenwai he saw a young lady waving to him. He is short-sighted, so he couldn't see her clearly. He jumped off his bike and went to meet her. He was rather taken aback, and stopped dead on the pavement when he saw a strange face.

'"Sorry! I thought you were waving to me." He was a bit embarrassed and smiled apologetically.

'"Well, yes! I was waving to you."

'"Really?" He was even more puzzled, and looked at her, perspired.'

'Perplexed. She means perplexed,' cut in her husband, suddenly alert. His chopsticks snapped in the air. Li Xiaohong glared at him. Her eyes widened in annoyance. I was sure by now that they were not grey but the delicate shade of a seashore at twilight.

'He was still perspired,' resumed Li Xiaohong pointedly. 'He couldn't remember where he had seen her. She was no more than twenty-four, with bright black hair, pink cheeks, rosy skin and big dark eyes.' She giggled.

'You have guessed that it was me! But Zhou Yong just shook his head and said again that he was sorry. I said softly, but in a gentle manner, "Don't you remember here, two weeks ago, near the bus stop, there . . ." Suddenly he remembered the quarrel and guessed that it was probably the young lady who had got into trouble that day. "It was really very kind of you," I continued shyly. I hesitated for a second, then added, "My parents know all about it, and asked me to thank you and invite you to our home. I've waited here every afternoon for you since, but didn't see you until now, which is nearly two weeks . . ."

'On hearing this Zhou Yong was even more embarrassed and didn't know what to say. At length he replied, "Yes, I'd be very pleased to come."

'A year later, Zhou Yong went south with the charming girl for his honeymoon!'

Down the Li River, amid Guilin's scenery, I floated the next day, eighty kilometres to the small town of Yangshuo, still thinking of and delighting in Li Xiaohong and Zhou Yong's story: it was the human reality of China, for which I had come in search. I was glad they had chosen Guilin for their honeymoon; their unlikely romance seemed very apt in this unlikely and unusual place, where everything was seen through a mirror, inversely. The mountains didn't so much rise up as seem to hang down, a landscape suspended from the sky by invisible threads.

The boat for which I had gone to so much trouble to get a ticket was a China Travel Service pleasure craft designed for decadent foreigners, and had troubled engines, emitting coughs and smoke. A cold lunch was supplied, featuring unappetising scraps of ham and dishes of fried peanuts which I ate moodily, washing them down with several miniature bottles of soft drink. Tourists leaned over the railings with camera lenses a metre long, taking pictures. One of them, an American in a stereotypical loud plaid jacket, accosted me with exuberant enthusiasm.

'You look Irish! As soon as I saw you, I said to myself, that guy is certainly Irish!' he boomed, leaving me at a loss for words and without the time to either deny or confirm his statement before he resumed.

'The Ring of Kerry. You been there? The Blarney Stone? You done that? I toured Ireland in 1979, it was *so great* staying in those bed-and-breakfasts, actually inside people's *homes*!'

'Really?' I replied frigidly. 'You make the Irish sound like some kind of tribal exotica.'

He guffawed. I thought he was going to slap his knee, but he did not. 'Ha ha! Tribal exotica! I like it. I'm from Kentucky. Know where that is? Just like the fried chicken! I've just been touring South-East Asia: a week in the Philippines, one day in Malacca, two days in Cowlalumper—know where that is?'

'Er . . . Well, I'm not sure.'

The American crowed happily, 'Cowlalumper, capital of Malaysia . . .'

'Oh, yes. Kuala Lumpur,' I suggested in my most upper-class British voice, driven to affect an accent I certainly did not normally possess.

'. . . Coupla days in Penang, Bangkok, Hong Kong. Now I'm in China, it sure is a great place, coupla days in Guilin, onto Shanghai, Peking . . .'

Overseas Chinese took pictures of each other and fell asleep after lunch in complete indifference to their surroundings, except for one old Hong Kong gentleman who chatted to me, and looked faintly horrified to learn I actually lived in China. He had struck up a conversation as I was copying out a passage from a book I had been reading, Thoreau's *A Week on the Concord and Merrimack Rivers*:

> Rivers must have been the guides which conducted the footsteps
> of the first travellers. They are the constant lure . . . to distant
> enterprise and adventure, and, by a natural impulse, the
> dwellers on their banks will at length accompany their currents
> to the lowlands of the globe, or explore at their invitation the
> interior of continents.

I liked that last phrase, 'explore at their invitation the interior of continents,' and I rolled it round on my tongue and wrote it carefully into my notebook.

'You are left-handed, I can see,' a voice had said. 'I think for the left-handed this world is really a clumsy one! It seems everything makes their lives uncomfortable—door handles, bicycle bells, buttons, scissors, can openers. Each day, these and hundreds of other items that were designed for use by the right-handed . . . But excuse me! I fear I am interrupting you.'

'Not at all. You seem very perceptive to have noticed such things. Perhaps you are left-handed?'

'No, no. In fact very few Chinese people are so. It would be corrected at an early stage . . . It is rather difficult to write Chinese characters with one's left hand, you know.'

'Yes, I do.' I had looked up at him, and had been disconcerted. He made me think at once of both Winston Churchill and Toad of Toad Hall: short and rotund, balding at the top, heavy jowls, and a voice like a rumbling butter churn—deep, rich, over-cultured and slightly monotonous. He spoke impeccable English, unusual in my experience for a Hong Kong Chinese, with an accent I associated with the playing fields of Eton rather than the far-flung corners of a moribund empire.

'My wife is left-handed, and so I have interested myself in this matter. Even language has always been unfair to the lefty. There are associations between "left" and "bad" in the minds of many persons. One greets another by shaking the right hand. In Latin the word for left is *sinister*, is it not? The same word in English means threatening, dangerous, evil.'

'Yes, and what about the French word *gauche*,' I added. 'It is invested with a derogatory connotation—awkward, clumsy, tactless.'

'Exactly!' He seemed clearly delighted by this addition to his knowledge. 'Quite right! The customs and cultures of many countries show such assumptions. In some African tribes the men insist that women prepare the food only with their right hands.'

'As do the Indians! In India it's rather rude to accept or offer anyone something with one's left hand, I believe, which is reserved for . . . er . . . reserved for . . .' My voice trailed off as I realised where my sentence had been leading.

'Yes, yes, I understand! And what about the ancient Greeks and Romans! They thought it was unlucky to hear thunder on the left.'

'And in Christian mythology Christ sits at the right hand of God, while the devil was cast into hell with the left!' I said excitedly, beginning to enjoy this impromptu dialogue.

'But nowadays, I think opinion is shifting to a more favourable point of view for the lefty,' said Winston with a shade (I felt) of disappointment. 'Tests have also shown that left-handed people are much quicker at using their left hand, than right-handed people their right. No wonder many famous table-tennis players and sportsmen are left-handed!'

'And in intelligence tests, left-handed people come out, on average, more intelligent than right-handed ones,' I contributed smugly.

'In fact, if you are left-handed, there is no need for despair!' summed up Winston Churchill in a comforting voice. 'For quite a lot of notable persons were also—Leonardo da Vinci, Michelangelo, Picasso, Raphael. And so even is England's Queen Mother!' he added triumphantly, as if to clinch the argument.

I knew nothing of the Queen Mother's left-handedness, and I had never felt despair at my condition—not, at least, my physical one. I stared out at the banks of the river where the mountains rose, crenellated against the sky like the ramparts of Gothic castles. Quoted in nearly every guidebook to China is a line from the nineteenth-century poet Han Yu, describing this river as being like a green gauze ribbon between mountains like blue jade hairpins, rather inaccurately I thought. Perhaps he was colour-blind; it seemed to me that the river was blue, winding its way in sweeping hairpin bends among mountains green-coated with vegetation. Huge clumps of lacy bamboo swayed hypnotically over the water, creaking like a ship's rigging; buffalo wallowed in the river, snorting and puffing in satisfaction; on flat rafts made from lashed bamboo trunks, locals dived to collect armfuls of long, green weed from the river bottom. Four naked children splashed at the water's edge, their bodies gleaming brown, hair splayed dripping across their foreheads; a muleteer with his animals ambled along the river bank. Humped mountains rolled past the moving boat like serried ranks of petrified tidal waves, as we drifted on through the interior of China.

On arrival in Yangshuo, the tourist groups were bundled off the boat, hurried up the main street lined by souvenir shops, put on air-conditioned buses, and driven back to Guilin with a precision and urgency that made the process seem like a military operation. Locals threw themselves hysterically at the disembarking foreigners, screaming of bangles and postcards, demanding money to be photographed with trussed-up cormorants on their shoulders. This daily hour-long tourist invasion had considerable impact on the village: menus in the tourist cafés were in English, and one could drink Horlicks and Nescafé and even eat with a knife and fork. In the evening, after the main tourist exodus, large numbers of backpackers still remained, and the locals sat out with them on the cooling streets, playing cards, eating, fanning themselves and watching the world go by. Old men with deeply wrinkled faces pulled contemplatively on long-stemmed pipes, gazing benignly at the foreigners. Street vendors cooked ears of corn over charcoal braziers, the embers winking red as dragons' eyes in the night.

The village had a very mediaeval air about it—narrow flag-stoned streets and sturdy stone houses—and indeed I suppose it had changed little over the centuries. Plastic replaced metal and clay in the market place, but otherwise a villager from the Ming Dynasty, or even the Tang Dynasty, might have felt at home among the old peasant ladies under wide-brimmed straw hats which made them look like animated mushrooms, in from the country villages with their produce. Farmers in dirty singlets, with sinewy carved-oak arms, slung sacks of grain onto the market scales, querulously debating prices, poking at the bags with suspicious fingers. In a wire cage a civet cat, with a long sensitive face and watchful eyes, waited to be eaten.

My eyes were constantly lifted in this village from the streets to the horizon, as if impelled by divine visions. 'The scenery around Guilin is the most beautiful in the world, but the scenery around Yangshuo is the finest of Guilin' goes the old saw, much referred to in guidebooks to the region. It is little wonder that it has inspired artists for hundreds of years. In traditional Chinese landscape paintings, mysteriously shaped rock forms rise out of a delicate mist, seeming to float in the heavens. The landscape depicted is not supposed to be realistic; it is meant to draw the reader into realms of Taoist imagination, by which philosophy these paintings were greatly influenced. I had always thought Chinese scrolls looked warped, the mountains seemingly all squashed up from the sides like someone's face pressed against a window. Here I seemed to be living, Alice-like, inside such a Chinese painting; here were those very domed mountains mushrooming improbably all around me, and looking just as unrealistic.

The landscape was indeed stunning, perhaps because it was more immediate than in Guilin; everywhere one looked there was a view. Huge pinnacles of limestone hemmed in the village and shot up from within Yangshuo itself, spectacular giant towers of stone, like something from another planet or a Spielberg film. It was a landscape so original it was difficult to describe; as the Song Dynasty writer Fan Chengda had commented, 'I often sent pictures of the hills of Guilin which I painted to friends, but few believed what they saw. There is no point in arguing with them . . .' Chinese tourist brochures took the plunge and described the mountains with their typical enthusiasm and delightful English as being piled up like the petals of a lotus blossom, and claimed they would 'make you feel intoxicant'.

The next few days were spent cycling, spiritually intoxicant, through the countryside around Yangshuo—the bicycle rented for the handsome sum of one *yuan* a day. I rode out to the appropriately named Moon Hill, which had a huge hole through its centre in the shape of a crescent. Up this hill I laboured in the intense heat, eight hundred steps and a stiff scramble to the summit, to find a Frenchman perched on the top like a broody hen. I knew he was French even before he spoke; he had those chic tortoiseshell frames of disproportionate size on his glasses, and was wearing a casual pastel-coloured T-shirt with 'Lacoste' written on it in green. He wore Italian loafers and the bottoms of his trousers were neatly turned up to reveal a length of white sock in the fashionable continental style. He looked like a character from a French television advertisement for yogurt, and had the same fresh good looks.

'Zer are many ladders,' he said phlegmatically as I panted to a halt beside him.

'Steps.'

'*Pardon?*'

'*Ce sont des marches*, steps. Not ladders,' I explained. The Frenchman looked at me suspiciously, as if I might be making fun of him, and did not reply.

I turned and gazed out at the scenery, wave after wave of peaks retreating into the distance until they were no more than a purple smudge on the horizon. Down in the valleys crawled reed-fringed rivers. Flooded rice paddies shimmered in the sun, and compact mud-brick villages huddled at the foot of the almost sheer precipices which rose skywards above them. A line of poplar trees cut across the flatness of the valley bottom, embossed against the eggshell sky with phallic prominence.

'I shall descend the ladder,' announced the Frenchman grandly, unfolding himself from his squat. '*Au revoir.*'

'*Au revoir,*' I said sourly, and then to myself: 'May you break your stiff neck on your damned ladder.'

Back down at the hill's bottom, a woman was selling drinks and postcards; more excitingly, my eye lit on the spine of a book—Chairman Mao's infamous Little Red Book. It had been out of print for years and I had searched Chengdu high and low for a copy. After some hard bargaining I became its owner for seven *yuan*. I asked the woman what she thought of Mao; she trotted out the old party line that he was a good leader but had made some mistakes, notably in launching the Cultural Revolution. Then she added, 'And he killed Lin Biao.' Lin Biao had been Mao's defence minister and his closest comrade-in-arms, who had officially died in a plane crash while fleeing to the Soviet Union in 1971 after supposedly plotting to assassinate Mao and overthrow the government.

'Shot down his plane,' the woman elaborated, lifting her arms skywards from her frayed cuffs as if firing at a brace of duck.

'And Deng Xiaoping? What do you think of him?' I asked boldly.

Her face clouded. 'Very bad man. He killed many students in Beijing.'

'Who told you that? Was it on television?'

'No, no. The television and radio tell us nothing, it's all lies. Some foreigners told me,' muttered the woman. She was getting uneasy at this interrogation. She fiddled with the items spread out before her, straightening the trinkets and shuffling through her postcards.

'And do you believe them?'

'Yes. And some people from the town'—she meant Yangshuo—'returned from the cities, where they were students. They told us many things about the turmoil.'

'Does everybody in the countryside know this?'

'Yes. They know now.'

I cycled off, contemplating this percolation of news into such a small village despite the intense and omnipresent government propaganda. My thoughts were suddenly interrupted by three men in the fields with a water buffalo, who called and gesticulated to me. I could not imagine what they wanted and, propping my bike against a willow tree, moved towards them, threading my way across a maze of tiny fields along the tops of the dikes surrounding the rice paddies. I arrived out of breath, flustered. The three men huddled around me, one of them old, old, his thin hands as yellow and wrinkled as mediaeval parchment. He fumbled in his trouser pocket.

'Cigarette!' he announced suddenly, making me jump, generously waving under my nose a gold and red packet as crumpled as his face. I put my hand over my heart in an age-old Chinese gesture.

'I'm not able,' I declined politely.

'Take it, take it!' He offered them to the other two men, who each took one. 'Take it, foreign friend!'

'Really, *bu hui, bu hui*. I'm not able. I don't smoke. It's very kind of you.'

The old man looked disappointed. I knew it was rude to decline a gift in China, especially one so generously offered. I suspected these men had simply wanted to see me close up, but I knew also that their gesture was part of the age-long Chinese hospitality to strangers. Freed from their pointless inhuman bureaus and ticket offices, or never having known them, like these peasants, the Chinese could be both generous and affable. I exchanged halting pleasantries, embarrassed for the first time in my life by being a non-smoker, before hurrying away.

The sky had darkened. It was the unpredictable monsoon season in the south of China. The rain, like threads on a loom, curtained the mountains, soon completely hidden in the greyness. I hunkered down under a huge and ancient banyan

tree, next to a tiny old lady with a face as eroded as the surrounding hills, who peered at me benignly from under her
coolie hat. I looked back at her but the woman did not say anything; I did not know what she was thinking. We squatted in
companionable silence until the rain stopped. I felt very happy,
entirely comfortable in the company of this Chinese peasant.
Shortly I got on my bicycle and rode off. Soon the rain began
again with renewed tropical energy, the steam rising off the hot
tarmac like a miasma, warm against my legs.

I arrived back at the hotel like a bedraggled dog, my pile
of fifty-*yuan* notes soggy and my passport unfortunately not
much better, the numerous multicoloured exit and entry stamps
running surrealistically across the pages. Only Mao's words of
wisdom remained miraculously dry. I tramped up the stairs and
stood outside my door, dripping. It seemed I didn't have my
key with me. The *fuwuyuan* or floor attendant, who was probably off in some dark corner reading a magazine, was nowhere
to be seen. This was maybe just as well; I confused the two
words *laoshi* and *yaoshi*, one which meant 'key' and the other
'rat', and I was always worried I would announce to someone
that my rat had gone missing. I hovered uncertainly in the
corridor, feeling cold and foolish, until the *fuwuyuan* appeared.

'Hello,' she said. I ignored her guilty look, so that she could
save face at not having been where she was needed.

'Are you German?' she asked unexpectedly. I stared at her.

'No. British.'

She looked puzzled. 'But the British always have umbrellas!'
She was grinning in spite of herself now at my bedraggled appearance. 'Only the Germans walk about in the rain and get wet!'

She opened the door of my room for me with a flourish, as
if pleased at her observation, and I sidled sheepishly inside.

I met the Frenchman again on my last night, in the streets of
Yangshuo near my hotel. To my surprise he said good evening
and stopped to speak to me. He was wearing another Lacoste
T-shirt, a pink one, pale and crisp as strawberry sorbet. After
the usual opening comments the conversation faltered to a
halt. I shifted from foot to foot.

'Did you know that if all the Chinese stood on boxes one metre high and jumped off at the same time, the force of them all landing would knock the earth out of its orbit?' I said in a nervous rush.

'No, I did not know.' I found the bland indifference of his tone, his lack of even feigned interest, shocking.

I gave a forced laugh, and cracked my knuckles. 'No. Yes, well.'

'I am going to the restaurant,' he replied in a querying tone of voice so that I realised after a moment, to my consternation, that it was an invitation.

'Oh! Well, *bonsoir et bon appétit*' I replied, pretending mis-understanding, fleeing down the street towards the river and peace.

That last evening in Yangshuo was beautiful. Fresh skies invented and destroyed frescoes of clouds, rose-tinted by the caresses of the declining sun, with the alternating beauty and cruelty of the artistic genius. At the river's edge, as dusk fell, I watched the fishermen set out, poling themselves along against the current. They fished by an ancient and unique method using cormorants; a string around the birds' necks prevented them from swallowing their prey, and they returned their catch to the boats. Periodically they were awarded a fish by their masters; then these handsome birds perched at the prows of the punts, preening themselves and holding out their wings to be ruffled in the night breeze. The huge rock chimneys across the water were gleaming in the moonlight, as unreal as a landscape from *The Lord of the Rings*. I sat at the river's edge with a bot-tle of beer, admiring the scenery as had the ancient Chinese poets over their wine cups. Insects spun erratically around my head. I drank my beer and listened to the night. Soon, as the tourist blurb had suggested, these hills made me feel intoxi-cant. The lights on the prows of the fishing boats gleamed dull orange, luring fish to death. The towering Manhattan of mountains jostled for space in the darkness, squeezing each other up into absurd shapes. In the dark sky, the moon was like a tear in the black curtain of the night, giving a glimpse of a luminous heaven.

city of snakes

A Chinese bus station at six o'clock in the morning is a scene straight from Eliot's *The Waste Land*, and Yangshuo's was no exception. Men, neither living nor dead, with their eyes fixed on their black-slippered feet, slumped patiently around the walls of the draughty waiting room that seemed to echo with lost memory and desire. An elderly woman with a corrugated face sat huddled in one corner, eating out of a paper bag hidden in her pocket. She would dip her hand in then slip its concealed contents into her mouth as if afraid of condemnation. She worked her jaws slowly and methodically, and did not look as if she were enjoying it. A row of ticket windows turned blind eyes on the scene, closed over with cracked wooden boards and peeling rusted paint, and on a wall was spread a map of provincial transportation routes, its grubbiness betraying any offer of adventure. Empty cans and fluttering scraps of rubbish stirred under the benches.

By seven o'clock I was ensconced on the local bus bound for Wuzhou. The mood changed suddenly, like the bewildering vision of the kaleidoscope through which I seemed to be viewing this nation. The countryside was a landscape to absorb and breathe, at once exhilarating and grand yet belittling and awesome. The water of the river was inky blue in the early light, divided by a gleaming streak of rippling gold sun, a mother-of-pearl sky and early morning mists making the fields as ethereal as a photo in soft focus. The figures of stooping peasants seemed to float between heaven and earth.

I was very uncomfortable and very hot, squeezed up against a local who could only have been a pig farmer and who ate sunflower seeds, spitting the shells onto the floor with a repetitiveness born of boredom. The bus driver blared his horn and crashed through the gears with true Chinese enthusiasm, drifting down hills in uncannily silent neutral, as if exhausted by his efforts. But somehow none of this mattered, for as the morning grew older I passed through what was perhaps the most beautiful countryside I had ever seen, a patchwork of maize, rice, bean, sugar cane, peanut and tobacco fields among the dramatic karst rock piles and sharply eroded pinnacles. Along the road passed buffalo and wobbling bicycles with squawking chickens hanging upside down over the back wheels, blue-smocked farmers with hoes over their shoulders, or women with full baskets of cabbages. Chinese peasants produce more rice, sweet potatoes, millet and barley than any other country in the world, but I was not deceived by the abundance or the picturesque landscape, created by generations of drudgery in the grilling heat of summer and equally gruelling dampness of winter. In the small villages locals stood about irresolutely among their spectacular geography, with the air of people waiting for something they know will never happen, weary resignation etched on their work-stained faces.

We stopped for lunch by the roadside, where a small shop displayed fusty packaged biscuits and sticky green drinks crouched under glass panes thick with dust and fingerprints. The locals and the bus passengers squatting by the side of the road watched me sadly, their faces devoid of all animosity or friendliness. I bought a bunch of finger-sized bananas and ate them furtively, almost apologetically. Eyes watched me as, feeling nervous, I peeled and consumed them, pressing their squashiness against my palate. I dropped the mottled peels by the roadside and returned to the bus, away from the watchfulness. It was uncannily quiet, like the last moments before a dreadful cataclysm. I stared at the seat in front of me. There was a tear in the plastic; yellow sponge spilt from it like pus from a suppurating wound.

Eventually the karst landscape fell away, replaced by wild rolling highlands, the valley bottoms a vivid grasshopper-green spread of rice paddies, with the odd misty sprinkle of delicate yellow rapeseed tucked in at random, as if grown as an after-thought. The greys and purples of the hilltops suggested the highlands of Scotland; closer at hand, entire hillsides terraced by generations of Chinese families dispelled the illusion. Finally the bus trailed sullenly into Wuzhou, rattling with exhaustion. In the first decades of this century Wuzhou, perched high on the riverbanks to avoid monsoon flooding, had been an import-ant foreign missionary post and riverine commercial centre with numerous trading companies, a Western hospital and a British consulate. Now it was a small industrial town, its only claim to being cosmopolitan its hovercraft link with Hong Kong.

I made my way to the bus station and joined the melee to obtain a boat ticket to Canton, barging and elbowing my way towards the counter among a crush of people swaying back and forwards. ('Beauty and gentlemen, that is the impression I get from British films,' a Chinese had once informed me, but I did not feel British here.) On reaching the window, I held on firmly to the ledge to avoid being swept away and, peering through the tiny aperture, yelled in Chinese 'I want one boat ticket to Canton, leaving tonight!'

Fortunately the harassed woman entombed behind the aper-ture was in no mood for debate.

'Eight o'clock?' she queried back, as arms pushed in all around me, thrusting money through the window and demand-ing a similar ticket.

'Good!' I replied.

A moment later I was clutching my stub of cardboard. I did not have to turn and leave; no sooner did I let go of the ledge than I was brushed aside by the struggling proletariat and swept helplessly out of the building into the town's crowded streets. Wuzhou was very Dickensian in appearance, with ram-shackle red-brick buildings and small cottage industries hidden down narrow alleyways blackened by soot and smoke. Grubby children scrambled over heaps of charcoal, conversing shrilly, while their mothers crouched over sewing machines, silently twisting cloth under the dancing needles. High along the river was an esplanade of beaten earth shaded by plane trees. People squatted under the trees, shirts and trouser legs rolled up in the heat, spitting and fanning themselves and staring at the foreign devil. One man stopped to scrutinise me and moved to the other side to get a better look; I stared back, but he was impervious. He had a lean and hungry look that had always made me uneasy, like those peddlers that importuned one with drugs in Bangkok. His hair stuck up in tufts and he had eyes narrow as button holes.

Rashly, I got out my diary and started writing in it in order to screen myself, but immediately drew a crowd of curious onlookers fascinated by my left-handedness and the outlandish letters with which I covered the page. I looked up at them, but nobody flinched or seemed embarrassed.

'Can I help you?' I asked sarcastically in Chinese, and then, 'I don't like you staring at me!'

But there was no response; perhaps my intonation or dialect was wrong and they thought I was speaking English. I could not concentrate on what I was writing. 'Wuzhou very Dickensian,' I scrawled. And then, 'Why are you looking at me, please go away.' My writing wavered irresolutely across the page. I shut my book with a snap. I felt oppressed and frightened.

This staring was to be the one thing with which I would never come to terms. I learned to live with the deferential politeness of Chinese acquaintances and the indifference and rudeness of bureaucrats, with the spitting and fetid public toilets and bad roads, with the sometimes incomprehensible attitudes. But I never managed to ignore the staring. It was bearable in the cities, but in the small towns and villages it often reached a crescendo of intensity. Infrequently it made me angry and aggressive, for I saw it as a violation of my privacy. More often I felt irritable and intimidated, even persecuted, under the constant scrutiny. Coming to China had given me a sharp indication of my own strangeness that I knew I would never lose, like a middle-aged woman who studies herself long and objectively in the mirror and suddenly realises she looks old. The thousand eyes watching me were the thousand new angles of my own self-awareness, and all the normality accepted since birth—in myself, in my society—was rendered outlandish. That was the thrill and the terror of China.

Finally, with relief, I boarded the boat and set off on the fourteen-hour journey down the Xi River to Canton. A long wooden platform divided by slats formed coffin-like beds in the cavernous interior of the vessel. Beside me an elderly lady sat bolt upright against her enormous cardboard box, which bore the legend *Handle with Care* in English and Chinese; I spent the first hour idly memorising the strokes of these new characters. With her was a young woman, seemingly her granddaughter, fumbling with a letter which she read over and over. She caught me stealing curious glances at her.

'Perhaps you think it is from my boyfriend?' she asked in English. She blushed and giggled slightly, whether with the enormity of the idea of having a boyfriend or in nervousness at speaking to a foreigner I couldn't be sure.

'No, not at all,' I lied courteously.

'In fact,' she continued, 'it is from my younger brother who is studying at university in Kunming. Reading his letter, I feel a pang of sadness. He says how he misses his mother, father and sisters. He says he has realised for the first time what loneliness is like. I feel strange in the change of feelings at the moment when people are together and apart. My brother and I always quarrelled like sparrows at home. I blamed him for being lazy, disorderly and for coming home late. I once told him angrily that he had better go to university in a place far from home so that he wouldn't annoy me any more!'

'And what did he say to that?'

'He laughed, and said it would be pleasant to do that, and enjoy his freedom. But now both of us begin to miss each other! And now my letters are full of concern for my younger brother. I tell him to take good care of himself, that I love him and miss him. I decide that I will treat him well when he comes home for the winter vacation!'

The girl folded her letter away, putting it into an orange bag. The boat chugged on slowly through the evening. Men stood around in their long-johns, brushing their teeth and spitting ostentatiously, and then lay down motionlessly on the hard boards, heads resting on their battered luggage.

'But please don't think I don't have a happy family, always fighting!' whispered the girl, as if confiding a desperate secret. 'In fact I am very lucky. My father is a kind man. He likes to help people who are in trouble. He always worked until midnight in order to benefit the workers. He retired last year, but he often goes back to his unit and gives the manager advice. He built a garden behind the house and planted several kinds of flowers such as roses, peonies, orchids and chry-san-the-mums.' She stumbled over the little-used word. I felt sleepy, listening to her whispering in the dimness like a dry wind through reeds. 'He practises *taiji* in the garden every morning. I like to sit there to read or knit.'

'I practise *taiji* also,' I said proudly. I felt a bit ashamed at my boast, but happy that by it I had appropriated a piece of China.

'I also have an elder sister. She is very clever and beautiful. Her eyes are very big! She is employed by a chemical factory. I advised her to take an examination at the film institute, because she always is longing to be an actress. I hope she will succeed! This is my grandmother,' the girl added breathlessly. 'She is eighty-five years of age, but just as fit as a young woman!'

As if aware that we were talking about her, the old woman smiled and nodded guilelessly, still sitting against her enormous box. *Handle with Care*. Outside, through the portholes of the slow-moving boat on which I was exploring the interior of the country, the evening had descended. The dark smudge of the landscape had mellowed to a deep purple in the low light, filling in the horizon like a theatrical backdrop, only its contours and muted shadows giving the idea of ridges, valleys and hills. I lay in my coffin, listening to the engines rumbling and the slow slosh, slosh of the water outside, as the boat passed into the shadowed night.

At first light I was awakened by the clatter of tin mugs and gargling as the Chinese washed. They produced towels from their bags, dampening them before pressing them against their faces and necks delicately, as though cleaning wounds. I felt dishevelled and disorganised, and watched in fascination. The Chinese were tireless washers, always scrubbing and soaping in never-ending ritual, like a ceremonial cleansing that absolved them of the day's hardship. Marco Polo had been fascinated too. He had noted how clean the Chinese were, bathing in cold water every day and washing before each meal; the public baths in Hangzhou, he claimed, were the finest in the world.

Centuries later, when Versailles was built by the French king as the epitome of Western civilisation, it did not contain a single washroom, bath or toilet. I felt unclean; I was a foreign devil. The Chinese thought white people smelt of dead bodies—hadn't I read that somewhere?

My companion was already awake, sitting up with newly brushed hair. She started talking as soon as she saw me stir, as if she had been waiting impatiently for a sign of life. Her grandmother was still propped against her box; I wondered if she had stayed that way all night. I wondered what was in her box but I did not ask, shy that my all-encompassing curiosity about China would be interpreted as prying.

'I have a good hobby, which is that I brush my teeth every night, while I have a bad one that I don't brush my teeth every morning!' My new-found friend laughed merrily at her own joke as she watched the rest of the passengers scrubbing themselves.

By this time the sun was visible and we had entered the Pearl River, which flows through Canton southwards to empty into the South China Sea between Hong Kong and Macao. We were passing through Guangdong Province, of which Canton, with a population of more than five million, is the capital. According to legend, five gods descended here in ancient times bearing rice stalks, as a symbol that the area would always produce in plenty. Guangdong is indeed a lush coastal province that yields three rice crops a year and an abundance of vegetables, sugar cane, wheat and fruit. The area is especially famous for lychees, I noted in horror, as I loathed the fruit. The Tang Dynasty Emperor Ming Huang had them relayed with all possible speed to his northern court, to have them fresh for his favourite concubine. The eleventh-century poet Su Shi wrote a poem entitled 'Lament for Lychees' about this practice, and the men who lost their lives in the breakneck attempt to transport the fruits northwards before they lost their freshness.

Gradually agricultural land gave way to ugly factories on the riverbanks, and we sailed upriver into the heart of the city. Because of this navigable river Canton (known to the Chinese as Guangzhou) became the gateway to China; the Indians

Boxing with Shadows

arrived there in the second century, followed by the Arabs and Persians. In 714 it was declared a foreign trade centre, and the area soon boomed after years of being a remote backwater to which disobedient court officials were banished. More than a hundred thousand foreigners, mostly Arabs, lived in Canton at that time. When the Portuguese received permission to set up a base at Macao in 1557, the British and other Europeans soon followed.

From the boat docks where in past times Arab dhows and foreign opium ships had berthed, I walked back along the river's edge for several kilometres to the centre of the city. Modern Canton began to develop in the 1920s, when the notorious sampans housing brothels, reeking of perfume, river water and opium, were cleared away from the waterfront along with their euphemistically named occupants, the flower girls, and broad leafy avenues in the French style were laid down. The esplanade along the river was now thronged with people, photographers, pineapple vendors, fortune-tellers with their charts spread out on the pavement, workmen, Chinese tourists, lounging policemen in crumpled uniforms. Eventually I arrived at the Guangzhou Youth Hostel on Shamian Island. I took a cold shower, washing off the grime of my boat journey, and lay down under a huge fan that whirred slowly from the ceiling.

Directly across from my own humble accommodation, as if in tantalising mockery, stood the best-known and most luxurious tourist establishment not only in Canton but perhaps in the whole of China. The White Swan Hotel (member of the Leading Hotels of the World), a joint venture of the Guangzhou Tourist Authority and a group of Hong Kong companies, was the last word in Western decadence, a hundred-metre-tall ivory-coloured skyscraper on the edge of the river, boasting everything from a swimming pool and closed-circuit television to an extortionately priced Japanese restaurant and European grill room. One could get one's hair styled, have a massage, dance in the nightclub, use the six-hundred seat conference hall, or wallow in a jacuzzi. I looked around it that evening, glad that I had showered and dressed decently. The locals trooped uneasily into the air-conditioned luxury, over the marble floors, and stared in disbelief at the sumptuous lobby complete with its own waterfall. They took photos of each other in ludicrous poses, standing on the hump-backed bridge in front of the cascade, before withdrawing; one night in this hotel would cost ten months' wages, while the price of a suite (with views east and west over the Pearl River) would keep them fed for a year.

Guidebooks for foreign businesspeople claim the staff at this hotel (all two thousand of them) are the best-trained and most efficient in all China, all able to speak three languages and dedicated to the happiness of each and every guest. Despite these claims and the hotel's opulence, however, the staff seemed just as surly and inefficient as anywhere else; perhaps I didn't look sufficiently business-like. When I bought a croissant in the much-vaunted French bakery, no change could be found for my humble ten-*yuan* note; in exasperation I took another croissant and a cream bun and told the unamiable clerk to keep the change. Hostesses tripped around in glittering *cheongsams* slit up the thigh, smiles painted on in pink lipstick. Jacketed servants opened the entrance doors after a slight pause that was like a slap in the face. But I was sympathetic. Their hesitation seemed to bridge some awful abyss between the egalitarianism promulgated by their government and the hard reality of foreigners' dollars.

This was the lesson of the White Swan Hotel, and of Canton. It was an uneasy city, a communist city of collective ideals that thronged with thousands of aspiring capitalists only wanting to serve themselves. It was a city suspended between two views of its own destiny, and in the eyes of the doorkeepers I saw it mirrored, in a flash of mixed hostility and acceptance.

Shamian Island, on which the White Swan Hotel and youth hostel were built, lay in the Pearl River, separated by what was little more than a ditch from the rest of Canton. There were no cars on the island and it was very pleasant and quiet, a secluded patch of old colonial buildings; it could almost have been a genteel, decaying suburb of London. The similarity was not coincidental; it was here that foreigners had been permitted to set up their trading houses in the eighteenth century, joined to the rest of the city by two bridges but otherwise strictly separated from the Chinese.

The British had come to Canton to purchase tea and silk, paying in silver, and had soon realised that a ready way to redress this trade imbalance was to sell vast quantities of opium, grown in British India, to the Chinese. The imperial government, however, prohibited opium smoking from 1729, and its cultivation and importation from 1800. An official edict closed Canton to the opium trade which was draining China of money and health, and Commissioner Lin, a government mandarin in charge of customs at Canton, wrote a letter of protest to Queen Victoria, asking that her subjects refrain from violating the laws laid down by the Celestial Court. But his plea fell on deaf ears, and the edict gave the British the excuse they needed to start what became known as the Opium Wars. Begun in 1837, the First Opium War culminated in the extortionate 1842 Treaty of Nanking (now Nanjing). Shamian Island on the Pearl River became a British and French concession. Hong Kong, an uninhabited and rather swampy island in the South China Sea at the mouth of the Pearl River, was ceded to Britain.

The Chinese have long memories. In Chengdu I had been told by a local that it was sometimes known as the City of Hibiscus; when I answered that I had not seen any such flowers, my informer had laughed. 'It was in the Five Dynasties Period,' she had answered, and the fact that that was in the tenth century and hibiscus had not been seen since did not seem to matter in the slightest. I had been reminded, too, by numerous Chinese of British perfidy during the Opium Wars, and had never been sure if they had been joking or serious in seeming to hold me responsible. Whatever the case, Canton was not the place to proclaim one's Britishness, and I skulked through the city slightly apologetically, as if atoning for the imperialist violence of my forebears.

I fled from Shamian Island and its English facades and took refuge in Canton's largest food market, not far from the Pearl River. There was a long street devoted exclusively to spices—sackloads of earthy-coloured powders and dried roots, herbs and grasses—as well as streets with the usual collection of meat and vegetables. Markets are the centre of Chinese life; half the urban Chinese salary is spent on food (as opposed to about one-fifth in the West). Each item was chosen with care to see if it was fresh. Women poked and prodded each potato or tomato, turning it round and holding it up as if suspecting it of being an imitation, and then haggled inexhaustibly over the price, holding up fingers in canny semaphore. I pushed through them, avoiding their swinging bamboo baskets.

Soon cabbages and slabs of pork gave way to more unusual buys, the wide range of animal species for which the southern Chinese cuisine is famous. 'The Cantonese will eat anything with four legs,' runs a northern Chinese witticism, 'except a table', and the proof was before my eyes in wire cages containing oddly silent cats and dogs. There were animals here with not just four but any number of legs, or none at all—numerous bird species and snakes, as well as basins of frogs and toads, eels, crabs and strange sea creatures. A beautiful wild feline lay cramped in a tiny cage, its white-freckled nose thrust trembling through the wire, hazel eyes flecked with gold. I stared at two scruffy grey dogs, sickened but fascinated. They looked unkempt and emaciated, and I wondered how much meat they would provide. Beside them in a box was a rare pangolin like a tattered parody of itself, half its scales missing. Snakes were available by the scoopful, entangled like licorice.

I had intended to try some of Canton's culinary exotica, and had even investigated the menu of its most famous snake restaurant on Jianglan Road, which offered thirty different dishes. One could eat snake braised, fried, boiled, fricasseed or stewed, stuffed with chicken liver, coated in shrimp paste, or simply chopped into cubes in the famous Dragon-Tiger-Phoenix Soup, which also contained cat and chicken (cat could be omitted for a cheaper meal). But the miserable conditions in which these creatures were kept in their market cages put me off. 'Birds in their nests agree / With Chinamen, but not with me,' Hillaire Belloc had written and I could only, after wandering through Canton's market, agree with him.

Back in my room I lay on my bed and thumbed through my guidebooks to find a restaurant with more normal fare. One could not actually eat the famous *chop suey* here, I knew; it had been invented in San Francisco during the gold rushes to use up leftovers, and could not be found in China. On the other hand, one could find crab meat and shark's fin consommé, I read. Fried duck web in oyster sauce in the Beiyuan Restaurant (telephone 333365). Pigeon in plum sauce. Roast pig skin. Chopped crab meat balls (which sounded particularly painful). Crab cutlet with pig's brain. One could eat all these delicacies in pagodas and pavilions, under bamboo and beside picturesque lakes, in restaurants with five floors and ten floors and ebony cabinets and roof gardens and tree-filled courtyards . . .

I stood at a street corner, sucking at a bowl of noodles from a peddler's stall. Now that the Chinese had enough to eat I did not understand this interest in freakishness, the desire to consume animal oddities. It seemed self-indulgently perverse. Sometimes I wondered if it were not a hysterical search for the good life, unleashed by a relatively prosperous present after centuries of semi-starvation: 'Look at me, I choose to eat expensive snake, which my forebears ate because they had nothing else.' In this respect the Cantonese were like Western yuppies who ate coarse bread and became vegetarians; the peasant food was a statement of their new-found economic freedom of choice, and maybe too it involved a nostalgic hearkening back to a simpler, less complicated (and romanticised) past. Whatever the case, this relish for the grotesque seemed very Cantonese. This was Snake City, where necessity had become indulgence, but where purpose did not seem clear.

I ate my bland and meatless noodles, and became entangled in an English conversation with a worker keen for practice. His name was Mr Lao. He had approached me sideways, in a skulking crab-like motion, and I thought he would ask me to change money—everyone did in Canton. But he did not. He told me instead of his father, retired from the army, who had been unhappy with his unaccustomed leisure.

'I became worried about him. If always living the empty life, he would become much older and his bad mood would affect his health!'

One day Mr Lao had seen an advertisement for Guangzhou Elderly University which would soon be enrolling students for new courses such as cookery, dancing, *taiji* and photography. He had persuaded his father to join.

'Since then he has been studying at this special university. He takes two courses, photography and drawing. From that time on he has changed. He is very eager. By diligent work, he can draw much better than before. Moreover, he is very satisfied with his lessons and interested in his new hobby. Every time he goes out he brings his camera to take souvenirs of the wonderful world.' Mr Lao nodded pleasantly, smiling.

'Thank you. Goodbye sir!'

He wandered off, satisfied that with this glimpse he had given me of his private life he had improved his English. I did not mind. I finished my noodles and stood thinking of universities for the elderly. I was tired of finding meanings in things. I thought, in a vague, desultory fashion, that these universities were a good idea. Then I went back to my room and lay down on my bed, thinking of nothing at all, and fell asleep.

Universities for the retired seemed part of the get-ahead attitude of the Cantonese. Canton is one of a number of specially designated Special Economic Zones along China's southern and eastern coasts, with regional economic autonomy and preferential investment policies. They were set up chiefly to promote foreign and Overseas Chinese investment in the People's Republic, using the incentives of reduced taxation, a plentiful supply of labour, and low operating costs. Canton had been the first city to be designated a Special Economic Zone, and although it had not progressed as rapidly as Shenzhen on the Hong Kong border, which was the most successful Economic Zone, growing prosperity was nonetheless evident. The city's main department store was not only air-conditioned but contained a wide range of electronics, stereos, hair-dryers, refrigerators, sewing machines, kitchen blenders and futuristic-looking vacuum cleaners. All these things were luxuries to the Chinese. I had never seen the likes of any of them in Chengdu, and I gaped like a Guangdong peasant at the displays (grandfather clocks priced at nine thousand *yuan*—six years' salary for a Chinese teacher! I thought wonderingly). Well-dressed middle-aged Hong Kong Chinese with fashionable hairdos, tall pale northerners looking slightly nervous in this city where they couldn't understand the language, shabby peasants in from the countryside for the day, all jostled for space at the counters. Along Beijing Road was a further range of enticements: a music shop selling flutes, cymbals and traditional two-stringed *erhu*; a traditional medicine store; a sports shop bedecked with footballs and jogging suits hung out like mediaeval banners in a banqueting hall; book stores; pet shops; barber shops; beauty parlours hung with posters of Chinese starlets. Industries produced ships, steel, cars, chemicals and fertilisers, sugar, machinery, clothes and textiles, canned food and rubber goods, as well as more traditional bamboo products, pottery, jade and jewellery. The shops bulged with a veritable cornucopia of goodies.

Somewhere in the back of my mind I had always imagined communism to be a grey nightmare of snaking bread queues and empty shops, as it was in Moscow. I was constantly surprised in China, not by the Chinese, but by my own narrowness of vision. In reality the newspapers often extolled the initiative of entrepreneurs, and suggested that making money might be glorious, as long as it were made in the correct spirit (to further the prosperity of China, not that of the individual). In the 1980s all urban Chinese had longed for the Four Big New Things (cassette player or radio, washing machine, colour television and refrigerator), but now shops also displayed compact-disc players, video machines, foreign cigarettes and freezers. Massive billboards advertising Volkswagens lined the streets. There were less than a million cars in all China, nearly all run by companies and factories, and I doubted that many private individuals in Canton could have afforded a Volkswagen. Yet it seemed clear that for some urban Chinese, at least, the time of the Four Big Things had long passed.

This certainly appeared to be the case in Canton, which was unabashedly consumer-oriented. Money-making was the new revolution. The Cantonese had a saying which summed up their attitude to life in general and living under a socialist economy in particular: 'If the traffic light is green, drive as fast as you can. If the light is red, drive around it.' In the end, when the wonder had worn off, these shops made me nervous; they presaged a difficult future. Advertising hoardings jostled for attention beside family planning posters, displaying the delights of Panda washing powder, Volkswagen Santanas, instant coffee and industrial products, including steamrollers. (I could not read the characters, and pondered in amusement on how one might promote the attractions of a steamroller.) Often I wondered if these advertisements were not also an eventual writing on the wall. Behind the statue of Mao in Chengdu, for several weeks, had hung a screaming blue advertisement for Tampax. It was an amusing but uneasy juxtaposition, for these new economics sat uncomfortably with political rigidity. Canton seemed to embody this new Chinese tug-of-war. Beijing was far away in space and spirit, and just down the road Hong Kong loomed as large as had the Great American Dream for the early settlers. One could (illegally) tune into its television and pay taxi drivers in Hong Kong dollars. Trendy adolescents, I discovered, liked to set their watches by Hong Kong time (an hour different from that of China, which ran on Beijing time, no matter how far away the capital was). Indeed Canton was in many ways a preview to the British colony—the roads might have been termed expressways, street names were translated into English rather than transliterated into *pinyin*, and the grey city was loud with neon lighting for Western products: Peugeot, Dunlop, Maxwell House ('Good to the last drop'), Slazenger and Shell. French perfume, Levi jeans and Benetton T-shirts were big sellers in this town, as they were in Hong Kong.

To arrive in Canton from Guangxi Region was like coming to a different country. The people were not only far better dressed and made no bones about accumulating wealth, but were darker-skinned, speaking swift, alien Cantonese. They were boisterously different, the Italians of China, talkative, lovers of good food, with a reputation for being passionate and volatile. Canton was their city, and reflected their character.

I thought one day to find respite from the bustle of Canton's streets in Yuexin Park, the city's largest, sprawling in the north of the city. I might have known better by this time, for Wangjiang Park, beside the university campus in Chengdu, was the only pleasant park I had visited in China. For the most part Chinese parks were more a source of local entertainment than a retreat to the outdoors for quiet relaxation. 'You glorify nature and meditate on her,' a Chinese had written two centuries before the birth of Christ, and then added, 'Why not domesticate and regulate her?' Here in Canton couples, screaming theatrically, rowed in rusting tin boats on a stagnant artificial lake, or took photos of each other standing in front of hideous statuary, or rotted their teeth on expensive American soft drinks, the whole circus accompanied by music piped over speakers—'Brown Girl in the Ring', 'Que Sera Sera' and 'La Vie en Rose' in shrill, unflattering Cantonese.

There was a swimming pool here, and a stadium that could hold thirty thousand people, all of whom now seemed to be crashing through the rockeries. An unused rollercoaster tottered in a twisting pile of metal like the spine of a stegosaurus in a provincial museum, the only quiet corner of the park, where courting pairs skulked under the iron, chastely holding hands and whispering, just as they did around the pond at Sichuan University. The six-hundred-year-old Zhenhai Tower, now housing the city museum, I could not find; perhaps I was just in a daze. To me the final outrage was the white horse painted with black stripes to resemble a zebra. The modern Chinese, one billion strong, had had little chance to develop any appreciation of solitude or quietness, or even of nature. In the end, this park made me feel exactly what it wanted me to feel—a curious onlooker with the world as a theatrical set, to be walked over and sat upon and concreted to make way for little booths selling Coca-Cola.

Sightseeing, especially visiting parks, I had already realised, was not a satisfactory part of travelling in China; it was frequently mechanical, almost obligatory and rarely culturally or spiritually fulfilling. Tourist sites, like parks, were mostly artificial, Disney World creations made to satisfy the Chinese delight in imitation and spectacle. They made me feel bored and restless, and slightly frightened of the never-ending flow of people. Few Chinese would ever have chosen to be alone in a park. As a solo traveller I frequently found myself an object of pity and concerned solicitude and curious stares that left me wondering if there was not something wrong with me. Now couples' murmuring seemed like a mockery, and every laugh was directed at me. I felt an urgent desire to leave Canton, maybe even China. For the first time I was homesick.

I emerged from the park with my nerves on edge, and unwisely headed for the nearby CAAC airline office. A counter proclaimed *Information* in English.

'Hello, do you speak English?' A shake of the head. '*Ni hui shuo putonghua ma?*' No, she apparently didn't speak Mandarin either, despite it being the supposed *lingua franca* among the Babel of Chinese dialects. The salesgirl made no other move to help but I stood pointedly waiting, and she trailed away to return with someone who spoke English.

'I'd like a CAAC flight timetable, please.'

'Don't have one.'

'Well, can you tell me if CAAC operates flights from Xiamen to Chengdu?' A pause.

'This is Guangzhou.'

'Yes, I know that.' I repeated my question.

'Don't know.' And then, making a supreme effort to be helpful, 'Try counter number three.'

Counter number three was the sales desk for Overseas Chinese and Foreign Friends, and after waiting in line for twenty minutes I made my inquiry again.

'We can't book that flight here, you have to go to Xiamen to do that,' said the pigtailed woman behind the glass. She sighed heavily, perhaps at my stupidity, perhaps in sheer boredom.

'I don't want to book a flight, actually, I just want to know if the flight exists!'

'I don't know. You have to go to Xiamen and ask.'

'But I don't *want* to go to Xiamen unless there's a flight to Chengdu! I have to be back there by the end of next week.' I felt a sinking feeling somewhere below my ribcage. This conversation seemed depressingly familiar.

'Oh, well, perhaps you should find a CAAC timetable.'

'Perhaps *you* should find a CAAC timetable,' I snapped crossly, almost shouting in frustration. She looked shocked at the suggestion.

'But we don't have one of those here!'

In 1985 the Chinese government began a Spiritual Civilisation Campaign in order to improve social behaviour. This consisted of the Five Talks (politeness, civil behaviour, attention to social relations, morality and attention to hygiene) and the Four Beauties (behaviour, heart, environment and language). It was clear to me, as I stamped crossly out of the CAAC office, that the Spiritual Civilisation Campaign had failed as surely as the Four Pests Campaign, which sought to eradicate sparrows, mosquitoes, flies and rats. Only sparrows were largely exterminated: eight hundred million peasants banged tin lids together on a certain morning until the sparrows, too terrified to land, died of exhaustion.

There were times when I felt like just such a sparrow, caught in the crossfire of rudeness, unhelpfulness or at best indifference of many Chinese; caught in a society that to a Westerner was sometimes ugly and cruel, irreconcilably alien; or, quite simply, overwhelmed by the sheer numbers of these people, smoking, yelling, fighting, sightseeing, pushing, crying, laughing, living people. 'I have often thought that if I were compelled . . . to live in China . . . I should go mad. I am terrified by the modes of life, by the manners, and . . . want of sympathy, placed between us by feelings deeper than I can analyse,' wrote Thomas de Quincey in *Confessions of an English Opium-Eater*. 'I would rather live,' he concluded, 'with lunatics, or brute animals.' Only the last sentence rang hollow; had de Quincey ever been to China, he would have found that the Chinese were as human as himself. And that was perhaps the most frightening thought of all. Looking around me in these streets and offices I saw myself multiplied a billion times, fighting for space and recognition, full of pent-up emotions and humanity that had no room for exposure. I shivered. I felt frightened. I knew that under similar conditions I might be as bored and unhelpful as the woman in the CAAC office. I wanted to run and run, away from this claustrophobia, away from seeing myself in every Chinese face, recognising that to understand these people I needed only to look into my own soul.

Later, wandering in the streets, I found quite a pleasant part of the city, the lanes too narrow for motorised traffic. There were no blocks of flats here, only the single-storey *pingfang* (literally, flat house) residences with enclosed courtyards, that characterised so many Chinese cities. It was surprisingly quiet, only the click of mahjong tiles and the trills of caged songbirds breaking the silence. The streets were flagstoned and divided by moon gates, those circular Chinese archways like the entrances to goblins' lairs; there were balconies with washing

hanging overhead, while at front doors women sat peeling vegetables and children agonised over Chinese characters, memorising their intricate strokes. Canton almost managed to make
itself agreeable in these back streets, but it was too late. I had
not really taken to this brash city and suddenly, irrationally, I
hated it.

Despite its energy Canton was an ugly city, its long roads
choked with traffic, the light half-blocked by flyovers. It was a
city of snakes and salesgirls, I thought crossly. Like Guilin,
much of it seemed to be half built, or half taken apart, like a
Lego house in which a child had suddenly lost interest. It was
a place without past or any indication of a real future, that
hung in a concrete limbo of uninspiring present. It was an
odd reflection in a city of urgent people and busy shops and
easy money, but its energy seemed without purpose, lost
in labyrinths of diverging philosophies. I thought Canton an
exciting place but it made me tired and uncertain, the way one
might be confused and exhausted by dizzying high-living
friends who did not know what they wanted from life. A schizo-
phrenic place, which lacked even charm.

I abandoned its confusion, took a plane and flew eastwards
over a creased landscape of desiccated hills and sluggish brown
rivers to Xiamen.

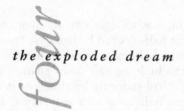

the exploded dream

All air travel is disorienting in its rapidity, wrenching the body sharply to a new destination, dislocating it from the lingering spirit which has no time to follow. The latter must be hauled back with a snap, as if pulled on an elastic, as one steps off the plane; the point of departure must be consigned to a past life, an incarnation that has no bearing on the present. At Xiamen airport in Fujian Province it was a shock to arrive to fresh blue skies, far away from the grey humidity and pollution of Canton. This was a different city, a new scene that shattered old generalisations, and the people even spoke a different language.

Fujian Province had long been on the front line of the ideological war waged between the mainland communists and Taiwanese Nationalists in their outposts only twenty kilometres across the water. During the 1960s and 1970s they had bombarded each other with artillery fire and incessant loudspeaker messages denigrating each other's modes of life and equally repressive governments. The Nationalists still often referred to the ruling communists as Red bandits and maintained China's capital was at Nanjing and not Beijing, which they stubbornly referred to by its pre-Liberation name of Beiping. For the mainlanders everything on Taiwan was so-called, including the so-called parliament in the so-called capital of Taipei, where so-called ministers ran a so-called government. The two sides agreed only on maps, on which the island and the mainland were the same colour and China was united.

Now, in the spirit of new *entente*, fresh ties were being forged between Taiwan and the mainland. They exchanged mail and sports teams, and set up joint-enterprise companies. Overseas Chinese from Hong Kong and the so-called Republic of China on Taiwan, with relatives still living in Fujian, streamed off planes at Xiamen airport. They were loaded down with toys, television sets and stereos—a new form of ideological propaganda—bustling self-importantly across the tarmac and into the arrivals building with the bonhomie of bulldozers, swinging parcels and bowling their shy Fujianese relatives triumphantly in front of them. Despite the fact that many of them would have scrimped and saved under what was, until very recently, their own dictatorship in order to thus impress their mainland cousins, they hauled their bulky cartons of electronic goodies with them like out-of-season Santa Clauses, displaying them as solid symbols of their sophistication and prosperity.

Wandering through the streets, I had trouble finding somewhere to stay. The only hotel I could locate was the Lujiang Hotel down on the waterfront, which had a torpid staff and pretentious marble lobby with prices to match. I was standing indecisively on the pavement when a Chinese popped out from behind me like a genie from a lamp.

'Are you looking for a hotel?'

'Er . . . maybe,' I muttered, being somewhat suspicious of unsolicited advice, which was often a prelude to black market dealings or inquiries about English conversation lessons.

'There is a hotel there,' said the man, pointing behind me at the Lujiang Hotel helpfully, as if I could have missed this elephantine carbuncle squatting on the harbourfront. He made no mention of dollars, and gazed at me in a friendly fashion.

'Ah, yes. But it's rather expensive, and there doesn't seem to be any other place for foreigners to stay.'

'I know a place, but rather far from here. We will go in a taxi!'

Moments later we were spinning along in a cycle-rickshaw. My companion was Xiao Li, a factory worker on his lunch break. There was nothing socially unacceptable about being a factory worker in China, and Xiao Li readily admitted to being one. If anything, it was a good deal more secure—and often

better paid—than working in an office or a university, where
the spectre of the Cultural Revolution was a reminder that
political disapproval was only a step away. A statement of pro-
fession always came early in any conversation with a Chinese;
China always had been, and still very much was, a status-
oriented society, and it seemed imperative to find out the social
position of a stranger so that one could behave in the socially
correct way.

Xiao Li had the quiet, contemplative face of stone bishops in
a French cathedral, and surprisingly slender hands—more
priest or pianist than factory worker. His family, he told me,
was originally from Shanghai. His grandfather had been a
prominent member of the Green Gang, a Chinese triad that
had dominated the city's opium trade, prostitution, gambling
and criminal circles. His father had moved to Fujian Province
after Liberation in 1949.

'I don't believe in Marxism and I don't believe in your
Christianity!' he remarked to me moments later. I laughed nervously, anxious about such an outspoken remark in public, but
no longer naive enough to be surprised by it.

'I believe in money! But I am in the Communist Youth
League,' Xiao Li added, looking at me impishly.

'You are very provoking, Xiao Li.'

'Well, what is communism? It is a dying thought.'

'"A dead time's exploded dream",' I quoted dryly. Xiao Li
was delighted. 'An English poet called Matthew Arnold wrote
those words in the last century, about an entirely different
philosophy—in fact, Christianity,' I added.

'Well, I think they are very appropriate to China today. Who
wants to help others by labouring in the fields or factory?' the
young man asked with rhetorical contempt. 'My great ambition is to make money, to be a businessman and earn three
thousand *yuan* a month! There is a Chinese saying: "With
money a dragon, without money a worm." I would like to find
a job in Shenzhen, or Guangzhou.'

'Well,' I answered doubtfully, 'I wish you good luck.'

Xiao Li was not the sort of person I had expected to meet in
a communist country, yet now that I had come to China I felt
he represented the disillusioned and rather cynical youth of his
generation. This was even more true in recent times. 'We will

say what the government wants us to say—we will toe the party line,' one of my Chinese friends was to tell me later in the autumn after two hours of his Political Studies class. 'But in our hearts we are just the same.' After the Tiananmen massacre and despite the ensuing propaganda and political re-education, many urban Chinese lost whatever faith they had had in the validity, and indeed legitimacy, of their government. The Beijing clampdown, like the Cultural Revolution for the previous generation, had shattered faith and Xiao Li was a product of it, sceptical of politics and anxious to make his own way in the world. He was too young to have remembered the old China, which gave the elderly so much pride in the achievements of their era; the communists had bequeathed him relative economic security, and now he demanded more personal satisfactions.

In a European youth Xiao Li's disillusionment and grudge against authority might have manifested itself in vandalism, football hooliganism or drug addiction, and in Russia he would already have been on the road to alcoholism, finding solace for his narrow life in a vodka bottle. Yet although the shops were stocked with spirits and wines, and opium poppies and marijuana grew wild in the fields of south-west China, the Chinese largely avoided such futile escapes. I had always been struck by the self-confidence of the young Chinese and the feeling of security they got from the system they simultaneously rebelled against, just as I had noticed how they felt secure in their work unit despite grumbling about the control it exercised.

'I have been abroad, you know,' said Xiao Li unexpectedly with quiet pride, interrupting my thoughts. His face lit up with satisfaction. 'I have been to the West!'

'Really?'

'Yes, I took the train from Beijing through the USSR, spending a few days in Moscow, and stayed two months in Poland. I was sent by our Youth League on a friendship exchange.'

'And what did you think of Moscow?' I did not want to puncture his happiness by suggesting Poland was not quite the West as I thought of it, especially as he had clearly been there during its communist days.

'Worse than China! People come up to you and ask if they can buy your shoes, your jeans, your cassettes, even your underwear!' He laughed at the absurdity. 'Nobody does that in China! I felt sorry for them. I gave a Russian a pair of my shoes. I hope he is happy! He will say, "A young Chinese fellow gave me these shoes." Imagine!' He looked at me, his eyes wide in simulated astonishment.

And Poland? Poland was quite wonderful, with beautiful old towns and countryside and space (maybe too much space—'So empty!' he said to me wonderingly) and all the splendours of the West, of which he longed to see more.

'And if you could go somewhere else?'

'To Paris, because it is the City of Love.' A pause.

'Do you want to go to Paris to find love? Or because you are in love now, Xiao Li?'

Xiao Li tittered nervously. It was a laugh that meant 'Why do foreigners ask these indelicate questions?'

'Love is like a ghost,' he answered cryptically. 'Everybody talks about it, but few can see it! It is another Chinese saying. And now we are arriving at the hotel,' he added, hastily changing the subject. We stopped outside a flight of steps leading up to a cavernous doorway. He paid off the cycle-rickshaw despite my protests, and found me a room after consulting with the lady at the reception desk. He was rushing back to work, he said.

'Can I meet you again? Maybe tomorrow?'

'I must work tomorrow. I will visit you on Wednesday, it is my day off.' He smiled at me shyly, and was gone.

The hotel Xiao Li had brought me to was certainly cheaper than the one on the waterfront. It was also rather neglected and particularly noisy, as I was to discover. Men shouted and argued in the corridors, banged doors, or yelled over cards in their room, disputing every hand with loud amiability. They turned their televisions up to maximum volume, so that they howled with distortion. I soon discovered, too, that my room was uncomfortably close to the bathrooms, and a constant stream of Chinese passed outside, clattering about and spitting raucously; the hawking began at six in the morning and continued until, bleary-eyed, I went down for breakfast.

Chinese hotels were noisy places and not for the faint of heart. Isabella Bird, one of those redoubtable Victorian women explorers who travelled extensively in the Orient, described in

Unbeaten Tracks in Japan a hotel on Hokkaido Island in 1880 that could just as easily have been in modern Xiamen, or anywhere in China:

> The people speak at the top of their voices, and, though most words and syllables end in vowels, the general effect of a conversation is like the discordant gabble of a farmyard. The next room to mine is full of storm-bound travellers, and they and the house-master kept up what I thought was a most important argument for four hours at the tops of their voices . . . but on inquiry [I] found that it was possible to spend four mortal hours in discussing whether the day's journey from Odaté to Noshiro could be best made by road or river.

I did not believe the Chinese were capable of whispering; certainly I had never heard any of them doing so, and I suspected that having a tonal language made it difficult to understand subdued voices. There were only slightly more than four hundred syllables in the Chinese language, though in a dictionary there were some twenty thousand different characters. The only way to differentiate one similarly pronounced monosyllabic character from another, therefore, was by the use of tones and context—difficult if one was whispering. In any case, the Chinese seemed to have little concern for what Westerners would consider the etiquette of community living, and saw no need to lower their voices. This was one of the paradoxes of China; although sheer numbers had produced a traditional philosophy of interdependence in a complex and tightly knit community, they had also produced an attitude in which others, especially strangers, did not really meet with respect as human beings. In the fight for resources and breathing space, that was a luxury few Chinese could afford.

The noise made me sleepless, but the other guests did not even seem to notice it. They appeared fresh-faced every morning for their rice gruel, shouting with renewed energy over the breakfast table.

Xiamen was a city of wide, quiet streets (quieter, I thought, than my hotel) and well-regulated traffic, making it a pleasant though, at least by Western standards, an unexceptional place.

It had all the modernities of the city I had just left—taxis, pedestrian crossings, air-conditioning, karaoke bars and well-stocked shops—but was seemingly without any of its crowds and traffic congestion. Unlike Canton it seemed a city satisfied with itself. In the town centre, at least, there were no flyovers and no half-assembled buildings, and the city had an assured and comfortable air, without pretension. Mobile hawkers' stalls along the pavements sold steamed dumplings, piled into pyramids like cannon shot. The acrid tang of incense, the stale smell of water, frying chicken, soy sauce—all the smells of China—were confused with exhaust fumes and the cold, metallic smell of air-conditioning outlets and a very un-Chinese suggestion of passing perfume.

Xiamen was a city of handsome buildings, tall and narrow, higher storeys built out over the ground floor and separated from neighbours by arches creating arcades running along entire streets in alternating—but extremely dingy—pastel shades of banana, mild green, burnt pink and eggshell blue. The stonework was brought to life by the summer sun, the edges of the buildings crumbling into nacre and ochre and smudged violet, shutters folded against the insidious heat like the petals of a flower. The entrances to the houses were surrounded by red and gold banners and the black ideograms of prayers to safeguard the homes for the present year, pasted up with the same easy assurance as party ideologies. The city reminded me of Penang, though in Malaysia the Chinese had raced around on motorbikes, in Levis and pink T-shirts. In Xiamen the Chinese still wore pea-green trousers and pedalled their Flying Pigeon or Shanghai bicycles, whirring like a host of migrating locusts along the city's roads. Cycle-rickshaws lumbered heavily in their wakes like cumbersome black beetles.

The Fujianese did in fact emigrate in large numbers to Malaysia and all South-East Asia, although an imperial edict as far back as 1718 had tried ineffectually to halt the exodus. It is thought that some sixty percent of the present population of Fujian have relatives living abroad. Many of the Taiwanese who fled the mainland at the time of the communist victory still ploughed money back into Fujian Province. As a result the people of Xiamen appeared more affluent and better dressed than in Chengdu or even Canton; the television was choked with slick advertisements produced in Hong Kong for such luxuries as refrigerators, air-conditioning, instant coffee and cars. Around the waterfront prowled hard-faced young men intent on black market dealings. They hung around in small groups, dragging at Marlboro cigarettes and scuffling playfully, James Dean expressions on their faces and combs in their tight jeans pockets, looks that spoke more openly than any I had seen in China of sex and money, those twin measures of modernity. They called at passing girls, flashing their expensive watches and their teeth.

Near my hotel was a large park which I visited often, fascinated in spite of my unhappy experience in Canton. In the early morning it was the gathering place for elderly locals, who practised *taiji*, played badminton and brought songbirds in yellow bamboo cages for a walk—a graceful moment of quiet movement, landscaped scenery and the rustling of bamboo canes. Released from the flattery of the early morning, however, the park was ugly, a collection of neatly paved and railed pathways leading to inelegant modern pavilions of concrete covered in hopeful paint. The absurd pagodas and little walkways gave the place the look of a badly sketched Chinese scroll in which, although the crags appeared wild and remote, they were in fact artistically arranged, the little figures at the bottom asserting human dominance.

At night the park was again completely altered. Vendors carved pineapples and stuck them on lengths of wood, selling them to passersby for a few *jiao*. Chinese pop music wailed loudly and spouts of water floodlit in lurid green and red soared geometrically from a huge, uninventive fountain in the park's centre, from the base of which fairy lights winked and blinked. Around and about wandered the wide-eyed citizens of Xiamen, inevitably taking photographs of each other against this ultra-modern landmark. I did not know whether the Chinese were so starved of beauty that they had to stroll around this unnatural monstrosity in the evenings for pleasure, or whether I was imposing my Western values on an alien culture. Maybe the Chinese *liked* this fountain, or maybe they simply had a poor grasp of aesthetics, the legacy of the Cultural Revolution and the socialist principles of art for practical purposes.

I did not resolve this question, but I returned to the park evening after evening in the same way that, as a child, one pokes and prods at a painful tooth. Perhaps I was becoming too cynical and accustomed to travel and new sights; I envied the people of Xiamen their spontaneous enthusiasm and ingenuous delight. The fountain left me feeling unhappy, but everyone else was eating ice cream and taking photos and smiling.

At other times, tiring of the park, I would wander through the dim-lit evening streets, sometimes slipping into a garish karaoke bar to marvel at the display of leather miniskirts and expensive watches. In one of these bars I met a lone Englishman. He was from Yorkshire, a representative of a shoe factory that had several joint-enterprise interests in the People's Republic. His eyes glowed with an evangelical light at the old dream of a market one billion strong, even though most of his shoes were at the moment exported back to Europe. He sat in a corner, propped against the wall, drinking Chinese vodka and reeling off investment and sales figures like good-luck charms for a prosperous future, in which Chinese clumped around their rice paddies like London bobbies in good British-style brogues.

'It's going to happen sometime! Even now, the Chinese are beginning to Westernise—karaoke bars, vodka, miniskirts, why not British shoes?'

'Karaoke bars are Japanese,' I said unhelpfully.

'Well, you know what I mean,' he replied, splashing more vodka into his glass and adding a thin trickle of orange juice.

I said I didn't.

'Use your eyes!' he said genially. 'It really surprised me, coming to China, just how really Western-looking the cities were—Canton, Xiamen, Chongqing. You know, the buildings, the taxis, the pedestrian crossings and whatnot.'

'I don't think they're *Western*. They're just *modern*,' I said sharply. I did not like people who claimed every sign of development for the White Man.

'Same, thing, isn't it?'

'Look, you can go for a weekend into the mountains of Sichuan, west of Chengdu towards the Tibetan border, and see little wooden buildings with sloping roofs and balconies and stacks of firewood under the outside stairs. Would you claim that these were Western, borrowed from some Tibetan vision of Swiss chalets?'

The Yorkshireman laughed. 'No, of course not. I mean, I haven't been there, but I suppose they just use the available alpine resources and build the style of house that best adapts to their environment.'

'Well, exactly! I couldn't have put it better. If you suddenly have a city with large numbers of people and traffic then a pedestrian crossing, for example, is also simply a convenient adaptation to the environment. It's not Western, it's just one of the many inevitable consequences of mass living and industrial development.'

'What about the buildings, though?' continued the Yorkshireman, unrepentant. 'Look around in this city. Traditional Chinese architecture is all crinkly roofs and gables and painted walls. Show me one in the whole of Xiamen! The houses are Western at least.'

'That's like saying traditional British architecture is all Tudor half-timbered houses with bulging upper storeys. It's just the same,' I said excitedly. 'Blocks of concrete apartment blocks and glass-and-metal offices are the only practical answer to the needs of mass housing and work space. If China had undergone the Industrial Revolution before Europe, we would have been saying all these things were Chinese today! I don't think those things have a culture. If they do, it's a culture of industrialisation and modernity that transcends national boundaries.'

'So you're saying the West hasn't affected China at all?'

'No. Even the government here follows an ideology conceived in the West. Apart from that, the West does hold out an enormous attraction for the people of developing countries as a role model in all kinds of fields, even down to the level of pop music and miniskirts. But I think there's a big gulf between economic influences and cultural ones. The Chinese look to the West and see development and modernity more than Western culture or ideas. Chinese cities may look "Western", and smug Westerners are lulled into the happy delusion that everyone wants to be like them. The urban Chinese may live in blocks of flats and drink vodka in karaoke bars and listen to the Carpenters, but in spirit and mentality they're as fundamentally different from Westerners as they were a hundred years ago.'

'Maybe people's mentalities are like their houses,' said the Yorkshireman with drunken cunning. 'Maybe they adapt to their environment too. In that case we'll end all end up with the same Western—or *modern* as you would say—mentality.'

'Maybe we will,' I said grimly. 'With a bit of luck I'll be dead by then; the world would be a stifling place.'

The Yorkshireman grinned a self-satisfied grin, pouring more vodka into his glass.

'But everyone will be wearing my shoes!'

One evening, looking out a restaurant window, I saw two cyclists crash into each other, both tumbling to the ground with the disjointed awkwardness of wooden puppets. As the second got uncertainly to his feet, the first landed him an unsolicited and vicious punch in the face, sending him sprawling once more. The Chinese seemed rarely to resort to violence, but when they did it was sudden, unpredictable and usually unwarranted. I saw no more, for the crowds closed in to stare with ghoulish curiosity, like a flock of vultures attracted by the possibility of blood.

The Chinese were avid starers, particularly when it came to other people's misfortunes. (One of the few consolations of being stared at as a foreigner was that the Chinese stared at other Chinese too, if they were doing something sufficiently unusual.) I found the speed at which bystanders closed in for the fight, like Romans on early Christians at the arena, rather sickening. I had little doubt they would have stood impassively watching the two antagonists beat each other senseless had the situation arisen—I had seen a similar staring crowd stand motionless over an accident victim bleeding to death in a Chengdu street.

When I saw Xiao Li again on his day off I told him about this as we sat drinking beer in a café. He laughed at my naive shock.

'You think we should be co-operative and self-sacrificing?' he asked mockingly. 'Good little Confucians, perhaps, not to mention full of the communist spirit.'

I flushed and muttered that of course I did not expect such a thing but, secretly, influenced by Western stereotypes, I did.

'You've heard of the novelist Lu Xun? He made an excellent discovery in *A Madman's Diary*, where he wrote about his inspiration by the two characters *ren ci*—mercy, mutual dependence—and their connection with another two, *ci ren*—kill one another.'

There was a silence and I sat in my chair, taken aback that my casual observation of the cyclists had unleashed such cynicism. Xiao Li turned his eyes on me quizzically. 'But I hope you don't think all the Chinese are so ruthless! It's a social aspect, I think, a way of survival. But we Chinese make real friends too!'

'Of course. Though yellow gold is more common than white-haired friends.'

Xiao Li laughed gently. 'I see you are familiar with our Chinese sayings. Then I will tell you another: "With friends, even water tastes sweet." Let's see how some beer tastes! We Chinese and you British have been acquainted for many centuries!' He sloshed some more beer into my glass.

'That was an acquaintance of yellow gold, too.'

'Well, we shall make amends for that. Cheers!'

'*Gan bei*!'

Xiao Li was right about the British. The people of Fujian, like the Cantonese, have a long history of contact with foreigners coming to China. Marco Polo painted an appealing picture of thirteenth-century Xiamen as one of the busiest ports in the world, full of Indian and Arab ships trading in fine pearls and precious gems, pepper, aloes, sandalwood and delicate porcelain. 'It is a delightful place,' he wrote, 'amply supplied with all that the human body requires; and the inhabitants are peaceable folk, fond of leisure and easy living.'

During the Opium Wars a British naval force seized control of the city, then known as Amoy. Xiamen was declared an open port by the Treaty of Nanking. The British were followed by the Japanese, Belgians, Danish, French, Germans, Dutch and Americans. Just as Shamian Island in Canton had been reserved for Westerners, in Xiamen these imperialist nations set themselves up on an island just off the coast of the city (which is itself located on a much larger island at the mouth of the Jiulong River). Gulangyu Island was established as a foreign enclave, with its own hospitals, churches, libraries and hotels, and was later officially designated as an International Foreign Settlement. Xiamen became once more a thriving port on the Taiwan Straits, exporting sugar, fish, fruit, paper, tobacco and tea.

'Though called *cha* in Mandarin Chinese, in our local dialect tea is pronounced *te*,' Xiao Li told me. 'I think it is where you found your English word. The British exported a lot of tea from China in the last century. They made us take opium in exchange!' (I was pleased with his use of 'they', not 'you'. No need to feel apologetic here.)

It was my last day in Xiamen. Xiao Li had called upon me at my hotel early in the morning, presenting himself rather self-consciously and apologetically, but I had been glad to see him. I was tired of wandering around the city on my own, and I rather liked him. Now we took a ferry, and went across to the former International Settlement on Gulangyu.

From a hill in the centre of the island there was a view over the town: biscuit-brown tiled roofs and dusty red brick; a peaceful place in russet and olive, small patches of fields sewn together by decaying stone walls and bordered by bamboo canes, fragments of a Van Gogh canvas. Beyond it was the narrow sea that separated it from Xiamen city, as smooth and flat as slate, written over by the wakes of small boats in unsteady hieroglyphic lines. Far below, tourists stormed straight up the main street like a physical assault, buying plastic souvenirs along the way. They panted up to the top of the hill where we were standing, taking photos of each other posing at the summit, before descending in a renewed rush of energy.

One had only to step off the main street, however, to imagine oneself the only visitor to the island. The smell here was quite different from in Xiamen—almost Mediterranean, the sharp heavy scent of dusty streets and heat, bougainvillea, dampened pavements and bedraggled eucalyptus giving a heady but barely perceptible under-tang; a sleepy, musty smell that drugged the senses. It was very quiet and peaceful, almost deserted, baking in the sun, the wide dusty plazas and shuttered shops and limp trees harsh in the heat. We sat in a small square, on a rough stone wall under a tree. Xiao Li's best friend had only yesterday celebrated his birthday, he told me. He had gone to see him, and found him eating birthday cake in a low mood.

'And when I asked him what was wrong he said that every year he dreaded his birthday because he was growing old. Actually, he is now only twenty-five!'

'A great psychologist once said that men are old by the age of twenty-five,' I commented.

'This psychologist was right! They are satisfied with their jobs, have closed their minds to new ideas by accumulating all those boring prejudices that they claim are principles. I think they have ceased to grow. The minute a man ceases to grow—no matter what his years—that is the minute he begins to be old.'

'And how old are you? Are you not satisfied with your job?'

'No! As I told you, I want to be a businessman.' He uttered it with the same faraway longing tones in which American boys claim they want to be astronauts. 'That factory I am working in now will really turn me into a robot. You must do what you dislike to do and stay, perhaps for your whole life, at the place where you are not willing to stay. That's the system of China, the socialist idea. I don't know how many gifted and ambitious people have been ruined by this system. I want to be myself, not a piece in a system. I hope before I am turned into a robot and become numb I make a timely escape! When I am old I do not want to be tortured by the fact that I have idled away my life.'

We walked on through the hot streets and sat in a restaurant, eating platefuls of chicken and peanuts and drinking Fujian beer. In China, I thought to myself, one of the norms of judging a person had long been whether he was obedient. But now that the urban Chinese were adequately clothed, housed, fed and educated, they saw neither reason nor need to kowtow to authority for survival. In giving them economic security, the communists had perhaps become hoist with their own petard and sown the seeds of growing individual autonomy. Having no worries about their next meal, many Chinese were asking themselves if the collective attitude were not the denial of personal values, and whether in the emphasis on mutual dependence their individual creativeness and originality were not being smothered.

I must have looked puzzled and uncertain, for Xiao Li asked me what was wrong.

'It's funny. I see your point of view, and I agree with you. I think the paradox is that it is the very system you protest against that has given you the opportunity to feel the way you do.'

Now it was Xiao Li's turn to look confused.

'What I mean is, this system has given the Chinese food and housing and medical care and all the things that give them the time and energy to think about what they really want. Forty years ago Chinese like you were only thinking of survival. It's your secure factory job that gives you the opportunity not to want a factory job! Does that sound stupid?'

Xiao Li looked unhappy. 'No . . . No, I see that you may be right. It is a paradox.'

'It's really a self-destructive system, isn't it? I mean in the literal sense of the term. As soon as it achieves, even to a certain extent, its aims, then there is no need for it to exist any more.'

'You are very cunning! Sometimes I think you are just playing with words . . . Anyway I am not ungrateful for what our leaders have achieved in the past. But now I am young and want to direct my own life. Certainly I think poorly of my friend who thinks himself old at twenty-five. Even Mao Zedong, a great man, became old in the end, and useless. But I hope that I shall be like Laplace, the French astronomer. Do you know of him?'

I shook my head.

'He died crying, "What we know is nothing; what we do not know is immense!" You see, there you have the real question of what is old age. Laplace at seventy-eight died a young man. He was still dissatisfied, still sure he had a lot to learn and do. Oh, my dear friend is only twenty-five!' His eyes lifted in pretended despair, and he laughed. 'Maybe communism has come of age, yes? But we young people want to go on, we are the astronomers looking to the future.' He fidgeted in his chair excitedly, pleased at his metaphor. He took my arm gently. 'Come, Brian, we will continue our walk through this town. It is a little like Europe, you have said. I can do as I like today, when I am here. Since we can't breathe the free air always, to breathe it sometimes is also a good thing, right?'

Only the drift of leaves like the soft movement of butterflies disturbed the sultry quiet of midday, the subdued murmur of voices behind closed shutters, the undulations of the hot breeze down shaded lanes. Narrow streets were lined by high walls, over which hung bougainvillea and slanting almond and lime trees. Behind the walls, silent behind wrought-iron gates surmounted by coats of arms, stood impressive mansions now divided into flats, dark-green shutters closed like sleepy eyelids over their windows. From several of the houses drifted the sound of pianos, the Toreador's March from *Carmen* and 'My Bonny Lies over the Ocean', the playing of which would have been unimaginable only twenty years ago during the Cultural Revolution. One could almost have slipped through a door to another century, layers of history emerging to haunt the shadowed streets, evocative, atmospheric, whispering of past intrigue, illicit rendezvous and greedy foreign plotting.

But this Western nostalgia for the past was the self-indulgence of people comfortable enough to sentimentalise. The Chinese had no nostalgia for history; it was too close and too harsh. They knocked down their old buildings and built modern replacements without regret. ('But it's so *old*,' my students often said in supreme contempt for some edifice I had admired.) I felt Xiao Li thought quite differently from myself. Gulangyu was his escape into a future that was not yet realised, and history was a dirty word.

It was attractive, this little enclave of prosperity and spaciousness separated from the cramped, shabby cities of the mainland by a narrow channel of sea, but soon we had to return to the other, more real China. We took the ferry back across to Xiamen in silence, watching the water suck and gurgle around the edges of the boat. Xiao Li went back to his factory and I to my noisy hotel, and the next day I flew back to Chengdu.

I was sad thinking about Xiao Li. One of the few drawbacks of travelling is this leaving of people behind, this abandonment of potential friendships and interesting other lives and possibilities. But I was glad to be going home. Home—it was minutes afterwards that I realised how I had used the word. I peered through the scratched aeroplane window down at the rice paddies of Sichuan Province, feeling tired but satisfied. It looked very familiar. As on the first night I had arrived in Chengdu, there was no warning of any city, no buildings and few roads, as the plane skimmed the green fields. As we came in to land the tables were still strewn with the remains of meals. The call-buttons didn't work but the flight attendants had vanished anyway, powdering their noses in the forward service area. I put my tray on the floor and pushed my table back into the upright position; I would have felt guilty ignoring the lessons learnt on a hundred Western flights. The Chinese man beside me looked at me askance, sweeping his empty packets, crumpled cling-film and empty cola can into a disordered heap in front of him.

The pilot must have miscalculated the altitude, for we plunged so steeply to lose height that I thought the plane would stick quivering, nose first, into the glutinous mud of the surrounding rice fields. Several of the ceiling panels came loose with a dull groan and flapped, exposing a jumble of wires like a rack of hanging noodles drying in a marketplace. I watched with a feeling of helpless and resigned interest as a smoke-like cloud seeped out from the joints in the ceiling (a normal occurrence on Chinese planes, I was to learn, and not smoke but water vapour from the air-conditioning). No sooner had the wheels hit the runway than the passengers, in their usual eagerness to get off (and on) any vehicle, scrambled to their feet and, pulling down boxes and bags, jostled towards the doors as the aircraft hurtled along the tarmac. They were in a hurry to get somewhere, these Chinese.

I sat in my seat, with my safety-belt buckled and my table in the upright position. I had arrived once more.

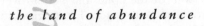

the land of abundance

five

According to traditional Chinese geomancy, still water facing a building means its occupants will make easy money. Though this was no doubt now branded a feudal superstition by the Chinese government, I was nonetheless reassured by this piece of lore—outside my flat at Sichuan University, in the centre of the courtyard onto which my windows looked, there was a stagnant pond. Fat orange fish swam in its murky waters. It was surrounded by a low wall of grey stone slabs, and from its centre rose an island of rocks sprouting dejected ferns and other unhappy-looking plants. Sometimes a kingfisher would visit it, sitting on the rocks like a brilliant fragment of pure colour, before flashing away in a blur of electric-blue wings.

Around the wall of the pond foreigners often congregated, chatting or waiting for a visitor or a partner to play badminton. There were some sixty foreigners living in the compound—mostly students studying Chinese language, politics, history or economics—in a tightly knit community sharing similar interests, where one made fast friendships and everyone knew everyone else's business and eventually got on everyone else's nerves. One of these was Hedvig, a Swedish student studying Chinese language and economics, who had already become a friend and with whom I talked and bickered over ideas and day's events. The pond was the trading post, the gossip centre, the meeting place around which the life of the courtyard revolved. People sat on their balconies in the warmer weather, peering down into the courtyard, calling to each other, leaning over to conduct animated conversations, or simply shouting for someone to check their postbox. I was drawn frequently and irresistibly onto my own balcony, where I spent long moments, often with my friend Hedvig beside me, leaning over the railings and watching the passersby, avid for something to happen. Our patience was rewarded shortly after my return from Xiamen; one day a Japanese student, cycling into the yard, failed to apply his brakes on time. His bicycle ran forcefully into the low wall of the pond and he fell over its handle-bars straight into the gloomy waters. He emerged, mud-covered, to the sound of our delighted cackles, as papers from his notebook spread slowly over the surface of the pond like geometric waterlilies.

The pond was an ugly and unimaginative creation, but it was the focus of compound life. In my mind it also became the geographical heart of the immense country I was residing in—China stretched out around it and centred upon it, just as the ancient Greek world had unfolded from the *omphalos* at Delphi. It was the centre of vast concentric layers: the court-yard, the campus, the city, the province, the wide immensity of China that I had imagined, and which had so intimidated me, on my first day in Chengdu. Now that I had made my first suc-cessful foray into China, the rest of the country beckoned, full of adventure, and filled me with excitement. In this vast land the pond was my reference point, my familiar home ground, and I greeted it with pleasure each time I returned from the mass of humanity that struggled and lived outside the quiet of the courtyard.

I was, in geographical reality, somewhere near the centre of China. Sichuan Province lay nearly two thousand kilometres from Beijing in the heart of the nation, and was no less para-doxical than China itself, at once impoverished and affluent, empty and overcrowded. Westwards of my pond the provincial borders were remote behind wild mountains and turbulent rivers, supporting a sparse population of Tibetans and other ethnic minorities living at subsistence level; much of western Sichuan had in fact been part of Tibet until the 1950s. On a clear day—which was hardly ever—one could see mountains on the distant horizon from the flat roof of my building; they shimmered like a snow-capped mirage far beyond the choking dust and concrete of urban China. Sometimes, in the centre of the town, one could see Tibetans from mountain villages, squatting on the pavements selling deer antlers, bones, dried mosses and other traditional medicinal remedies at extortionate prices. They were scruffy people, with handsome rugged faces, proudly dressed in big boots and colourful jackets tied around their waists with multicoloured sashes. They had dangling turquoise earrings and daggers and gold-capped teeth. To me they looked impossibly romantic, but the Han Chinese averted their eyes and wrinkled up their noses, hurrying past.

On the eastward side of my pond, into the Sichuan Basin and Yangtze River valley, was squeezed one of the densest rural populations on earth—one hundred million people in a lushly fertile agricultural zone that had been irrigated since the third century BC and was still China's greatest rice-producing area, yielding a quarter of the nation's supply and earning the province the nickname Storehouse of Heaven or Land of Abundance. Supported by rich soils and a humid, subtropical monsoon climate of plentiful rainfall and mild winters, the Sichuan Basin produced not only rice but rapeseed, tobacco, wheat, tea, fruit and vegetables (especially sweet potatoes) and had a surplus every year, exporting all over China. Sichuan was famous for its sugar produced in Neijiang, its oranges and tangerines from Jiangjin, its wine from Luzhou and Yibin on the banks of the Yangtze River, its medicinal herbs from Xichang deep in the south of the province, and of course its silk.

The countryside around Chengdu was a landscape of bizarre trees straight from a Dr Seuss story, of modest mud-brick villages crouched under gargantuan bamboo clumps, and of blue-smocked farmers working knee-deep in fertile mud. On some of the drier land grew fields of wheat, interspersed with patches of tobacco, rapeseed, swollen squashes or gleaming red tomatoes. But flooded paddies predominated, and twice a year the young rice shoots flourished with a startlingly brilliant emerald colour. Rice fields were a constant source of pattern and beauty—flat, lush lozenges of patchworked green around the city of Chengdu, a crazy-paving of fields far out into the countryside, and flights of monumental tiered steps and generous contours up in the hills around Dazu to the east. Everywhere tiny but relatively prosperous villages floated in a chequered sea of square and rectangular iridescence.

Built of mud bricks and grey slate, usually around a central
duck pond, Sichuan villages were always a bustle of activity:
women sitting on their doorsteps weaving baskets or preparing
vegetables, children scampering around or fishing in the local
streams, men sawing planks of wood, washing down buffalo
or hoeing in the fields. Later in the autumn, in front of their
houses, women would thresh wheat in large, circular shallow
baskets, tossing the grain in the air to let the chaff blow away
in the breeze in a timeless gesture. It was my romanticised view,
this rural beauty, as I pedalled slowly down the rutted country
lanes on my bicycle. This threshing of grain and planting of
rice was back-breaking work, and the older women shuffled,
bent over, eyes fixed on the ground from which they had
harvested such abundance and such pain.

Chengdu, urban island in a sea of rice fields, was a great and
ancient city, once the capital of the independent State of Shu,
and at that time named Brocade City for its successful silk and
brocade trade, its products exported westwards along the Silk
Road, as Xiao Han had mentioned on my first day in the city.
The Temple of Marquis Wu lying off the ring-road in the
southern part of the city is a reminder of that time, commem-
orating a famous military strategist and prime minister of Shu
who lived in the second century. (The temple is now under
state protection, its preservation assured by Chairman Mao,
who sent political cadres there to study the writings of the
ancient prime minister.) In 316 BC Emperor Huawen of the
Qin Dynasty brought Shu and the neighbouring Kingdom of
Ba under his control and later, in the Yuan Dynasty, the two
places became a province named Sichuan. Chengdu—the name
means Perfect City—became a link between central and south-
west China. Since then it has been the commercial, administrative and educational centre of the province, and indeed of all
south-west China.

Sichuan also became a cradle of culture; Sichuan opera is
famous throughout the country, and many renowned Chinese
poets came to the province in ancient times. There is a park in
the western suburbs of Chengdu devoted to the memory of the
Tang Dynasty poet Du Fu, with a model of the thatched

cottage at the site where the poet is said to have lived. One of his poems describes a fierce autumn wind which tore the thatch off his house. He lies in bed while the rain drips down on him through the roof, and dreams of owning a palace with ten thousand rooms 'Where all the poor on earth could find welcome shelter / Steady through every storm, secure as a mountain!' Much of Du Fu's poetry is concerned with social injustice, the evils of war and the hard life of the people, so his verses were still in vogue in communist China. Mao Zedong (himself a rather fine poet) had visited Du Fu's park and had left a sample of his calligraphy there in praise of the Tang writer. After such a seal of approval the reputation of Du Fu could only continue to flourish.

Even in Du Fu's day Chengdu was large, described in one of his poems as a city with a hundred thousand households. Modern Chengdu is not Sichuan's largest city (that is Chongqing, an industrial centre on the Yangtze River to the south-east), but it has a population of over one million in the city proper and a further six million in the 'metropolitan' area, which extends into the countryside. As in most Chinese cities, Chengdu's long history is not immediately apparent, though it can be hunted out down back streets and alleyways. Wenshu Monastery, tucked discreetly down a lane near the railway station, is another site that dates from as far back as the Tang Dynasty. It is one of the most thriving temples in China, being not only the headquarters of the province's Buddhist association but an active centre of training for monks. It also serves excellent vegetarian food in its restaurant, and I often went with Hedvig and other friends for lunch and a stroll around its quiet buildings and gardens. But such places are exceptions. Many Chinese cities were destroyed during the war against the Japanese, and much of what was left has been built over by much-needed socialist housing projects. Most of Chengdu's old buildings, though spared during the war, were demolished during the 1960s to make way for its growing population. The Exhibition Hall, behind the Mao statue in the centre of the city, is a monstrous Soviet-style building of heavy pillars and hard lines, built on the site of the ancient palace of Sichuan's viceroys which was destroyed during the Cultural Revolution and was reputed to have been one of the finest buildings in China.

Despite its sometimes stifling architecture, Chengdu was a city very much alive, bursting with human energy. Chengdu's charm lay not in its monstrous buildings but in its people, crowding the streets and animating the markets, and I often cycled around the city's back streets, marvelling at the new and familiar sights. For many Chinese it was an outdoor life, a life of bicycles exposed to all weather, of restaurants open onto the pavement, of outdoor snooker games and outdoor shopping, of girls washing their hair at the tap in front of their house, of little children peeing in the gutters, of the evening meal being eaten squatting by the side of the road, bowl of rice in the one hand and chopsticks in the other. Chinese homes were often small and overcrowded, dimly lit with low-energy light bulbs, and Chinese mothers sat outside with their children, knitting or peeling vegetables while chatting to the neighbours.

On campus too it was an outdoor life. A Chinese university was not all hard work and Marxist doctrine. Like students anywhere, those clever or careless enough could get by with less study than was formally considered necessary, and nearly all of them bent the rules. Like students anywhere, they lay on the grass, played the guitar and sang songs out of tune, skipped class for a 'doctor's appointment', or sat in teahouses avidly watching lurid Chinese soap operas or *Singapore*, an imported foreign equivalent. Movie screens were often set up on the playing fields, and students sat on chairs under the night sky for an evening's entertainment. In the evenings too they often played illicit games of mahjong in their dormitories (mahjong was against the university regulations, as it encouraged gambling and was a waste of time), or listened to sentimental pop music from Taiwan and Hong Kong, or went out with their friends to cafés to gossip and argue and drink Green Leaf beer.

With the onset of a warm autumn the river had lost its treacly brown colour (though not its distasteful smell) and sparkled in the sun, and the few cafés along its banks were filled in the evenings with chattering university students. The most popular of these was the Bamboo Bar, which I had glimpsed on the morning of my arrival, and one evening Ping and Pong arrived at my flat to take me there.

'An exciting thing has happened to me,' Pong claimed as we settled at a table on the river's edge. 'It is the story of a letter. When I was a junior student at Sichuan University, last year, I had a short article published in the *China Daily*. Ten days later, I received a strange and unexpected letter from Beijing. It was from an alumnus of Sichuan University. He had studied here from 1952 to 1956. When he read the *China Daily* one day, he saw two familiar names. One was Sichuan University, his *alma mater*'—she used the Latin words with casual ease—'and the other was Zhang Rong—my name, but also the name of his daughter. He couldn't help writing to me, though a much younger alumnus. Coincidentally, his daughter and I were born in the same year. After her graduation, his daughter was assigned to a military college to teach English. Yet for her first year, she didn't teach in class. She was assigned to a grassroots unit in Qinghai Province.'

I had already heard about Qinghai, a vast region of desolate grasslands and rugged mountains in the heart of western China from which the Yellow River emerged. It was a Siberia full of labour camps, a distant place to which a Chinese would be assigned with feelings of dread. In fact this daughter had liked Qinghai. She had stayed there a year, teaching troops and describing to her father her military life among the yellow crops and snowy white mountains. Her father had written to Pong, telling her the story.

'She made a lot of friends, and lived happily! Who can imagine, to find happiness in Qinghai. Really I admire her spirit! Since then, we have been writing to each other in English. Both of us are getting to know more and more about each other.'

I was a bit confused by now. I did not know who was writing to whom in this tangled story of penpals. But I smiled encouragingly at Zhang Rong (I still thought of her as Pong), and drank some more of my thin Chinese beer, and watched the light slowly fade over the river. I liked stories of coincidence and improbability; they suggested a pattern and a destiny in human fate that I did not otherwise often accept.

'My new "uncle" concerns me very much. He often wishes to encourage me when I am pessimistic. Although he is well versed in English and French, his major was Chemistry. I long to go to his hometown and meet him. The thing I would like to do best is take a photo with him and his daughter in front of the Gate of Heavenly Peace. It is a very famous place.'

Pong's voice faded to a wistful silence, and we all stared companionably into the river. Ping was unaccountably quiet that evening, but I supposed she had heard this tale before. Chinese pop music sounded faintly from inside the bar, and there was a sudden peal of laughter from a table nearby, a high, fluting laughter that trilled like the cry of a songbird out of the darkness, as if saluting the autumn.

I got to know the Chinese who was to become my best friend when he presented me with a snake.

Wang Ming was a student in the new classes I had started teaching on returning from the summer holidays. But I had well over a hundred new students—forty in each class—and until that time had barely noticed him. I knew he was from Jiangsu Province in the east of China and from an impoverished background, but little else. He seemed a quiet and unassuming student, short, with glasses and a dark skin that was considered unattractive by the Chinese—it was fashionable to be pale. He seemed little more than an average student and I had only had the most general and brief conversations with him until the day he gave me the snake.

It was alive, in a basket with a lid on it, and he told me he would come around to my flat that evening and cook it. As an introduction this seemed both bold and unconventional. I gaped at him and agreed, taking the basket gingerly between a finger and thumb. I hung it over my handlebars and cycled back to the Panda Park, putting the basket on my balcony before heading off for a vegetarian lunch at Wenshu Monastery with Hedvig.

'Would you like to come to dinner tonight?' I asked her as we pedalled along by the river. 'One of my students is coming too. We're going to have snake.'

'Oh! Er . . . fine. Where are you going to get the snake?'

'I've already got it,' I said airily, as if I had just popped down to the supermarket and bought half a dozen. 'It's in a basket on my balcony.'

'Oh,' said Hedvig again.

'We'll have to kill it first, though,' I added with studied casualness as we continued cycling northwards through the city.

Some time later, having had lunch, we returned to the university campus and Hedvig came up to my flat for a coffee. She went to look at the snake, but the snake was gone.

When she saw the empty basket Hedvig gave a shriek that nearly burst my eardrums and retreated to the door of my flat. 'Help, help!' she yelled frantically as if the house were on fire, turning around blindly and nearly knocking me senseless against the wall. 'Oh, Brian! My God, help, help! The snake has escaped.'

'Escaped!' I echoed.

'It's not there any more, I can't see it. My God, I was walking around the flat and it could have been anywhere, on a chair or something.'

'It might have dropped down on you from the light,' I said maliciously. Hedvig clutched my arm.

'What are we going to do?'

'How do you know it has escaped?'

'I went right onto the balcony, didn't I?' said Hedvig indignantly. 'I lifted the lid off the basket and it wasn't there.'

'And then you gave a few shrieks and ran off,' I pointed out disapprovingly. 'How could it escape when the lid was still on the basket? That's what I'd like to know.'

'Well really,' countered Hedvig. 'I don't think this is the time to conduct research into the versatility and cunning of serpents.'

'Well, in any case it's only a snake.'

'You go in and catch it then.'

'Perhaps we should just wait for Wang Ming to get here. After all, it's his snake.'

'Brian! It could go anywhere.'

We crept cautiously back into the flat. It looked innocently empty, and very quiet. There were, as usual, a great many newspapers and magazines strewn haphazardly around the room, and for the first time I realised what a good hiding place they would make for snakes.

'God, it's going to spring out on us. Maybe it's hanging from the ceiling and will *strangle* you,' said Hedvig in her rich Swedish accent.

The snake was not hanging from the ceiling; it was curled around the leg of my sofa. Out of the basket it appeared far larger than I had first thought—a good metre and a half, a brilliant emerald green with yellow flecks down its side.

'A boa constrictor!' claimed Hedvig, goggling at the beast in amazement.

'It is not a boa constrictor,' I said with some calm now that I had located the snake. 'They're much fatter than that. That's a skinny snake.'

'It won't be skinny after it has crushed your ribcage and devoured you.'

'I don't think they have boa constrictors in China, anyway.'

Hedvig seemed a little disappointed at this. She studied the snake and then sighed in deep Scandinavian gloom, 'It's probably one of those damned poisonous things, mambas or something.'

'Don't be silly,' I said, like a disapproving memsahib. 'It's not a mamba or a boa constrictor. You wouldn't give a poisonous snake to someone without warning them.'

'Well, if you're so convinced, please go ahead.' Hedvig waved graciously towards the snake. I approached it cautiously with a broom, prodding and sweeping it along in the direction of the balcony, where I could at least imprison it until Wang Ming came.

The snake slid onto the cold tiles of the balcony and I slammed the door. We both peered at it through the window as it slithered towards the railing and stuck its head out, tongue flickering as if testing the air.

'It's going to jump,' said Hedvig, digging me sharply in the ribs.

'Snakes don't jump,' I corrected her crossly. Just then the snake seemed to gather its coils together and in one impressive movement leapt clean off the balcony. I wrenched the door open and leaned over the railing.

There was pandemonium when, as if from nowhere, the snake landed in the middle of the courtyard, scattering assorted foreigners to the four winds.

'Stop that snake!' I bawled. 'It's mine.' I grabbed Hedvig, who was wailing like a deranged banshee, and shoved her down the stairs ahead of me. Down at ground level a nervous gathering of people circled the snake, which lay as if momentarily dazed by its exploits. I was asked what I was doing with a snake.

'It's a present,' I said grandly. 'I'm going to eat it.'

This announcement was greeted with a suspicious silence, during which one of the Japanese students appeared with a spade. He brandished it above his head and seemed ready to smite the serpent with it.

'Hey! I have to eat it.'

'You're not going to eat it alive, are you?' asked Hedvig. 'I mean, you have to kill it *some* time.'

'But it's a present. And it's supposed to be *fresh*. What's Wang Ming going to say if he comes round and finds his snake battered out of all recognition and lying dead in the courtyard?'

Clearly the Japanese could not keep up with the flow of my excited English. He was leaping up and down hysterically and finally he brought the spade down on the snake, fortunately hitting it only a glancing blow that stunned it long enough for us to sweep it into a bucket.

Later that evening Wang Ming did indeed come to my flat. With me he seemed shy and a little nervous, but he picked the snake up by its tail and brought it down with a resounding smack against the side of my metal bathtub. Then, using my Swiss Army knife, he slit it clean along the belly, splashing blood around the walls. My bathroom looked like an abattoir and Hedvig retreated to the living room, muttering darkly in Swedish. Wang Ming plucked out the gallbladder and offered it to me. I declined politely. He popped it into his own mouth and washed it down with a shot of fiery Chinese liquor.

'Good for the health,' he observed. Seeing my stunned expression he flashed me a smile. 'Virility,' he added. The delicacy—or perhaps the alcohol—seemed to give him confidence and he suddenly became loquacious, chatting to me about his family and childhood. He chopped the snake into bite-size sections and flung them into my cooking pot of boiling water, adding herbs and chicken. Over an hour later the soup took on a yellowish tinge, with a raft of unidentified scum floating on its surface.

'Delicious, Brian,' said Wang Ming, having tested it with a spoon.

And to my surprise, so it was.

Many students spent a great deal of time in their dormitories, and Wang Ming, as we became friends, often complained about being bored. Their lethargy was due to limited recreational facilities, as well as the lack of extracurricular activities organised by the university. Students also had limited funds, and could not afford to go drinking often in the bars and cafés.

Student dormitories were not conducive to inspiration. The corridors were unpainted and dingy, and at meal times unbearably crowded as students pounded up and down the stairs with bowls of rice and fried cabbage. The rooms, small shoe-box oblongs, were of unadorned concrete. Two sets of bunks lined each wall, looking more like shelves than beds, with thin grey mattresses over a plank of wood. Above each bed ran a narrow shelf holding a few books and any other possessions including clothes, some of which were also kept in students' trunks. Down the centre of each room ran a long, narrow table (chipped and scarred and scribbled over by generations of students) and a few stools, with just enough room to pass on either side. Some of the window panes were broken and naked light bulbs hung sullenly from the centre of each ceiling. The electricity was turned off at eleven o'clock at night, and there was no heating, nor any fan for the humid summer.

Students were allocated a dormitory and roommates from their own department on arrival at university, and could not change rooms for any reason. Many of them confessed to not getting on with one or more of their seven roommates, and empty classrooms or the library were the only alternative to the cramped spaces and noisy rowdiness of the dormitories, which seemed a reflection of the poor social position and the indifference, bordering on contempt, in which the government held intellectuals. On the other hand, many Chinese friends admitted to me that they often enjoyed the noisy, chaotic, friendly atmosphere of their rooms, in which they knew everyone else's business and there was always a game of cards or mahjong to join. They often gazed around my flat with slightly nervous awe, and asked if I were not lonely.

Some of the students were so busy with extracurricular activities, however, that they were rarely in their rooms and their work fell into the background. Not all of them were bored, such as one student who was the department chairman of the student union, the organiser of Sports Day, an announcer on the university's television channel and the head of its radio broadcasting station. ('I am also a dancer and a very nice pop singer,' he told me once. 'I like John Denver and Kenny Rogers. But my favourite thing in the world is my girlfriend. We love each other tenderly.') Others, more academically minded, read frequently and omnivorously in English as well as Chinese—poems, novels, history, linguistics, geography and any other subject they could lay their hands on. They held discussion groups and attended open lectures given by visiting and resident foreign academics, and some of them translated short stories for literary magazines. 'One of my hobbies is reading poems,' a friend told me, an intelligent and timid young man, small and thin with a scattering of freckles across his nose and already with flecks of grey in his hair. 'Reading the poems, I feel the beating heart of the author, I can feel the beauty of nature and human beings, and I become happier and happier. I try all I can to read books so as to enrich my knowledge and enlarge my eyesight.'

Enlarging or improving one's eyesight, a much-used student phrase directly translated from the Chinese, seemed to include widening one's horizons, being open to different points of view, and developing one's abilities. Many students took the chance of the relative freedom outside the classroom to travel around Sichuan Province, indulge in their hobbies, be happily lazy, or practise a new sport, particularly swimming, as there was an Olympic-sized pool on the university campus. I too was busy enlarging my eyesight, for I played table-tennis regularly, changing to a Chinese-style grasp after a friend commented dismissively that my European hold on the bat, my fingers curled possessively around the handle, looked as if I were strangling a chicken. I was studying Chinese, too. And I was turning my hair black and acquiring the ability to break pencils without touching them; I was practising *taiji*.

Mr Jing, my shadow boxing teacher, was a small, slight man in a blue tracksuit and Adidas sneakers. He hopped nimbly among the assembled foreigners with restrained energy, urging us to be relaxed and graceful in our movements. He seemed to possess an arcane depth of knowledge, talking of the earth's energy and natural forces with quiet assurance. He had beady eyes. He spoke only Chinese, and I sometimes needed whispered translations from Hedvig and the other Swedish students around me. The teacher would stand facing us, then delicately lift his arms, extending them in front of him as if making an offering to the gods, spreading his hands and twisting his wrists slowly with controlled grace so that his palms faced the heavens. I would copy him, waving my hands carefully in the air, usually provoking a spiel of unintelligible admonition from the teacher.

'What's he saying?' I hissed. My Chinese was improving rapidly, but the rarefied language of the mysteries of *taiji* was proving too much for me.

'He says your arms are at the wrong angle, and you are too clumsy. All movements should be like the flowing of a stream.'

I closed my eyes in order to concentrate, wiggling my hands in front of me with gentlemanly caution, as if dabbling them in water, as I raised them slowly to shoulder level in the opening motion.

'Body straight, knees slightly bent! Chin slightly in!' commanded Mr Jing in Chinese.

'Body straight, chin down,' whispered the Swedish girls in unison as we progressed slowly with our lesson.

'Now lean backwards and downwards as if about to sit, move your weight to your left leg, raising the toes of the left foot and turning them outwards before placing the whole foot firmly on the floor, then bend the left leg and turn your body around to the left, shifting your weight now to your left foot and make a gesture in front of your chest as if holding a ball, make sure your left hand is on the top, then move the right foot to the side of the left foot, toes on the floor, while looking at your left hand. These are movements ten, eleven and twelve.'

'God, how many movements are there?' I asked, tuning into the last part of the teacher's instructions.

'A hundred and seventy-four,' said Hedvig, floating with serene elegance from foot to foot.

'Well, what did he just say? I got lost in the middle.'

'Oh. Well. Pretend you're sitting down, move your left foot outwards, shift weight from left to right leg.' She progressed with her movements, lending them a graceful Scandinavian air I found enviable.

I squatted down, hopping clumsily from one foot to another like a toad on a hot rock as the teacher moaned in anguish.

'Teacher Johnston! Teacher Johnston! Slooowly, slooowly.' It was his only word of English.

I slowed to infinitesimal movements.

'Slooowly, slooowly!'

Shadow boxing was indeed a slow sport, an exercise of incomparable grace and beauty. Classical Chinese writings on *taiji* compared its movements to clouds floating in the sky, or to reeling raw silk from a cocoon or, as Mr Jing had said, to the flowing of a stream. The secret was to find the correct balance between lightness and vigour to achieve fluidity of movement without inertness; the Taoist complementary principles of *yin* and *yang* meant that one had to unite stillness and motion, strength and gentleness. All those old men and women pirouetting silently by the playing field and in the parks made it look deceptively easy. In fact, for the first few weeks I took lessons my muscles ached, and after an hour's practice I was physically exhausted. *Taiji* also demanded deep abdominal and rhythmic breathing and great concentration on every movement made, as it was mental as well as physical exercise. As the weeks progressed I learnt more movements: white cranes flashing their wings, strumming the lute, grasping the bird's tail, parting the horse's mane on both sides, waving hands like clouds. But I never achieved the elasticity or style that these names indicated, or that I saw every day in the streets and parks.

Chinese cities were at their best very early in the morning. At six or seven o'clock, soon after the sun had risen, the grey concrete of the New China took on a rosy tint, and the soft light of morning sifted its harsh lines and geometry to a blurred haze. It was at this time, too, that people practised *taiji*, emerging into the streets to stand silently as ghosts under the trees along the river to perform their mysterious ballet. *Taiji*, it is said, originated over eight hundred years ago, taught by the gods in a dream to Zhang Sanfeng, a magician and producer of elixirs, and it was one of the few traditions the Han Chinese retained. It seemed to be an affirmation of cultural heritage, and it had an aura of the supernatural and the dreamlike, despite the fact that the story of its origins had been debunked; they were now fixed (according to the government) five hundred years later in Henan Province, where it began as a martial art devised to resist foreign invasion and to encourage peasant uprisings.

The government now actively promoted *taiji* as a physical culture; there was much evidence to indicate that it was of considerable benefit to general fitness and in the prevention of cardiovascular, respiratory and metabolic health problems. It was one of the most common sights in China, but for me it never lost its sense of mystery and strangeness, and nothing was more beautiful than to watch a group of pensioners in black slippers and shabby sweaters, synchronised in a perfect, slow-motion dance of curves and sweeping, silent, elegant rhythm.

All the scenes of Chengdu, the mundane and the unusual, the remarkable and the ordinary, I took in with eager pleasure. Always exhausted by the crowds, the staring of many Chinese and the novelty, I would in the end be drawn back to the peace and calm of the university campus, and I would cycle home, relieved to see the old familiar pond with its rocks dripping, its half-hearted fountain and its placid, carp-filled waters. It was a return to the starting place, a coming back to the imagined centre of China, the still point of a turning world, where I could ponder the sights of the day, secure in my surroundings.

The Chinese, had they known about my almost superstitious attitude to the pond, might have approved. If one could sum up a civilisation in a single word, one could well claim that the fitting word for China was 'home' or even 'centre'. It represented a geographical reality and a state of mind. The Chinese called their nation *Zhong-guo*, the Middle Kingdom or Middle Country; the character for centre, *zhong*, was a square slashed clean through the middle by a bold vertical stroke.

In 1601, in the last years of the reign of Elizabeth I of England, a Jesuit missionary called Matteo Ricci set up a small mission in the Chinese capital, and brought with him some European maps. These puzzled the Chinese for they thought that the earth was flat and that their own empire was squarely in the middle of it.

> They do not like the idea of our geographies pushing their
> China into one corner of the orient . . . the geographer was
> therefore obliged to change his design . . . he left a margin on

either side of the map, making the Kingdom of China appear right in the centre. This was more in keeping with their ideas and gave them a great deal of pleasure and satisfaction.

Europeans today who travel to America and suddenly find their continent has been shunted off to the far right of the map will understand the seventeenth-century Chinese reaction. All countries have an egocentric mentality, but it seemed particularly developed in the Chinese. Their long centuries of geographical isolation behind some of the most rugged landscape on earth had created a culture with a dislike of outside influence, with ideas of centrality expressed in their philosophies and cultural attitudes.

Such concepts were still very much in favour, for they were encouraged by the communists. One of the communists' most important and worthy achievements had been to unite the country after centuries of foreign intervention and decades of quarrelling warlords into a single entity, a nation that could stand up in the world. It was a powerful achievement, and one that fitted comfortably with the idea of the Middle Kingdom. Splittism, revisionism, factionalism, individualism, liberalism and deviationism were big bogeys for the government, words often bandied about in horror when they published reviews of the nation's history; centralism, collectivism and of course communism were favoured. These words were full of the flavour of socialist rhetoric, but often they contained a taste much older and more firmly entrenched. These were traditional attitudes of mind, always turned towards the centre, the fulcrum of power.

These attitudes and philosophies were useful enough as a rough guide to the Chinese mentality. Like any guidebook, however, such rules of thumb were often misleading. The neat little classifications included in the many books I had read about China I was now finding sadly inaccurate. Almost everything in China was full of rich historical and traditional meanings and symbolism, not all of which was clearly understood and interpreted by foreigners. In any case, I did not see a need to try to cram every observation of China and its people into prearranged boxes all neatly labelled. It was rather condescending to think the Chinese could be so easily explained and classified. Such notions were important, but I had already realised that they only went part way in explaining the many individuals that made up this collective country. The pattern of a kaleidoscope seemed in the same way satisfyingly complete, but it did nothing to explain how each coloured piece had fitted into the whole.

And so I pedalled around the city, and practised *taiji*, and sat by my pond, plotting more journeys as the last few weeks of term drifted to a close. I wanted to go south once more, and seek out more contradictions, more parallels and paradoxes, more mystery. Yet these were views I thrust on the country from the outside. More than that, I wanted to understand things from the inside, the way the Chinese saw them, and steep myself in the ordinariness of China.

Like a child before Christmas, I counted off the days to the close of term with excited anticipation.

by black dragon pool

six

During the peak travelling period in China, twenty days before Spring Festival and twenty days after, six hundred million people take to the railways, the air, the roads and the waterways to join their families for Chinese New Year; the railway network alone carries a hundred and twenty-five million passengers. It was, therefore, with some relief that I found myself with a ticket for train 321 to Kunming, and early in January I set off southwards to Yunnan Province for the winter break.

My hard sleeper carriage on the Chengdu–Kunming express consisted of eighteen compartments open onto the corridor, each containing two triple bunk-beds of hardboard coated with plastic, with pillow and blanket supplied. There was a short black shelf-table, bucket seats under the windows in the corridor, and imitation blue velvet curtains which hung limply, serving as convenient substitute towels for those emerging from the washroom. Hopeful signs, complete with cartoon drawings, warned passengers not to smoke in bed or spit in the corridors, but blue cigarette smoke already filtered through the carriages in the huge, lazy drifts of a French Gauloise advertisement as I climbed on board and settled in.

Across from my bed a slight, middle-aged woman clambered lethargically into the top bunk, squashed up against the ceiling like a narrow coffin. She had a tired, lined face; her hair hung lank and lustreless about her face. She seemed to have given up on the world; she lay on her bunk with hands clasped over her stomach like an effigy in a churchyard, locked away unmoving in her own tragedy. Underneath, two young men sat side by side, holding hands, drinking Green Leaf beer and laughing softly, muttering to each other of foreigners. As the journey progressed, loudspeakers supplied music and announced forthcoming stations in sharp, high-pitched staccato, warning passengers to gather their luggage in time, and doling out mind-numbing statistics on the distance travelled and distance remaining.

Early the next morning a belligerent woman attendant pulled the coarse grey blanket unceremoniously off me and away; I looked out the window to see southern Sichuan bathed in sunlight. The terrain was fragmented and rugged, and tunnels (over two hundred of them) were frequent, giving the passing scenery an unreal appearance, flashing from dark to light like a slide show: a man in blue standing forlornly at a tiny railway halt with a yellow flag; a river sliding under a grey bridge, the shallow braids of water weaving patterns across the pebbled riverbed; rolling mountains dotted with graveyards. Few of the passengers cared to peer out the grimy windows at this spectacular, fleeting landscape—perhaps they had made this journey many times before. They sat on their bunks swinging their legs and gazing resignedly in front of them, sipping without enthusiasm from chipped, tea-filled jamjars. Their movements were tight and economical, as if wasted energy had to be accounted for at the end of the journey to some heavenly overseer—small, surreptitious sips, elbows tightly in against their chests like young children learning table manners. They snapped the lids back on hurriedly, preserving the warmth of the tea.

One of these tea drinkers was Zhang Hua, a translator for a trade company. He was from Xichang, he said, a town on the train line in the southernmost part of Sichuan Province, over five hundred kilometres from Chengdu. I knew the place, having spent a long weekend there with some friends in the early autumn—the capital of Liangshan Yi Nationality Autonomous Region. The Yi were the fourth-largest ethnic group in China, with a population of over five million scattered through southern Sichuan, Yunnan and Guizhou Provinces. They had maintained an aristocratic and slave-owning society until 1958, and spoke a Tibeto-Burman language. They were largely a rural people, so the majority of Xichang's population was Han Chinese, like Zhang Hua.

Zhang Hua had a surprisingly lavish breakfast, courtesy, he told me, of his girlfriend. He produced smoked duck, roast beef and spring rolls filled with spicy vegetables which he offered around before delving in himself, sucking noisily on the duck bones and discarding them carelessly out the window. A railway attendant passed along the corridor with a metal cart filled with polystyrene boxes of rice and limp, colourless vegetables. Zhang Hua waved him aside scornfully. I drank coffee—boiled water was supplied in flasks—and looked meditatively out the window, watching flocks of goats, blurred white like snow patches against a windswept mountainside.

Some time later Zhang Hua said to me, almost apologetically, 'When I was a child, I was told that all Westerners have blue eyes made of precious stones. That's why they are so rich.'

He laughed genially. I was rather taken aback; I did not like being the subject of someone else's childhood fantasy. I watched Zhang Hua packing his belongings, and wondered how these foreigners with gems in their eyes could be rich without also being blind. Zhang Hua said goodbye; we had arrived at Xichang. I said goodbye too, rather self-consciously. I avoided looking at him now with my blue eyes.

'Are you familiar with Xichang?' a new passenger asked me hopefully as the train drew out of the station. 'It is the place of my birth, though I now live in Kunming.'

'Yes, I know your hometown,' I said, explaining that I had visited it in October.

'Really? I think it is not so interesting for a foreigner,' replied the passenger with true Chinese modesty.

'Oh, yes, yes it is. A lot of foreigners are interested in China's minorities. I found the Yi people in Xichang very colourful, though very shy. Though I saw few of them,' I added thoughtfully. 'They don't seem to like town life very much.'

'They are a dirty people,' said the passenger disparagingly, wrinkling his nose in demonstration. 'Only washing at certain festivals.'

'Well, I like their clothes,' I said crossly. 'All those blues, scarlets and yellows. I like the way they dress—broad sashes and tassels and spectacular headgear. They have a very interesting history.' I was beginning to sound like a tourist blurb, but I resented his attitude. He didn't look especially clean himself. He was picking his teeth with a grimy fingernail, I noted.

'Luckily we have abolished their feudalistic slave society.'

'The Han Chinese are really rather drab, compared with China's minorities,' I replied rudely. 'Boring, in fact.'

The man who came from Xichang but lived in Kunming said nothing. He seemed to shrink inside his crumpled jacket. He looked out the window and swallowed some tea from his jar. I wondered if I had offended him. I wanted to snatch the jar off him and hurl it out the window. I turned away, gazing out across the countryside.

Some time later, just before midday, the train lurched into Jinjiang, a large railway depot and shunting yard on the border of Sichuan Province. It was a rough place, full of angry-faced young men preying on bewildered travellers for easy money. From here it was a ten-hour bus ride through the mountains of Yunnan to Lijiang, my destination. Dukou, a large town of smoking industries and ugly quarries scarring the barren landscape, was soon left behind, to be followed by isolated farming communities and rice paddies tiered up from valley bottoms in regular steps.

Next morning, the fresh air and sunshine of Lijiang were intoxicating, making me feel almost light-headed after the smoggy greyness of the Chengdu winter. Lijiang sprawled in a mountain valley, the new part of the town geometrically ruled with wide, straight streets lined with functional concrete buildings (People's Post Office, Children's Cultural Palace, People's Department Store). There was a statue of Mao Zedong on the main street in his characteristic pose, a bent right arm upraised as if pegging out washing. With the coming of evening, loud-speakers entertained the entire town with classical Chinese music and announcements so distorted that I, at least, could understand none of them; they howled as meaninglessly and eerily as wolves on the Russian steppes. In the square around Mao, young men idly played pool in the dying light, scarcely speaking.

Historically, Yunnan Province was one of the China's most recent acquisitions, having been absorbed into the empire a mere seven hundred years ago. For centuries after that it had remained an undesirable place where political embarrassments had been sent to cool their heels. Kunming, its capital, had long been a backwater, a journey of months from Beijing. Only the flight of many intellectuals and professional people to Yunnan during the Japanese occupation of eastern China opened up the city to industrial growth, and today both the city and province are thriving. But in remote Lijiang the Chinese walked along with heads shyly averted, as if aware they didn't belong to this isolated corner of the Middle Kingdom; spawned in the central reaches of the Yellow River far to the north-east, what right had they to these wild and barren mountain valleys? Here, only the local Naxi women seemed at ease, with their stout frames and feet splayed as a Swiss peasant's, hands clasped comfortably over their stomachs, their faces as wrinkled as the mountains that cradled them.

No one is certain from where the Naxi originate; they claim they are all descended from Tabu, an Adam hatched long ago from a gigantic egg. Whatever their source, Lijiang has long been the centre of the Naxi minority, whose kingdom reached its zenith in the seventeenth century, controlling trade between China and Tibet. But there are few Tibetans here now, and the Naxi have been shunted into a historical backwater. Now they number only a quarter of a million, and though they speak their own Tibeto-Burman language, their unique script, developed more than a millennium ago and written on insect-proof bark, is dying out; it can only be read by a few religious leaders.

There were a number of Yi, too, in Lijiang, in from their remote villages further up in the mountains. The Yi women flounced through the streets in ankle-length layered skirts in purple and red that made me think of Spanish flamenco dancers. Their desperate shyness seemed contradicted by their startling multicoloured head-dresses, which gave them the intimidating dimensions of Amazons. It was hard to tell who was more fascinated—I by the Yi or they by the foreigner, as they peered blushing from underneath their hats. One old Yi farmer in a dark, tattered cloak stared at me with mouth agape from the pavement as I sat in an open-fronted restaurant eating an evening meal.

The Yi claim their ancestors were nourished by the blood of a divine eagle; the *charva*, or cape made of felt which Yi men wear over their shoulders, is meant to make them resemble these heavenly birds as they stride along, material flapping in the wind. This belief was hard to accept at that moment; the old farmer looked more like a raven from a fable, of rather battered aspect, observing a new species from the top of a tree and unsure of how to treat it. To me in that moment he was a metaphor for all China: a poor man, frozen in time, clinging with pride to the tattered remnants of his culture but simultaneously fascinated by a West he found difficult to reconcile with his present existence. It was a moment of deep meaning, full of portent and foreboding, as this man hovered uncertainly, as if choosing his own future, and I stared back, aghast at its significance.

Our eyes met, our looks wavered, and he was gone, winding his way in a bundle of black into the night, leaving a trail of questions.

The old town, where the Naxi lived, had a quite different character from the new, Han part of Lijiang. Cobbled streets were lined with old homes, half wood and half grey stone, with overhanging eaves and tiled roofs; most opened into a central courtyard filled with potted shrubs, limp washing and discarded boxes. The streets were alive with markets and commerce; Naxi men shouldered their way through the crowds, some with magnificent hunting falcons on their leather-gloved wrists, their faces tanned dark by the mountain sun and wind. But only the women still wore traditional dress—blue shirt and trousers and a blue or black apron, the whole often topped off by a Mao cap which, in its matching blueness, was an almost unnoticed anachronism. A sheepskin hung down the women's backs to prevent chafing by the heavy baskets they carried from the fields, supported by a headstrap. Seven embroidered circles on their capes symbolised the stars; the sun and moon, larger circles, were now rarely seen among the younger Naxi.

At night, Orion and other stars lay sprawled across the sky above Lijiang; the river glittered as if with mercury. I stared up at the stars in exhilaration after the almost permanent greyness of Chengdu. The old village was particularly atmospheric under moonlight: gables against an indigo sky, chinks of light showing through wooden walls like an Impressionist painter's orange brush flicked haphazardly across a dark canvas. The wooden houses were like cottages from a Grimm fairy tale; I felt that a Naxi woman might beckon me inside, to push me into her oven or to feed me with fresh sticks of gingerbread. I strolled around this fairyland at night, cats recoiling in alarm before dissolving into shadows, meriting their reputation as the familiars of witches.

After the evening stroll it would be time to return reluctantly to Lijiang's Guesthouse Number One. The square, concrete room in which I was staying, the lower half painted in hospital green, the upper in faded, flesh-coloured orange, reminded me of all I disliked most: pistachio ice cream, apricots, school cafeterias. The high-pitched, almost hysterical Chinese laugh took on a new significance here; the institutional colours, the heavy old-fashioned furniture and the weighty bars across the narrow wooden-framed windows (looking out on a winter garden of dead trees) gave it the uncared-for look of a run-down mental asylum. A naked light bulb dangled from the centre of the ceiling on a cord long enough to hang oneself with; isolated noises resounded from other rooms, but no one seemed ever to walk the long, haunted corridor. This impression was re-inforced by a journey to the bathroom, a long march along endless corridors in aquamarine and white. By the time one arrived one felt one had indeed become insane; the corridors converged endlessly ahead, like the nightmares of old men in post-modernist Eastern European novels.

'*Ggubbu bbeu*,' I muttered to myself one night, lying on my bed. '*Ggubbu bbeu*.' It was Naxi language, and according to my guidebook it meant, 'I am going to Lijiang.' Their language seemed bewildering to me, and I did not really know how I should pronounce *ggubbu bbeu*. I rolled it around my tongue contemplatively, as if testing its flavour. My guidebook also told me that Naxi society was formerly matriarchal. Traditionally, men were child rearers, and often lived with their parents even after marriage, while women were independent and in full charge of business matters. Women inherited property; the town's affairs were controlled by its female citizens.

After a while I gave up my guidebook, listening to the sinister silence of the corridor outside. I said '*Ggubbu bbeu*' once more, *sotto voce* like an asylum inmate, and pulled the blankets up around my chin.

The star attraction of Lijiang was Dr He Shixiu, who lived in a nearby village and practised traditional medicine in his Clinic of Chinese Herbs of Jade-Dragon-Snow Mountain. The few foreigners I met in these parts urged me to go and visit him, as one might visit a museum in Beijing. Doctor He spoke English and welcomed all foreign visitors, I was told, for whom he apparently had a visitors' book complete with comments and photos. He would regale me with stories of learning English from Second World War airmen (who refuelled here on their route from India to Kunming), his meetings with Joseph Rock, a famous botanist who lived in Lijiang for more than twenty years prior to the Second World War, and his experiences during the Cultural Revolution. One could rent a bicycle and go to visit him. He pressed packets of tea on departing guests, while suggesting a small donation might be appropriate, I was warned.

'He met George Bush, while Bush was stationed at the American Embassy in Beijing!' said one German tourist triumphantly. 'A very interesting man.'

I imagined He Shixiu might be like one of those ancient mandarins who peopled the China of my childhood imagination. I had imagined such old men to be sages well versed in occult powers, with wispy beards that fell uncombed down to their knees, and fingernails long as shoehorns. They lived in pavilions teetering on the summits of high mountains, and wore long golden gowns embossed with dragons, with wide sleeves that gracefully draped down to sweep the floor. But now, faced with the fascinating reality of China, I had lost interest in these quaint ideas from my past. Secretly I was not interested in the Clinic of Chinese Herbs of Jade-Dragon-Snow Mountain, and having met George Bush was no recommendation to me. I did not wish to beat a track to the doctor's door along with every other tourist in Lijiang.

Renting a bicycle, I set off along rutted tracks and out into the countryside, through mud-brick villages populated by pigs and dogs dozing in the sun. I did not go in the direction of the village of the good Dr He. I had been advised by the receptionist at my hotel, who had knocked off knitting long enough to consider it, that if I wanted a nice cycle in the countryside I should take a lane leading off to the left immediately after the prison. As most buildings seem to look like prisons in China, with high walls and a guarded entrance, this was ambiguous advice. (I found it on the way back, ominously silent behind barbed wire.) Soon I became lost among the patchwork fields; the track deteriorated into a series of narrow footpaths along the tops of the irrigation banks, across which I was forced to stumble with my bucking bicycle, hauling it over a chessboard of channels and waterways under the by now surprisingly hot sun. This was a different experience from Joseph Rock's; he had been carried in a sedan chair and had travelled the countryside accompanied by a long caravan including, among other things, a gold dinner service, a seven-branched candelabra and half a dozen servants.

Still, my own hardships were perversely enjoyable, I thought as I yanked my recalcitrant bicycle out of a rut in the hard earth, for I knew they would become the fond memories of tomorrow. Besides which, the sky was blue, the corn long harvested, and the dead branches of willows clawed the air in a hypnotising motion—there was poetry in all nature.

The most beautiful poem of Lijiang, when I eventually untangled myself from the fields, was a park that lay at the far end of the modern town—Heilongtan, or Black Dragon Pool, a blue lake surrounded by reeds and trees and several monastic buildings dating from the Ming and Qing Dynasties, including the quaintly named three-storey Moon Embracing Pavilion. It was the Western image of China so rarely found in reality: tall wooden pagodas with turned-up roofs, arched bridges over lakes, and elegant trees like Chinese patterns on a Wedgwood plate. In the distance reared snow-capped mountain peaks. It was a far cry from the busy parks of Canton and Xiamen, splendidly peaceful and drowsy in the afternoon sun, the crumbling stone and peeling, painted eaves of the religious buildings conveying an atmosphere of perpetual peace—stone, wood and water, people and nature in perfect symbiosis as recommended by Taoist philosophy, once practised in these temples.

In the evenings, I could sit in this park for hours; it was a landscape made for solitude and twilight contemplation, for lovers and suicides and meandering old men with their lonely memories. But the only people here were a few young students, walking slowly along with their books held in front of them, reading aloud as if dictating to secretaries under the denuded trees. Down by the lake's edge, one could be carried away by the eternal fascination of water, the cross-hatching of ripples on the surface, the gentle sucking and gurgling which drew one in with irresistible hypnosis, the ceaselessly shifting blue shot with primrose yellow and purple by the dying sun. It could have been that I was the only person left in the world. Looking into the blueness of the endlessly shifting lake, one could imagine how easy it would be to slip into the water, insinuate oneself into its infinite anonymity and vanish for ever. But I did not. In fact, sitting there on a green wooden bench one evening, I suddenly felt a profound and unexplained happiness:

> You may ask why I come to live among green hills;
> I smile without answering, my heart at peace.
> Peach blossoms float away with the stream;
> There are heavens and earths beyond the work of men.

So wrote Li Bai in one of his most famous poems. This is the reason that I travel, I thought; for this I endure the nightmare marathons of Chinese buses, the discomfort of life on the move, for these moments of undistilled beauty.

At that moment there was nowhere else I would rather have been than alone on that peeling wooden bench in the mountains of Yunnan, looking across the lake where the rest of China waited, still an enigma, in the darkness beyond.

On the road from Lijiang to Dali, the sides of the hills were covered with graveyards, the tombs leaning like old teeth on the brown gums of the fields. It was a barren landscape of red soil and frozen fields and ditches, peasants standing, wrapped in cloaks, over insubstantial fires by the roadside, faces pinched with the early morning cold. The valley bottoms were a pattern of corrugated fields within a grid of earthen walls, seasonally planted with spring onions, cauliflowers, cabbages and potatoes. The villages looked tidy, the large houses solidly prosperous behind high walls, yet at a roadside stop a beggar woman with a small boy importuned the passengers, thrusting out scrawny arms. The Chinese turned away in embarrassment, leaving the woman to scavenge for peel, as bright as an accusation in the dust, dropped from their tangerines.

Dali (the name meant 'marble', for which the area was famous), though lower than Lijiang, was still two thousand metres above sea level, on the shores of a lake high in a mountain valley. It was the centre for another minority nationality, the Bai, though in most respects the Bai were difficult to distinguish from the Han Chinese, as they spoke a very closely related language and used Chinese characters when writing. They did, however, wear brightly coloured minority costumes in pink and scarlet, with jaunty bonnets. Dali had been continuously inhabited since the eighth century, when it became the capital of Nanzhao, a powerful kingdom which at its height comprised much of Burma and parts of Laos and Thailand and was able to keep the encroachments of the northern Tang Dynasty government at bay. It remained independent, controlling the trade route between China and India, until it was defeated by Kublai Khan's army centuries later.

Dali Number Two Guesthouse was as little inspiring as Lijiang Number One Guesthouse. It was a vast echoing concrete monstrosity, overlooking a dusty basketball court where young men lounged, cigarettes dangling from their lips, like a scene out of *West Side Story*. In the evenings I was to discover these same young men lounging naked in the cramped bathroom, filling the air with steam from the two showers, brushing their teeth, slapping themselves with towels and ogling foreigners with unfeigned curiosity, much to my embarrassment.

Inside my room a notice gave advice on 'How to maintain social order and ensure guests' security'. This included the prohibition of exploding or poisonous items, gambling, heavy drinking, 'lighting fires and laying goods' and 'living in a mixed state'. The notice ended with the enigmatic statement: 'When the public security officers and defenders show their identification initiatively, they can't refuse to be checked and make troubles. Thank you for your cooperation.'

Outside the hotel, Bai women prowled in the street, whispering 'Change money?' in the same hoarse voice that is heard all over China, hawking silver bangles and pocket knives, marijuana seeds as small and grey as the pellets of an airgun, and red-and-green earrings which (they claimed) belonged to their great-grandmothers and were very precious, very antique. But they were not insistent, content to be distracted by a private house being built by a local who, I was told, had made money from a market garden, selling the azaleas, camellias, pomegranates and other flowering bushes so common in the town. Workmen stood around in groups, smoking in short, nervous jerks, while a few of their mates worked overhead on the wooden supporting structure, banging joints together with unwieldy, oversized mallets and without the aid of a single nail. Long strings of crackers were tied to the last roof beams, exploding noisily as these were raised up, spilling cardboard casings and clouds of acrid, oily blue smoke, ensuring good fortune for the building.

The houses of Dali, like the one being built, were mostly in traditional style, with walls and floors of stone and roofs decorated with wooden gables and painted eaves. All that remained of the ancient city were the two massive north and south gates. The nearby three Chongsheng Pagodas at the foot of Mount Changshan were the only other structures of note. Pagodas were not, as many people assumed, home-grown Chinese; they originated in India, but like everything else of value from abroad had been quickly assimilated into Chinese culture. The tallest pagoda in Dali had sixteen storeys, more than any other in China. The other two pagodas were somewhat newer, built during the Five Dynasties. Unlike the major structure, which was hollow and square, these were octagonal and solid. They were handsome buildings, among the oldest surviving in south-west China.

While Lijiang, only six hours further up the road, was as yet virtually unchanged by tourism, Dali, despite its lack of real tourist sights, had become the haunt of budget travellers since its opening to foreigners in 1984. There were far more tourists in the streets of Dali than I had tried to avoid by not visiting Dr He, I soon realised. With the slightly bovine and vacant look of people long on the road, they had tossed hair and scruffy clothes. They sat in the cafés and exchanged information about the latest black market rates or tourist bargains, or repeated their potted personal histories with the glib patter of a vaudeville performer who retells the same stories night after night to an indifferent but polite audience. They tried to outdo each other with travellers' tales, yet despite their experiences their conversations remained, for the most part, remarkably uninteresting.

Thoreau, in *Life without Principle*, wrote: 'We rarely meet a man who can tell us any news which he has not read in a newspaper, or been told by his neighbour; and, for the most part, the only difference between us and our fellow is that he has seen the newspaper, or been out to sea, and we have not.' But in Dali, even that advantage was lost; everyone had been out to sea, like met with like, and it was only annoying and demoralising to find that others too had been in the jungles of Thailand, or the ghettos of Calcutta, or had been teaching English in Kyoto, Taipei, Shanghai or Hong Kong. Where once I had imagined I was unique, intrepid, I was suddenly revealed in Dali to be part of a whole world where only the most *outré* experiences were deemed worthy of note. I had temporarily dropped out of mainstream society—but to where? In Dali I suddenly realised I had merely fallen into another society, equally riddled with its own conceits and rules and prejudices, of travellers and expatriates thirsty for originality and yet secretly afraid of unfamiliarity. Many of the travellers in Dali seemed bored, smoking cigarettes and shifting restlessly from café to café (and eventually country to country) in a fundamentally unenergetic search for adventure.

These travellers brought with them one advantage, from my point of view: a demand for Western food. I felt guilty, but after a year of rice I felt I had earned it. I sat furtively eating steak and chips, pizza, banana pancakes and fresh milkshakes as I pondered on travellers, watching them with a detached amusement, as if I were not one of them—although, unnervingly, I knew I was. At times it seemed quite untrue to me that travel was a part of education, that it broadened the mind, for some of the travellers in Dali appeared fundamentally disinterested in the places in which they had travelled. They pounced on those oddities (the Chinese eat dogs, the Chinese have no concept of privacy), eagerly grasped because they highlighted the heathen strangeness of a distant and misunderstood race, and gave the observer a feeling of indulgent superiority without having to delve below the exotic surface. (Although I remembered the dogs in the market at Canton, I had never met a Chinese who had eaten one, and many of them wrinkled their noses in disgust at the idea.) They followed their Lonely Planet guidebook as assiduously as a preacher follows the Bible, stopping in the same hotels as other foreigners and eating in the same restaurants, hoping the menu would be in English. They discussed bus fares and their most recent hassles, as if hardship and the saving of a few dollars justified the journey, and triumphed over saving a few *yuan* at the expense of an impoverished local. When it was time to buy a plane ticket, however, they flashed their American Express cards and set off to some other piece of paradise.

Suddenly I felt that these itinerant Westerners—and I could not, after all, dissociate myself from them—could be just as interesting and unusual as the Chinese. Perhaps we were to be admired for giving up our comfortable lifestyles and the materialism of home in exchange for a precarious and often uncomfortable life on the road; this was, after all, an education of sorts. But at the same time our egocentrism was revealing to anyone who bothered to listen; we were people preoccupied with our own pursuits and adventures, living inside the cocoons of our own personalities yet offering glimpses of the society from which we were formed. Our self-centred, self-indulgent lives seemed so different from the lives of the Chinese. This was the flip side of the coin, the result of wide freedom and vaunted individualism, too much choice, too much indifference to others. Point, counterpoint: the Chinese were mirror images of ourselves, and to journey among them was to look at new reflections of my own society that gave me new awareness.

There was one interesting person in Dali, though he was not a foreigner. He came into the café late one night, when only I and the owner were left sitting among the dimness of empty plates and stale cigarette smoke—a novice monk in a long, dark-blue smock with white puttees wrapped around his legs. His hair was close-cropped and he wore glasses with ugly black frames. He looked about thirty-five, but he said his name was Zhang Xiangyang, so he couldn't have been more than about twenty-seven; Xiangyang means 'looking at the sun'—the sun being

Mao, and the name surely given during the Cultural Revolution. He was the only Chinese I had seen in this particular restaurant, but he was completely at ease and self-assured; he ordered a Nescafé—an expensive drink—and lit a Mild Seven cigarette, imported from Japan.

Having settled in, he initiated a conversation by asking me where I was from. He was from Anhui Province, but studying at the Buddhist seminary in Shanghai, one of the few places in China that trained monks. When did he come to believe in Buddhism, and how, I asked. He smiled rather vaguely.

'But I don't believe in the religious precepts of Buddhism . . . Some years ago I read a story about a hermit in former times. It made a very deep impression on me. I wished that I, too, could find a clearing in a forest, and then make a thatched home. That would be enough. Every morning after getting up, I would take a stroll along the little path, breathing fresh air and listening to the birds, then I would go to my garden to water the flowers and pull up weeds. After that I would return home, infuse a cup of tea, and read some history books. This would make me think profoundly.

'But of course'—he waved his cigarette dismissively—'such an existence is not possible in our China. I wanted to be far from the crowds so as to avoid the hypocrisy, fraudulence, hostility and all the vices of mankind. That is why I am studying Buddhism. Perhaps the monk is the freest person in China; he can travel from temple to temple all across the country, he has all the time in every day to do as he pleases.' He smiled at me without irony. He seemed very calm and detached, almost remote.

I smiled back at him. His was a response to Chinese conformity which I had not yet come across. In him the old cliché about the Chinese—minds regimented under authority— became once again a nonsense; here was a man who tried his best to make his own destiny within the restraints which bound him.

'The only reason for which I might change my mind,' he concluded, 'is if I meet a beautiful girl! For of course monks are not allowed to get married!'

He grinned again, impishly, looking young for the first time. I stared at him, intrigued, with frustration—I could see he was growing tired with this questioning. Just one more thing I wanted to know: where did he get the money to buy his Japanese cigarettes? He looked back at me, a flicker of amusement in his eyes.

'From foreign tourists. I sold some calligraphy to foreigners, in Kunming. Foreigners have much money, I think. They paid too much! But I must enjoy the best cigarettes. When I become a full monk, no more smoking will be allowed!' He grinned broadly, puffing a cloud of grey smoke into the air, where it writhed and twisted indolently.

The café owner was stacking away the chairs, the lights going out one by one. I went out into the street, footsteps sounding as loud as castanets on the cobbles.

The apprentice monk padded away silently into the shadows, cigarette smoke following him, looped in the air like the vanishing grin of a Cheshire cat.

kingdom of the peacocks

Red earth, white and blue skies, green vegetation: that was Yunnan Province through the windows of a bus, as simple and absolute as a child's drawing. 'The road is a winding and scenic one,' a Chinese tourist guide had told me in Kunming, the provincial capital, where I had spent a few days after leaving Dali. 'So when you drive or travel through that road you will be able to enjoy fertile fresh green rice paddy waving in the breeze, wonderful landscape, beautiful valleys and various plants along the road, such as tobacco, corn, tea plantation, potato and so forth.' The landscape did indeed become increasingly fertile as we crawled southwards. Wide valleys, as green and lush as magazine advertisements for Philippine Airlines, were terraced into steps and framed by the drier tans and russets of the mountains.

I was now heading to Xishuangbanna, a journey less than eight hundred kilometres south from Kunming but taking over two long days by road. A Japanese boy had sat beside me on the bus, wearing Levi's Red Labels and a peacock-blue sweatshirt. He had carefully rolled up his down jacket, squeezing it into a neat silver cloth holder and attaching it by a clip to his shoulder bag, on which was hanging a slim flashlight and a metal water bottle. Opening the bag, he had lifted out a plastic case containing a neat row of boxed cassettes, one of which he had selected and inserted into his Walkman. I had watched, fascinated, feeling scruffy and disorganised, until he went to sleep, falling against my shoulder. He was scarcely to move for the rest of the journey, except to replace his cassettes in his Walkman, slotting them in with slow carefulness the way a bored teenager might put bread into a toaster.

The first evening was spent in the one-horse town of Gang Zhuang, dirty and scruffy as are all places where people merely pass through, spending a night at an impersonal hotel. A few flaking houses with piles of disintegrating junk sitting outside them, an empty, hopeful-looking noodle shop, a few dusty chickens, all presided over by a couple of old crones perched on wooden stools in the road as if they had sat down for a rest coming out of the Ark and had never bothered to get up again—that was Gang Zhuang. But the valley in which the village stood was richly green with fields of rice and rustling sugar cane, farmers and buffalo struggling knee-deep in black treacle mud, and stooping women weeding pumpkin patches against the ochre sky of a dying day.

After a disturbed night in a hotel resounding hollowly with noise, it was on towards Simao, passing farmhouses as isolated as castles, surrounded by their moats of flooded terraces. The Japanese student, who had now migrated further down the bus, seemed to share my desperation over noisy hotels; he leaned his head back and pounded his forehead with his fist for over half an hour, stopping only to take swigs from a Pepsi Cola can.

It was on this section of the journey that I fell into conversation with a young Chinese woman who introduced herself by her English name, Elizabeth. I had ceased to be surprised by meeting so many people who spoke English; they converged on foreigners with the desperation of a drowning person sighting a raft, eager for practice. Often these conversations faltered to an embarrassing halt after an exchange of pleasantries, and sometimes I was stumped by incredible questions ('Excuse me sir, what is the difference between turmoil, disturbance, upheaval, tumult and commotion?') but occasionally students came along who spoke excellent English, and then conversation was sheer delight. Elizabeth—not surprisingly, it turned out that she was an English teacher—was one of these.

'In China,' she said after having gone through the standard introductory exchanges, 'it is taken for granted that a woman has already done more than enough preparation for her future by graduating from college. She should learn to be a tender, hard-working wife. The only thing for her to do is to take care of her husband and child, and to do most of the homework . . . I mean, housework.' She laughed nervously. Despite her self-assurance I did not think she had spoken to many foreigners, and she spoke carefully, as if afraid of startling a wild animal.

'I think that's too unjust for women! We have the same ability as men. So last year, I spent four months working for the entrance examination to become a postgraduate. I gave lessons during the day at my college, and stayed awake until late at night over a pile of books. The result didn't disappoint me! I passed the exam and proved to myself that I have the same ability as any man. Why shouldn't I continue my studies? I think I have made the right choice.'

I gnawed on my bar of chocolate—Lucky brand, made in Shanghai and, I had long ago discovered, the only palatable chocolate in China. Elizabeth had fallen silent; somehow she reminded me of Xiao Li, the factory worker I had met in Xiamen.

'There is a Chinese poem,' said Elizabeth after a while. 'I don't know if you know it. It goes something like this:

> How sad it is to be a woman!
> Nothing on earth is held so cheap.
> No one is glad when a girl is born,
> By her the family sets no store.

Such a traditional view is terrible! As a modern girl, I try to be active, not passive; self-confident, not easily controlled.'

Later in the journey, assuming she was married as are nearly all Chinese women at her age, I had asked what her husband thought of her becoming a student again.

'Most people think that girls should be quiet and sweet and get married! I don't have this traditional idea. I am not married yet! You know a Chinese saying, perhaps: "Marriage is like a circle; those who are not married want to step into it, while those who are already in the circle, want to step outside!" I am in no hurry to enter the circle. Whenever the thought occurs to me that I will marry, bear a child and then live peacefully and dully for my whole life, like other girls do, I feel very frightened and restless. I just can't help dreaming of a different life. So many things I want to have a go at! In fact, in many aspects I try to be boyish. I like to play with the boys, that is more challenging.'

I raised my eyebrows. I was always amused by this Chinese use of the verb 'play', which they translated directly from their own language. I have come to play with you, demure college girls would say when I opened the door of my flat. But Elizabeth was unaware of the slightly salacious connotations of the word.

'Most of the time I have a great desire to be a winner. For example, last week I played cards with three other boys. I became the centre and the winner, they admired and envied my technique of playing. I got great satisfaction, for I am aware that if I can beat the boys, I can beat most of the girls. This kind of victory attracts me a lot. It encourages me to continue. So that same afternoon, I defeated two boys at table-tennis!

'I always hold the idea that men and women are equal. I want to prove that through my own behaviour. Maybe people think I am peculiar. Oh, why care about what others say? But do I have the courage to be an unusual person? Is this good or bad? I don't know. I am not sure. But I am trying to be unique. Uniqueness is my destination.'

My own destination, less dramatically, was reached on the third morning from Kunming when the bus entered Xishuangbanna, a vast region of remote valleys and low, forested mountains bisected by the Mekong River. It used to take a year to get to Beijing from here; it would still take a week overland, though a new airport had opened in Jinhong, the regional capital. Xishuangbanna, covering a mere fraction of China's total land area, nonetheless holds a quarter of its faunal species (including the country's last remaining elephants and tigers) and a third of all China's birds, such as the rare great hornbill and the more common Chinese laughing thrush, popular as a songbird and often seen in cages across the country.

Xishuangbanna is also home to two dozen ethnic minorities, with names like aliens in a science fiction novel: Dai, Hani, Zhuang, Yi, Hui, Miao, Bulang, Lahu, Wa, Yao, Jinuo and Bai.

Among them they make up two-thirds of the local population. Minorities, once referred to as the Barbarians of Four Directions by the Han Chinese, were promised a measure of autonomy when the communists came to power in 1949, as well as assistance in maintaining their languages and cultures. These fraternal considerations were not realised, however. After 'liberation' by the People's Liberation Army in 1950 Xishuangbanna suffered religious persecution, imposition of the Han language and customs, discrimination against ethnic groups and the transplantation of large numbers of colonising Han Chinese. This was followed by the Cultural Revolution, which disgorged Red Guards into the region and left the smoking remains of desecrated temples and a smashed minority culture, just as it had done in Tibet. Now Xishuangbanna is an autonomous region, with relative independence in local administration for the minorities; temples are reopening and the traditions of the tribal peoples being revived. But this is not a miracle rejuvenation; it is a cosmetic mask over the brooding face of Han supremacy.

Jinhong, the only sizable town in Xishuangbanna, had the air of a colonial city; perhaps not surprising, for although it had been part of China for eight hundred years Xishuangbanna was, in some sense, a colony. As recently as the nineteenth century it was the scene of a struggle for imperial domination between Britain and France. Jinhong was occupied by five hundred British troops before both powers decided to leave the area, with Thailand, as a buffer zone between the interests of the British in India and Burma and those of the French in Indochina.

The streets of Jinhong were broad and lined with massive oil palms. Oversized for such a small place, the boulevards appeared empty, as if built for the parade of a conquering army. There were hospitals, schools and impressive government buildings ('Foreigners are not allowed on the grounds of government offices' announced a stern notice on the gate in red capitals) to justify the presence of the Han masters. The guest-house, too, felt colonial; here the spirit of Somerset Maugham seemed to linger much more than in modernised Malaysia or Singapore. Foreigners and Han Chinese lolled indolently on rattan chairs, sipping beer under the spectacular swathes of bougainvillea in imperial purple, rust orange, scarlet and white, while quiet native women in wide coolie hats swept the gravel pathways and tended to the frangipani. There were mosquito nets and large fans over the beds, and flasks of boiled water in every room. The occupying power had even brought its own sports; local boys played badminton and table-tennis, so beloved of the Han Chinese, with the same enthusiasm as youths from Corfu to Colombo played cricket.

But the real life of Jinhong was not in the guesthouse nor even in the broad modern streets; it was hidden in the Dai villages on the town's outskirts among the banana groves, where wrinkled black pigs with grotesquely squashed faces rooted among the rubbish for food. It was the wooden houses and women in sarongs, I felt, that really belonged to this landscape of banana trees and muddy brown rivers. Although much of the Dai's history remains unknown, they are clearly linked to the people of Thailand and Burma, sharing their smooth brown skins, laughing eyes and handsome looks. In Jinhong their wooden houses were perched on stilts and had high, steeply sloping roofs pulled low over the windows; hinged wall panels folded back to trap the breeze. They looked very picturesque hidden among the banana groves, but the tropical beauty was only superficial. Many of the houses were poor and shabby, sanitation was of the most primitive kind and rubbish was strewn about indiscriminately. Hens, goats and children ran around the dusty streets in equal numbers. Dai women shuffled about in tight, short blouses and printed sarongs, protected from the sun by straw hats or towel-wrapped headdresses as if they had just emerged from the shower. One is considered ugly among the Dai unless one's teeth are capped with gold, and when the women grinned they displayed glittering yellow molars. Several Buddhist temples dotted among these villages testified to a strong revival of the religious practice virtually destroyed during the Cultural Revolution, and young monks in orange and saffron robes and running shoes made purchases at wayside stores. In the evening they cycled round Jinhong in chattering groups, robes hitched high, grinning as they drifted sluggishly past.

Continuing through the villages, one came out on the flat land by the river banks. Outside the village these were lined with rubber, pineapple and tobacco plantations, interspersed with cinnamon, licorice and cocoa; near Jinhong they were intensely cultivated with private patches of peas, beans, corn and potatoes. Women in colourful sarongs, gaudy as flamingos, stooped to their weeding. During the afternoon the sun was very hot, and buffalo snorted and blew languorously in the water. The Mekong River, low at this season, was brown and sluggish, the banks in the evening dotted with little boys flying kites made from newspaper and sticks. Banana trees were everywhere, their leaves enormous, oval-shaped, seemingly dark green, yet when the sun caught them they turned a delicate yellow-green and one could see the ribbed pattern of veins standing out as if carefully inked in by a controlling hand.

The hotel boasted a terrace overlooking the fields and the Mekong, which descends from the Tibetan plateau, like so many of the great rivers of Asia, and flows through Yunnan into Laos and Cambodia, to empty into the ocean at the southern tip of Vietnam. I sat on the terrace and had meals with some friends from Sichuan University I had run into; we dined off sticky black rice, vegetables in peanut sauce, surprisingly tasty fried moss, and chicken in herbs and spices—traditional fare of the Dai. We kept a look out for Crim, the legendary monster of the Mekong said to devour people and cattle, but all we saw were women, ankle-deep in the water, silently panning for gold, searching for a thrilling glitter of tiny grains among the grey sludge at the bottom of their pans. Above their bent backs the veils of twilight sifted the harsh glare of day to a mellow, opalescent blue. Bats hunted overhead. Soon the evening sky was full of stars, the moon like a fragment of tinfoil; the chat drifted back and forwards in the balmy tropical night of this lost, peaceful corner of China.

Chinese New Year, the culminating day of the Spring Festival period, was early that year, falling on the 26th of January. Celebrations for the New Year had made a comeback; during the Cultural Revolution the tradition, like so much else, had been disparaged as superstitious. At midnight crackers and fireworks burst into action, resounding like salvos from the *1812 Overture*. The Chinese invented gunpowder two thousand years ago and fireworks some four hundred years after that, and have been using them with gusto ever since. In Jinhong it sounded like a battle was in progress: dull mortar-like crumps, the staccato machine-gun rattle of strings of crackers ensuring a New Year free from evil spirits—the noise was deafening and exhilarating and slightly frightening. Fireworks sparked briefly overhead in green and red chrysanthemums of colour, but there were so many that the sky was constantly alight in a blizzard of fiery snow. Sparks and empty squibs showered down and wreaked playful havoc among the shrieking population, who surged away from them in a circle as if conducting a strange tribal dance. A man walked down the centre of the road, casually trailing a string of crackers behind him. They banged and sparked until it seemed that the figure was a devil, dancing down the street with sparks flying from cloven hooves. The streets were drenched in a whirligig of fire, overhead was a scatter of jewelled explosions, a symphony of light.

No sooner had the last bang died away than everyone seemed to turn as one and vanish into the night, leaving me alone.

Early next morning I set off to Damenlong, the bus crunching over abandoned fireworks cases and blackened strings of crackers. Seventy kilometres and three hours on a dirt road south of Jinhong, and only eight kilometres from the Burmese border, Damenlong had the air of a town at the world's end. Two wide, dusty streets at right angles to each other comprised the Chinese part of the town. Enrobed monks were playing pool out in the street and men squatted along the shop fronts, picking their teeth and gazing vacantly at the gloomy bottle-filled stores across the road. Pigs and cows rooted along the rutted street surface, and under the sole tree five women crouched around a twig fire, cooking vegetables. This was the last stop on the road to inhospitable Burma, a dead-end village where locals stood in the street speculating on what might be happening elsewhere.

There was little entertainment in Damenlong. In the evening—every evening, I soon realised—young men played pool under naked, dangling light bulbs; televisions sounded, muffled behind closed doors. Perhaps they were content, these people, despite the emptiness of their lives, unable to imagine any alternative except through the flickering unreality of their television screens. The only hotel was a shabby, concrete building, the bowl of the silent fountain in its courtyard filled with stagnant green water and topped by a concrete peacock (the symbol of Xishuangbanna) on an island of rock. Around the peacock's neck was tied a long bamboo pole with a bent television aerial on its end; here, also, the television itself blared incessantly through the evening like the last desperate ravings of a dying person.

In my room I found one of the many leaflets produced by the Chinese government on a wide variety of topics. This one was a decade old, entitled *Forty Firsts in China in 1983*. I lay on my bed, listening to the roar of the television, and copied some of the points into my notebook.

> 2 The *Selected Works of Deng Xiaoping* outsold all the other nine best-sellers in China during 1983. All in all 54,850,000 volumes, in de luxe, paperback and popular edition, were put on sale.

> 3 Gu Xiulian became China's first woman provincial governor when she was elected governor of the east China province of Jiangsu on April 30 at the first session of the 6th Provincial People's Congress.

The manager's metal-heeled shoes clicked along the verandah like the *hyoshigi* of Japanese theatre that announce impending doom. I could hear them tapping past my door and down the concrete stairs before disappearing into the distorted noise of the television program.

> 5 In 1983, China reaped a record 387,275 million tons of grain. This surpasses the target projected for 1985 in the Sixth Five-Year Plan.

> 8 The Beijing Stock Rabbit Farm, the largest modern farm of its kind in China, was completed and it started breeding rabbits in March. It can raise 3000 pure-bred rabbits and supply 60,000 young rabbits annually.

Somewhere there was a mosquito, emitting a high whine. I could not see it against the grey wall, already pockmarked with the squashed remains of a hundred other insects. The folds of the mosquito net hung down limply from the bedposts, smelling of damp.

34 Chinese athletes in 1983 won a total of 39 gold medals in
   eleven events at world championship contests. This is the
   largest number of golds they bagged in a single year.

The sound of the television was now a massive rumble like
an approaching avalanche, perhaps an approaching avalanche
of Chinese government statistics that would overwhelm me in
a great tide of yellow leaflets, I thought fancifully, until I could
struggle no longer and went mad in this place at the end of the
world, muttering to myself of Five-Year Plans and rabbit
farms.

I snapped my notebook shut and moodily threw the leaflet
onto the floor.

During the day, young monks brought a splash of colour to the
town, gaudy in marigold-orange, saffron and crimson or pink.
Sometimes they walked with the edges of their robes pulled up
chastely over their heads; then they looked like Indian women
in saris walking to market.

I walked to the top of a nearby hill which sported one of the
monks' white plaster temples, the Flying Dragon White
Pagoda, constructed in 1204, where eight small stupa surrounded a taller central spire, the whole punctuated with nich-
es for images of the Buddha, decorated with pieces of mirror
and approached through an elaborate system of low walls to
deter evil spirits, which could not turn corners. The stillness
was absolute except for the tinkle of temple bells in the light
breeze.

The view was richly green, the valley bottom punctuated by
palm trees as obtrusive as exclamation marks. In the background the mountains of Burma were blue against a white sky.
The village below looked like something out of the Wild West,
almost as though it should be seen in black and white, like an
old cowboy movie shown late at night on television—it had the
same middle-of-nowhere look, the same wide main street and
dust and shopfronts.

Further on, up in the forests on these low, rounded hills, the
intense silence was almost overpowering, broken only by the
lazy whirring of an insect or the crackling of falling twigs high
in the tree canopy. Every plant appeared as in a distorting

mirror: huge ferns with fronds fully two metres in length; poinsettia bushes the height of an adult, a glory of deep green and scarlet leaves like a displaced fragment of Christmas; violets with leaves like saucers. The forest was a confusion of geometric shapes: evenly spaced ivy leaves on rotting tree carcasses; platter-shaped banana leaves in emerald green; circles and ovals in browns and khaki bisected by the straight lines of lianas and hanging roots and the verticals of bamboo.

This was another world, a world of unlikely plants and faintly sinister undergrowth that cracked and stirred uneasily, disturbed by my intrusion. All around me in the vegetation creatures were struggling for survival, hunting and being hunted, in an unseen violence. I pressed through the forest slowly, afraid to disturb its secrets.

One afternoon there was a knock on my hotel door, and when I opened it an earnest-looking young Chinese was standing there. His name was George, he claimed, and he wanted to practise his English. Would I mind chatting to him for a while? Rather taken aback at the boldness of his approach, I acquiesced, though I was becoming increasingly tired of English conversations, most of which were banal and exhausting, eked out in poor English that obliged me to speak slowly and with great deliberation. George, though, had majored in English at Changsha Metallurgy College, I was relieved to hear, and had then been assigned to an isolated lead-zinc mine where he taught elementary English in the factory's middle school to the children of miners. The job was boring, the town remote and the conditions far from satisfactory, but he had worked there for eight years.

'I also got rather a poor salary!' George added, as an afterthought. But in 1993 he had taken part in the postgraduate entrance examination of a university in Kunming, and had succeeded in getting a place to study translation theory.

Behind his thick glasses and rumpled hair George was an interesting man, and a talkative one. Although he looked very young, I had worked out from his history that he must have been well over thirty, older than most of the Chinese I got a chance of speaking to. I told him about Elizabeth, the woman

I had met on the bus, wondering if they were at the same college. He did not know her, but George in his turn was surprisingly vocal about the status of women in China. In prerevolutionary times, he told me, it was taken for granted that women were inferior to men: they were not allowed to appear in front of strangers, their feet were bound, and they were financially dependent on their husbands.

'Their husbands could have concubines, and if the wife was in poor health or sterile, she could be divorced without lawful procedures. They had no right to be educated, nor had they any political rights. Perhaps you know a Chinese saying: "Women must obey their fathers before marriage, their husbands after marriage, and their sons after their husbands' deaths."'

'Yes. And wasn't it Confucius who said that only women and ignorant men were difficult to educate?' I asked him.

George nodded, and went on to explain how sexism was expressed in classical Chinese characters. Many characters which had once contained the radical meaning 'woman' were invested with uncomplimentary meanings, such as 'jealous' (*du*), 'hypocritical' (*wei*), 'treacherous' or 'crafty' (*jian*) and 'obscene' or 'lewd' (*ying*), said George, as he scrawled the characters on a sheet of paper.

'It all formed an immense, unconscious prejudice. Even today, in fact, there is no woman in Chinese political circles who approaches a Thatcher, Bhutto or Aquino. The government admits that in many rural areas, female babies are abandoned, or even drowned, after birth. Girls graduating from university or college usually get assigned the poorest jobs . . . Since the founding of the People's Republic, great progress has been made with regard to women's equality, but we still have a long way to go.'

I was curious about what made George so fervent about women's equality. Most women among my students, though they complained that women bore the majority of the housework and had fewer opportunities for a good job, seemed to have little concept of the real issues involved in women's liberation; nearly all men dismissed it with a laugh. It turned out that George had five sisters, but though I suspected there was something more to it than that he changed the subject. When he came again on another evening, however, I asked him which woman he held in greatest regard.

'My mother-in-law!' he replied. (Was he serious, I wondered briefly? Did the Chinese make jokes about their mothers-in-law?)

'She doesn't get up until ten o'clock. Before that, she sits in bed and has a nice cigarette and a cup of tea, and plans everything she is going to do.

'"It is said the price of salt will rise, I must tell the older daughter."

'"The younger granddaughter is pregnant, I must go to the market and buy some milk formula."

'"Why has the older son-in-law not handed in some money for the month? If he comes I'll . . ."

'I cannot be sure if she is eighty or eighty-five,' laughed George, 'but she looks like a woman in her fifties. She is quick in thinking, wise in planning, sharp in quarrelling, lucky in games like mahjong. She never travels outside the town, nor cares what happens outside it, yet she always tells the neighbours the adventures of her children or her two sons-in-law. She doesn't know the names of the president, or the prime minister, or the Party secretary, but she knows Deng Xiaoping well.

'"Oh, that short guy," she will say, "I like him."

'Anyhow, she is a happy, pleasant and kind mother-in-law, not worse than those of my colleagues!'

On Sundays even Damenlong had its moment of glory. It came to life as the surrounding hill tribes, even from over the Burmese border, arrived in town for the weekly market. Even the Hani, wary people rarely venturing into towns, emerged from their hidden villages in the rolling highlands. They are of Tibetan origin—according to their own more picturesque folklore, descended from frogs' eyes—the women dressed almost entirely in black, with a short skirt above the knees and brightly-patterned leg-warmers. They looked sturdy and fierce, an impression reinforced by their betel-stained teeth, red as blood, and their elaborate head-dresses heavy with metal and coins, often Burmese or Vietnamese. Their warrior-like appearance intimidated me slightly, but they were not unfriendly; they smiled and sometimes said hello in Mandarin, inspecting me with a puzzled gaze, but briefly and rather disinterestedly, before turning back to their business.

For the half-dozen Westerners in Damenlong it was minority hunting for its sensation value. The few foreign tourists
descended on the village market and stalked the locals with
their offensive cameras. It was a kind of voyeurism, like peering through the curtain of someone's bedroom—the subject
was offended, but the tourists got a vicarious thrill. Quaint little people, with their heavy ornamented head-dresses and gold-
capped teeth! The monks shied away, startled at the sight of a
camera lens, but the tourists only waited until they cautiously
turned around again. Click! A handsome photo of delicate,
anxious eyes and strange robes, taken against the wishes of the
subject, the world appropriated by imprisoning it within the
frame of a Kodak film.

'Doing the markets' was like watching a movie—the characters had no past, nor any future, but existed only for the time
one was watching. Like much tourism it was a divertissement
and a superficial pleasure. One knew nothing, and cared less,
about these people's lives and modes of being, and was satisfied only if the entertainment and novelty value exceeded the
cost and discomfort of getting there. People claim they travel
to improve their mind, but many often care only to amuse
themselves.

Travel, I suspected, sometimes served only to confirm old
prejudices, and some travellers returned home basically unal-
tered, with nothing to show for their efforts but a collection of
photographs and a few tales to tell over the dinner table.
Travellers said much to justify their journeys, but like any
indulgence—drinking, reading, smoking, watching television—
it dulled the senses and was often but a distraction, a pleasant
means of filling in time, as I well knew myself. The real voyage
of discovery consists not in searching for new landscapes, but
in having new eyes. Every place is unusual, even one's own
back yard, depending on how it is viewed. For me, I hoped
travelling was not so much a black line on a map, detailing the
exotic places visited, as a journey into my own self, as I recon-
sidered my shifting perceptions and values to which my travelling had given new angles and dimensions. But in Damenlong
I became restless, divining the pointlessness of tourism, wondering what I was doing here and whether I was any different
from the other foreigners. I hated and admired travellers for all

the things I hated and admired in myself, and sometimes I thought my travelling a mere filling-in of time, an idle escape from the ordinary commitments of life.

After the weekend I returned to Jinhong. The bus was searched by Public Security officers looking for 'big smoke'—opium smuggled over the border from the notorious Golden Triangle of northern Burma and Thailand. After they descended from the bus we trundled on up the road, leaving Damenlong behind in a cloud of exhaust fumes, hanging heavily in the air like a reproach.

I smuggled nothing but my photographs and stolen memories.

One might say that the days back in Jinhong settled into a rhythm, if that did not suggest something planned and struc-tured according to a specific goal. It was two weeks of the life so admired by Pinocchio—eating, drinking and entertaining myself, living the life of a vagabond. Although Jiminy Cricket sourly warns Pinocchio that those who follow such activities usually end up in hospital or prison, nothing so extreme befell me. Every day in Xishuangbanna seemed like a Sunday after-noon—indolent, purposeless, languorously drifting to a close with no goals ahead and nothing achieved but a balm of spir-it. Breakfast was at nine o'clock, just as the sun was struggling out of the early morning mist—a leisurely affair of toast and boiled eggs, banana fritters and coffee. Then the sun was at an ambient temperature to relax outside in a wicker chair, soak-ing up the warmth and turning the pages of my book. A late lunch, and then it was the hour to retire inside to the coolness, my pen gliding drowsily over notebook and postcards. As the day cooled off, I would stroll through the town under the para-sols of the feather-duster palm trees towards the ice-cream ven-dor, past groups of squatting men playing Chinese chess on the pavements, old men sitting crinkle-faced in the sun, women in turbans sitting by piles of unripe bananas. A few other people like myself drifted idly along like flies exhausted by the heat of the long afternoon, moving slowly as if almost swimming through the oncoming evening.

Eventually my footsteps would lead me down to the river, where I would sit in quiet contemplation as the light turned gold, almost as thick and palpable as honey. The palm trees appeared to change colour with the sky until they were black as splashed paint against the indigo horizon. These were my favourite moments, these ambiguous minutes between day and dusk, as I perched on the river banks and listened to the slow gurgle of the water which was black and glimmering like a glass, darkly. Dinner, and it was night to the scraping of cicadas; another day well spent. I did not care how the hours drifted casually by; no loud clock shattered my days into frantic pieces, and only the slow-wheeling sun marked off passing time with quiet and undramatic inevitability.

Down on the banks of the Mekong, on the last night in Xishuangbanna, I sat watching time slip by. The heat had gone from the day and there was a little breeze. Small children threw stones into the river, leaving the white smear of a noiseless splash, like a film without a soundtrack. The river, sliding southwards towards Vietnam, was so smooth it appeared varnished by the rays of the golden sun. The opposite bank was steep, cliff-like, topped by a ragged line of banana palms like a paper cut-out, or candles stuck on top of a crumbling brown fruitcake. Behind, the domes of equally crumbling hills were red, patched with green. It was an unspectacular landscape, but intensely calm and peaceful; even the swooping swallows were silent as ballerinas in the purple sky, fading to yellow at the edges like a crumpled old parchment.

It was one of those intense moments of absolute peace, when the viewer and the landscape seemed to become one, when all time stood still and all dilemmas, though unresolved, became unimportant, insignificant. All around, people were laughing and crying and living and dying, but I felt momentarily above and beyond all earthly desires and concerns and seemed to get a glimpse of heaven. Nothing was mediocre; even the children moved, enveloped in the last rays of the sun's golden glow, like immortals.

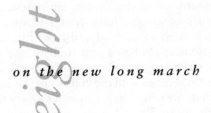

on the new long march

The pig brains, pink and slimy, sat on a plate in the middle of the table. There were four of them, each about the size of a tennis ball, and pale-blue veins ran in patterns over their surfaces like river tributaries inked on a map. They were expensive, and great delicacies. I knew that very shortly I would be asked to eat one.

'Please, Brian. Please take one of these pig . . . How do you say, inside of the head?'

'Brain,' I said faintly. 'A pig's brain.'

My friend Chen Ling scooped one up dexterously in her chopsticks, and announced that she would cook it for me. She put it into the pot of boiling stock that was simmering over a flame in the middle of the table.

I was back in Chengdu again, having extended my contract with Sichuan University for another year. I had been invited to the home of one of my postgraduate students, to meet her family and have dinner. We were eating hotpot, a Chinese meal designed along the same lines as French fondue. A wok sat in the middle of the table over a burner, containing a soup made from meat stock, with a layer of melted lard over the top to keep it very hot. Spices, including opium shells, Sichuan pepper and chillies, gave this celebrated dish an especial fame in Sichuan for its fiery taste.

After a few minutes Chen Ling fished around with her chopsticks in the red liquid for my pig's brain. When she lifted it out and set it in my bowl I saw that it had changed colour. It was grey now and soggy, like a grotesque ball of congealed

125

porridge. Everyone was looking at me and encouraging me to eat. Chen Ling's mother watched me, pleased that a foreigner was dining in her house. She had gone to a lot of trouble and expense to prepare this meal, and the table was weighed down with dishes of raw potato slices, cauliflower, spring onions, mushrooms and varieties of fungus, lotus root and spinach stalks. There was also pressed ham, dried and fresh fish, and liver. There was cow stomach, bubbled and rubbery like the plastic sheets used to wrap fragile objects for the post, and duck's blood, processed into cubes with the consistency of jelly. It was quite possible that more than half a month's salary had been sacrificed on this meal. The Chinese appreciate good food. When they meet each other they don't ask after each other's health or comment on the weather like the British. They say 'Have you eaten yet?'

I swirled the pig's brain around in the mixture of sesame oil, garlic and ginger in the bottom of my bowl, as one was supposed to do before eating anything taken from the hotpot. Now it was grey and soggy and oil-coated. I lifted it up cautiously in my chopsticks and took a bite out of it.

Everyone looked at me encouragingly, Chen Ling and her parents and her elder brother, and her brother's girlfriend, and her sister who was a CAAC flight attendant.

The lump of pig's brain slithered wetly down my throat.

'Very nice,' I gasped as casually as I could.

'Oh! Have another one,' suggested Mrs Chen happily, generously spearing her chopsticks towards the dish of remaining brains.

'*No!*' I almost shouted. 'I mean, no. Please let everyone enjoy the taste. Your son, perhaps, and yourself.'

The rest of the family did not need any further encouragement, and transferred the remaining food to the hotpot with alacrity.

'What do you think of our Chinese chopsticks?' asked Chen Ling's brother. 'I see you are good at using them.'

The Chinese often observed that one was good at things, unable to grasp that a foreigner could have been living like the Chinese for the last year, eating Chinese food ('Have you tried our Sichuan food?' I was asked by one student about six months after I had arrived in Chengdu), using chopsticks, riding a bicycle and speaking some of the language. They also, in the same spirit, often told foreigners the most obvious pieces of information about China, as if worried that they might never have heard them. This mental block had always puzzled me.

'Well . . . I think they're very suitable for eating Chinese food.' I did not really know what to answer, for I did not really think anything about chopsticks. 'They are also very elegant,' I added with sudden inspiration.

'We have been using chopsticks for more than a thousand years. We have a very long civilisation, in fact.'

'Yes. Three hundred years ago Europeans were still eating with their fingers, you know. No wonder the Chinese called us barbarians!'

There was a nervous titter around the table, and Brother Chen's girlfriend goggled at me wide-eyed, as if I had said something particularly shocking. Then everybody lapsed into silence again, and ate. Confucius commented that a gentleman should never converse while eating, and the modern Chinese still do not bother much with making polite conversation over the dinner table. It is a cultural habit that is a little bewildering to foreigners, who are often invited to banquets as the guest of honour and then (or so they imagine) ignored throughout the meal.

Mrs Chen brought in a dish of eels. Although they had been slit along their length, they were still wriggling convulsively on the plate. Mrs Chen lifted up a tangle of them and dropped them into the hot oil and stock, where they thrashed about before being boiled to death. I stared in horror. In fact I rather liked eels, and they were certainly better than pigs' brains. But while I was eating them I could see their little fellow victims out of the corner of my eye, writhing about in their dish with their stomachs cut open.

Beside me Chen Ling was still munching through her pig's brain. She was the only one of her family who spoke English, a postgraduate on an American Studies course and an unassuming but very intelligent woman. When the rest of the family started an animated discussion among themselves I turned to her and we chatted about the progress of her course. She was studying Hemingway, Fitzgerald. The course was also big on black American authors and studies on American Indians that showed up the darker side of the American dream.

Chen Ling had just been reading Jack London, whom she said had influenced a Chinese writer, Wang Fengling, who had written some short stories about wolves. It appeared that in Wang's stories the emphasis was on social relationships and the obedience and loyalty which the dogs owed to their masters, whereas in London's stories that loyalty was always tenuous and ultimately selfish.

'I thought the contrast represented some of the contrasts between the two cultures,' summarised Chen Ling.

'Yes, I think those contrasts do exist.' My mind was not really on the conversation and I was trying to shake a wriggling eel off my chopsticks. My mouth felt as if it were on fire and all around me the conversation in Chinese seemed to grow louder.

'I mean, Americans *are* basically selfish,' said Chen Ling. 'Though of course, not only—all Westerners too!'

She uttered this with such strong conviction that my mind suddenly snapped to attention. I bowed mockingly in her direction and thanked her. Chen Ling giggled.

'Well, not necessarily as individuals, but as a society. As you know, in Chinese the character for "family" or "home" also appears in the word for "country" and "everyone". Everything does turn very much on social relationships, whether in family or country, which in the end are almost the same thing. But Westerners are much more individualistic. I think their country might only come second place to their own desires.'

A little later she summarised, in what I thought was one of the best observations I had heard in China, 'Westerners like to try and alter the world and things about their society to suit themselves and their own wishes. We Chinese, on the other hand, tend to alter ourselves to suit society.'

We lapsed again into Chinese, and general conversation with her family. I boiled a few more slices of potato, which were my favourite part of the hotpot, coming out crisp and spicy. Apart from pigs' brains I liked hotpot very much, finding it a tasty and convivial meal. Even Chinese meals, I thought, in which dishes were shared from the middle of the table, seemed more in tune with a central and socially responsible attitude than the individual meals of Westerners, with their separate plates and servings.

I tucked her comments away; when I left I would write them in my notebook. Chen Ling's mother gave me some eels in a plastic bag, which she said I could eat for my lunch. I hung them over the handlebars of my bicycle, and they squirmed all the way back to the Panda Park.

Chengdu, historically a great centre of trade, was a bustling city of markets and shops, all of which were less than half an hour's bicycle ride from Sichuan University. Although I had been living there some time I had not become tired of pedalling around the city, for each time I went out I saw something that I had not come across before: a bird market, a teahouse tucked down a side alley, a tiny shop selling Tibetan sashes and bronze vessels. During my second year in Chengdu, as the weeks slipped by in a steady flow, I found hidden places—parks, temples and quiet tree-lined back streets—that I had never seen before.

My bicycle was my trusty companion on which I explored the town at my leisure. There were long waiting lists for new bicycles, from which foreigners were exempt. Despite the crush in the streets only one in ten Chinese possessed a bicycle, and it was a coveted item and—depending on the brand—a status symbol. The Phoenix and the Flying Pigeon, or any brand from Shanghai, were particularly desirable; local Chengdus were rather downmarket. When I bought my bicycle during my first week in China I had no wish to jump the queue, nor any need of a status symbol—my golden hair and foreignness were symbol enough for the Chinese. I had bought a second-hand bicycle in the market, a rusting and dilapidated affair, which as the months progressed had increasingly become held together by pieces of wire and string but which still had not fallen apart.

At first, all that time ago, cycling had seemed like a particularly hazardous survival course, especially at night, for there were hardly any street lights and bicycles were not fitted with lamps. Owing to the large numbers of cyclists, easily blinded, it was forbidden for trucks and cars to drive with their headlights on. Drivers only switched them on at full brightness, with maniacal excitement, at moments of uncertainty, so that one ended up pedalling along either in pitch darkness or enveloped in a sudden explosive white glare. During the day such problems were replaced with others, especially the sheer quantity of bicycles, which wobbled and careered and whizzed along with little regard to any highway code. Speed demons were an unexpected shock, zooming up from behind and over-taking with centimetres to spare, and one always had to keep an eye out for cyclists emerging from side streets with blithe indifference to right of way. Crossroads without traffic lights were a free-for-all, and wherever there were traffic lights they appeared to be viewed more as a suggestion than a requirement.

All was chaos, but would have been complete anarchy if not for the Women with the Red Armbands. These old ladies, usu-ally retired, policed the streets, their symbols of authority a red cloth tied around their arm and a red plastic megaphone clutched in one hand, through which they could berate offend-ers. They skulked among bushes at the sides of roads, particu-larly at traffic lights, and at the first sign of disobedience to the rules of the road rocketed out into the streets like disturbed grouse, yelling triumphantly.

Those who tried to jump traffic lights, who hitched lifts on the backs of bicycles, or who were missing a bell or a bicycle permit could fall victim to the Women in the Red Armbands. Such unfortunate people would find the backs of their bicycles suddenly gripped in a powerful hold as these old women hung on with the tenacity of limpets, forcing the offenders to stop and fining them on the spot. Those who ignored the yells of these ancient Amazons and pedalled swiftly onwards—and few had the nerve to do so—would be intercepted by accomplices on the far side of the intersection. There was no escape. Loss of face was terrible for, with particular craftiness, punishment lay not only in a fine. Those caught in wrongdoing were obliged to wait by the side of the road until they had caught another offender. I lived in constant terror of the Women in the Red Armbands, for my bicycle left much to be desired. Not only was one brake not working, but my bell—bells were particular targets of wrath—had not functioned since the day I bought my bicycle, except by banging it sharply with my fist, an adap-tation I felt the women would not appreciate. I lived in.fear of being grappled to a standstill by one of these ladies, for for-eigners were certainly not immune to their ministrations. One of my fellow teachers had been stopped three times for not having a bicycle bell, and had recounted her run-ins with these keepers of public order at great and hilarious length. I remained nervous, and had visions of finding myself one day dancing about the road in unhappy punishment, trying to waylay another criminal cyclist.

That spring in Chengdu I was constantly puzzled by conflicting pictures of the Chinese, pictures that sometimes fitted into traditional stereotypes but often did not. The Campaign to Learn from Lei Feng, launched in March and continuing throughout the spring, seemed an indication of the Chinese collective spirit and a denial of individuality, but in April another event seemed to overthrow everything the Lei Feng Campaign stood for.

Lei Feng was one of the model citizens the Communist Party held up for admiration and emulation. He was the epitome of the ideal Chinese, the son of a poor peasant family who devoted himself to performing services for the people, happily surrendering his individuality to his devotion to the nation. (He was also, not by coincidence, a soldier of the People's Liberation Army, or PLA, and the campaign was part of the long-continuing attempt to rehabilitate the image of the army after the Tiananmen crackdown.) Lei Feng cared for his ageing parents with filial piety, sewed buttons on other comrades' clothes, swept floors without being asked, and finally met his death in an accident in the 1960s. (A not terribly glorious death—he was crushed by a telephone pole which had fallen over when an army truck backed into it by mistake.) Lei Feng was arguably more a communist creation than a real man, and it was suspected that his 'diary' was largely the creation of the Ministry of Propaganda, but embroidered or not his character stemmed from a long history of Chinese heroes who devoted themselves to others. The statesman Fan Zhongan wrote in one of his famous essays, entitled 'Yueyang Pavilion', that he admired those officials who could only find enjoyment in life after everyone else had found enjoyment—and that was as long ago as the Song Dynasty.

Red banners appeared overnight around the campus and city like an advertising blitz, festooning trees like abnormal spring blossoms and proclaiming their messages across gateways and doors. *Learn from Lei Feng!* they screamed. *Learn from the PLA in Political Education and Ideological Work!* And another, supposedly a quotation from Lei Feng himself, *I Want my Limited Life to Serve that Limitless Cause, the Revolution!* They added a festive air to the university, like bunting hung out for a street carnival. Lei Feng's plump face grinned down from innumerable artists' impressions. Often he was depicted in his army uniform, cradling a machine-gun with an expression of infinite innocence on his face, surrounded by garish red peony roses which seemed to float like ectoplasm around the back of his head.

On the Monday morning the campaign began I saw Xiao Han, the woman who had met me on my arrival in China, leaving the Foreign Affairs Office with a host of her colleagues, all with brooms over their shoulders, setting off like the Seven Dwarfs to work.

'Xiao Han, what are you doing?' I called out in surprise.

'I'm going to learn from Comrade Lei Feng!' she replied vigorously, flourishing her broom in the air. Upon which she burst into song, among the resonant words of which I could make out, in my still struggling Chinese, 'Lei Feng' and 'socialism'. That day Xiao Han brushed the streets, sweeping the dust from one part of the road to another with inspired diligence. The next day she cut grass.

'What did you learn from cutting grass?' I asked Xiao Han one evening as she returned to her office, weary from her labour.

'I have learned to help others.'

'And how does cutting grass help others?' I queried wickedly, wondering what the regular university gardeners were doing in the meantime. Xiao Han only laughed, which I interpreted as meaning she was embarrassed, and that I should have had more sense than to ask the question. But she never doubted the validity of the spirit of Lei Feng, and she flung herself into each allotted task with enthusiasm.

Throughout the next few weeks I often came across my students pruning hedges or digging trenches by the sides of the paths. They too were learning from Lei Feng, which, as Wang Ming pointed out, was, at least for a few days, better than sitting inside a classroom learning English grammatical theory. I asked him the purpose of these trenches. Were new drains being laid?

'I have no idea,' said he with happy insouciance, leaning on his spade and grinning at me in a flash of white teeth. 'Anyway, I am sure they have no purpose. Middle school students will come here tomorrow. They will learn from Lei Feng by filling in the trenches again!' He laughed heartily.

'In any case Lei Feng wasn't as poor as everyone thinks, giving away all his possessions to help others,' said another of my students standing nearby. 'He had a colour television!'

'Nevertheless one must admire him,' admonished another classmate. 'Really I think young people have a lot to learn from Lei Feng. For example, yesterday as I dismounted from my bicycle at the gates, my books and papers fell out of my basket. Well, immediately a young boy helped me to pick them up! I was so surprised I forgot to say thank you. But I think it is because of the Lei Feng Campaign. Normally no one would help in such a thing. I think we can learn to be more considerate.'

Wang Ming and the other student grunted, whether in agreement or contempt I wasn't quite sure, and dug their spades into the earth again.

I tried to imagine a young Westerner making such a comment, without much success. By Western standards Chinese heroes, striving to maintain social order and sacrificing themselves for others, were do-gooders (the word in English is significantly pejorative, for no logical reason). As Chen Ling had pointed out to me when I had dinner at her house, a Chinese hero is exactly someone like Lei Feng—a model soldier and model socialist who maintains the status quo—while in America a surprising number of famous historical figures are bandits or people outside society, such as Jesse James and Davey Crockett. Lei Feng was regarded by foreigners with amusement as a person who was a far cry from the romantic heroes of Western imagination, who more often than not broke through the bonds of respectable society to express their individual desires or search for adventure. Such amusement was misleading because to the Chinese the ethos Lei Feng upheld was an important one. The foreigners who found the Lei Feng

Campaign vaguely laughable—which included myself—only highlighted the basically individualistic nature of Western society and many of its ideals.

I was still opposed to generalisations. In fact, I sometimes felt like a rat in an experimental maze while in China; just as I thought I had reached the centre of the puzzle, the walls and passages shifted and I had to start all over again. Yet the Lei Feng Campaign made me think once more of Chen Ling's comment, which seemed a valid one. Coming to China was indeed in some ways like looking at myself in a mirror, and I did not always like what I saw there. The Chinese, not without reason, often thought Western ideals selfish, and in China I frequently wondered where, in my own society, one drew the line between selfishness and freedom, rights and responsibility.

In April one of China's most famous stars came to give three concerts in Chengdu. His name was Cui Jian, and I had never heard of him. My students, wild with excitement, eagerly told me all about the young singer, and I went to the shops and bought his latest cassette. By Chinese pop music standards Cui Jian's songs were fairly advanced—he was the only mainland Chinese to produce rock music, which sometimes also bordered on the punk and contained elements of reggae. Certainly it was a far cry from the usual synthetic sentimentality in which many Chinese and Overseas Chinese pop singers indulged. His music was inventive and his lyrics were not only about love but about unhappiness and social inadequacies. They were full of youthful disillusionment, confusion, and resentment against authority.

The excitement had begun at a party given by one of the American teachers in her flat. She was famous for her parties, which she gave regularly and which were almost guaranteed successes, crowded with foreigners and their Chinese friends from colleges all over Chengdu. On this night I was dancing, and the flat was crowded with people, when four Chinese arrived. Or rather, it appeared to me that one was hustled into the room by the other three, who stood around him like those hatchet-faced men, pretending to be innocent bystanders, one sees around American presidents. The hostess greeted the hustled one with some animation. He was rather nondescript, wearing a dull-green Mao tunic and the heavy boots much favoured by punks in Britain. He had rather heavy jowls, I thought, and in fact was altogether quite plump by Chinese standards. The only striking thing about him was his long hair—I had seen few Chinese men with long hair.

After a while I suddenly realised that all the Chinese guests at the party were behaving in rather an odd way. They kept looking over towards the newcomer and talking about him, and some of them went up to him, their faces full of awe. I called Wang Ming over.

'Who's that guy that has just come in?' I shouted in my friend's ear above the music.

'Cui Jian!'

'Who?'

'You know, Cui Jian.'

'No, I don't know.'

'He's a very famous Chinese singer. Maybe the most famous among young people,' replied Wang Ming. 'Of course everyone is very excited. It's as if Michael Jackson arrived at one of your parties at home! Really they can't believe their luck at meeting him.'

I looked over at Cui Jian, who was now dancing rather unimaginatively in the middle of the floor. I could not imagine anyone more different from Michael Jackson. Certainly he did not look very exciting in his scruffy Mao jacket.

'What do you mean, *they*? Aren't you excited?'

'I don't like his music,' replied Wang Ming, who enjoyed being different.

'He's not much of a dancer anyway,' I said disparagingly. 'I dare you to go and tell him he's a hopeless dancer.'

'OK.'

My friend, always slightly excitable and eccentric, did not need much convincing to rise to a challenge. Once I dared him to smash my best porcelain bowl (thinking smugly, no Chinese will ever do that) and he promptly picked it up and threw it against the wall. Now he went up to Cui Jian and I saw them talking. Then he came back over to me, a big grin on his face.

'Well?'

'Yes, I told him he was a hopeless dancer.'

'What did he say?'

'He said it was true, he was sorry that he wasn't very good.'

Suddenly I felt very foolish. I did not know why I had put Wang Ming up to such a childish prank, only to have my pettiness exposed by what I thought was a mature and reasonable answer. It was some kind of elemental urge to criticise those more important or famous than oneself. In fact Cui Jian appeared a very ordinary person, who unlike American rock stars seemed to dislike the adulation of his fans. He spent the remainder of the party standing against the wall. Someone put on a piece of his music, and he stood there rigidly, looking embarrassed, as if it were the national anthem. He left unobtrusively before midnight.

When I thought about it, and as I learned more about Cui Jian, I rather admired him. He walked a delicate tightrope between self-expression through his music and government disapproval, and was often in trouble with the authorities because of his lyrics. Both his new album and his current tour were called *Rock and Roll on the New Long March*, and as even the title indicated he maintained a very precarious attitude that often verged on disrespect for communist ideals and history. His title song, 'Rock of the New Long March', was a satire on the Long March and its historical glorification, and also contained veiled references to the Tiananmen demonstrations and the 'rifles and bullets' of soldiers. Other songs gave voice to the confusion of young Chinese, who often felt they were lost in a twilight world between old-style communism and new possibilities, yet paralysed, incapable of exploiting the change, brought up to obey and feel responsible to society. The world of the young Chinese who listened to Cui Jian's music was no longer the perfect and easily explainable one put forward by communism and the example of Lei Feng, but more complex and puzzling, in which many young people wished to find the way on their own. But if they were now being given slightly more freedom to make their own lives under continued economic liberation, and if the government were encouraging them to stand on their own feet, these were advantages they were incapable of manipulating.

Not surprisingly the government kept a close watch on Cui Jian. Perhaps the most amusing and significant praise of him came from one of my students when I asked her if she had enjoyed his concert.

The Chinese were not just the product of ideological pressures encouraging them to conform and submit, nor did they all adapt themselves willingly to society as Chen Ling had suggested to me. All people were forced into conformity by social, economic and cultural pressures, whether in China or the West. What made people individuals was the way in which they faced up to these challenges and forces and struggled to overcome history. Like the youths in Cui Jian's lyrics, many of the real Chinese were on a new Long March and had an increasingly ambiguous attitude to their country and people. 'I close my eyes and find nobody but myself,' said one of Cui Jian's songs. 'I open them to find no past. I've nothing to say, nothing to do. I hold up my head, do nothing but stride forward, I open my mouth, do nothing but shout loudly. I hate them, I love them.'

Cui Jian finished his concert with the song most popular among university students, 'I Have Nothing'. Although ostensibly about a broken love affair, reading between the lines this song treated China's youth as a lost generation who were utterly destitute of material possessions and who had no hope of a satisfying future. Nearly all my Chinese acquaintances—even Wang Ming, despite his professed dislike of Cui Jian's music— knew the words of this song by heart. This tune too started quietly, almost with menace, as long-held notes droned in the background behind the raw, distressed tones of Cui Jian's voice. He stood in a spot of white light in the middle of the darkened hall, a plain figure in a worn jacket, with an electric guitar around his neck. Anyone could have identified with him; he was the boy next door. A pipe joined in to play a lament, almost Irish in its haunting sadness, as he sang of a broken love affair and how he was left without anything at all. Suddenly the music became louder and livened into a steady rock beat as the song imagined what the future could be if only his girl would come back to him. What was this song about: the poverty of the Chinese, the betrayal of communism, a shout for freedom? It could have been all or any or none of these things, but meanings lingered and teased with great subtlety under the surface of the words. Now the people in the crowd were jumping and waving their arms in the air, holding aloft bland faces of Chairman Mao and scarves and flags, blowing whistles and singing along. At the end of the song the music faded away to nothing.

There was an immense silence in the hall that seemed to last for an eternity before the cheering broke out.

Two days later, in Xian, live performances by Cui Jian were banned by the Chinese government.

University terms in China were impossibly long: two semesters, each of nineteen or twenty weeks. It seemed an age since I had returned from Yunnan at the end of the winter, tired and happy to regain the reassuring quiet of my pond and the comforts of my flat and a familiar city. The spring passed and I spent the summer in South-East Asia. Back in China and embarked on my fourth term, my spirits started to flag at the thought of the ten weeks of work still remaining as another dull winter closed in with heavy grey skies. Then suddenly, at the end of October, the *waiban* proposed a week away in the mountains of northern Sichuan.

The *waiban*, or Foreign Affairs Office, was in charge of the foreigners at the university. The *waiban* staff cosseted and danced attention on the foreigners, resolving problems, hosting banquets and paying teachers' salaries in thick bundles of tattered five-*yuan* notes, but they also controlled us and expected us to do as we were told. 'You are tired, you will have a rest,' Xiao Han had told me on my very first day at the university, and I had been foolish to dispute the instruction. A few days ago she had said, 'There is a trip to northern Sichuan, and you are invited.' I had grown weary of *waiban* trips—mostly weekends to areas of interest around Sichuan Province—which, though offered in a genuine spirit of goodwill, involved all those features of guided tours that I disliked and resented. I had, however, long been wanting to visit Sichuan's northern border, a wild region of famous scenic beauty virtually closed to unaccompanied foreign travellers. In any case, one way or the other, my indecision was irrelevant. I knew these Chinese invitations by now—they were really veiled commands.

So I said yes, and I went.

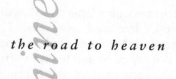

the road to heaven

Li Bai, one of the greatest Chinese poets, wrote that the road to Sichuan was harder than the road to heaven. There were once mountain passes into the province so narrow that loaded mules could not pass on them, and if by mischance two mule-trains met some of the animals had to be shoved over the edge of the cliff, as they could not even be turned, let alone pass each other, on such restrictive tracks. 'So steep and narrow,' wrote Li Bai, 'One man could hold this pass against ten thousand / And sometimes its defenders are not mortal men / But wolves and jackals.'

Now, as the bus clawed its way up into the valley, I thought it must surely have been a road like this on which the Tang Dynasty poet had travelled. The scenery along the river was smudged brown like an old sepia daguerreotype, but with none of its nostalgia or romance; it was a harsh, rocky valley of ravines and cliffs, with crude stone buildings at irregular intervals along an unsurfaced, rutted road that bounced and crumbled into the high mountains of northern Sichuan. The villages of the Qiang minority were easy to pick out, with their slim towers rising high from strategic points along the road. Now mostly used for storing grain, these former watchtowers were prominent reminders of more violent times in the history of Sichuan and its minorities. This had once been a wild and lawless place.

After a nerve-wracking ride we lunched at Maowen, a grubby minority town of harsh, concrete public buildings and a makeshift market, where beancurd lay like congealed wallpaper paste on trestle tables, poked and prodded by women in blue aprons. Then it was on into a sunlit valley, a landscape of frothing rivers and empty mountains:

Peak follows peak, each but a hand's breadth from the sky;
Dead pines hang head down into the chasms,
Torrents and waterfalls out-roar each other,
Pounding the cliffs and boiling over rocks,
Booming like thunder through a thousand caverns.
What takes you, traveller, this long weary way
So filled with danger?

It was a day's agonising journey from the populous Sichuan Basin to Songpan, an alpine town perched in the remote mountains along the northern provincial border. There were thirty of us in the bus, some twenty foreigners and ten Chinese from the *waiban* of Sichuan University, including two of the cooks who worked in the foreigners' dining hall. Most of these Chinese were freeloaders, taking no part in the organisation or supervision of the trip for which the foreigners had paid, but I did not resent their presence, for these perks were an important supplement for low Chinese wages and an integral part of life under communist restrictions. As the bus ground on and on into the evening the Chinese fell silent and finally asleep in the front seats, mouths agape. Soon the early alpine night had descended, and late in the evening we arrived at Songpan. Cramped and sore, we hobbled off the bus and were shepherded into our hotel, a shabby, ice-cold building of echoing rooms and dormitory beds, the best in town.

Roosters were, I discovered the next morning, inescapable in Songpan, beginning their demented crowing at dawn and continuing with undiminished energy until lunchtime. Hedvig, by now a firm friend and also along for the journey, called them screaming chickens, adding a certain Swedish poetry to the language. Breakfast was warm soy milk, boiled eggs and deep-fried fritters sprinkled with sugar, discovered in a little stall down a side alley from the hotel. Apart from roosters Songpan was quite a pleasant town. Nearly half its population was Hui, a Moslem minority that had come to China in the thirteenth century as mercenaries with the armies of Kublai Khan. Linguistically, culturally and by now even racially they were indistinguishable from the Han Chinese; only their religion set them apart, and they wore snowy white skullcaps above their blue Mao tunics. The rest of the people were Han or Tibetan, smilingly courteous and friendly. Their eyes turned quizzically but without hostility or intrusion on the aimlessly strolling foreigners, as we threaded our way through the crowded market streets, fingering Tibetan scarfs and lengths of embroidered material. It was the kind of staring that did not intimidate me, friendly and not annoying.

I liked these Chinese middle-sized country towns, always more traditional and human than the cities. In Songpan much of the old surrounding walls still stood, punctuated by three massive gates, an impressively thick bastion enclosing an energetic town of old stone and timber houses and farms in a huddle of narrow lanes. Horse-drawn carts trundled slowly through the markets, and smoke spiralled up lazily from the chimneys. I saw a dog approaching along the street, a brown mongrel with a shaggy tail that waved menacingly in the air like a challenge, but it trotted past nonchalantly and away. *Modern Shop* said a rusty sign in English over one store off the main street, boarded up with yellow planks of warped wood, paint flaking. The alpine rusticity of the town reminded me of Switzerland, where I had spent most of my childhood: stacks of freshly cut wood, timber houses with eaves pulled down low like woolly hats over the windows, cobbled paths. It was a cruel trick, these fragments of home in an alien land, but the trick was of my own making. I looked into my past for reassurance and measures of normality: scenes of China squashed awkwardly into the limited frames of my own mental parameters, rendered meaningful only by being seen through the distorting lens of my own society. I felt nostalgic and a little homesick.

If there was one thing that did not remind me of home, it was the smell of China, for public toilets in Songpan, as elsewhere, were places to avoid. While the Chinese had a high level of personal hygiene and their cities were relatively clean, the same could not be said of their public toilets, despite the fact that they are central to daily life. Many Chinese do not have bathrooms in their own homes, and use the communal toilet of their work unit or block of flats, or the public toilets situated at nearly every street corner in Chinese cities. In both the town and the city the waste from these toilets gathers in huge pits and is taken away to be used as fertiliser on the fields. This use of a natural resource is admirable and might have appealed to the Swiss urge to recycle, but the cesspits in which the waste fermented would certainly not appeal to their sense of alpine cleanliness. It is easy to find public toilets in China; when one walks down a street in which a toilet is located, one is assailed by the nauseating smell from a distance of several hundred metres, which grows steadily stronger as one approaches and reaches the proportions of noxious fumes as one enters. Chinese toilets are filthy and very public, often consisting of little more than a long trough set in the floor, over which one squats at will. In this respect the public toilet in Songpan was no different from those elsewhere, though at least blessed with a urinal, which I made haste to use before I fainted from the smell. I was standing there holding my breath and gulping faintly when a Tibetan strode in and came to stand beside me. He looked as if he had just walked down from the remote mountains. He had wild, scruffy hair and a deeply lined, walnut-brown face with flat cheekbones, and he wore traditional Tibetan dress, with a handsome but rather grubby scarlet jacket and a long dagger thrust through his belt. He looked at me sideways.

'Do you speak German?' he asked me in heavily accented English.

'Er . . . yes, a little,' I returned in cautious surprise. The Tibetan switched into German immediately, speaking with casual fluency.

'And where do you come from?'

'Switzerland,' I mumbled vaguely, as I happened to be thinking about it. 'Geneva.'

'Ah! A beautiful country! I spent four months in Zurich,' said the scruffy Tibetan, hitching up his trousers.

I turned abruptly to look at him.

'I was there on business, setting up a company. I was in Geneva for a couple of days, too.' He pulled down his jacket and smoothed it out, straightening his dagger. 'A pleasant city, with a big fountain beside the lake, I seem to remember,' he added contemplatively. Then he turned and strode out, and was gone.

I stood staring after him, mouth agape. I wondered fleetingly if he was joking, but the fact that he spoke such good German weighed heavily in his favour. I would like to have known what business he was conducting, and why he was now here, in this remote place. I wondered if he too saw any resemblances between Songpan and a Swiss alpine village.

I ran out into the street after him, but he had vanished as completely as if I had imagined him, an improbable manifestation of my nostalgia and homesickness.

The second day of our trip was foggy, an indiscriminate greyness like the Tibetan *bardo* where souls linger after death, waiting to be reborn. Our coach heaved its way up the mountain and when, suddenly and unexpectedly, we burst out of the mist, it was indeed like a rebirth—brilliant sunshine in a splash of blue sky flawless as an imperial silk banner, five-thousand-metre snow-capped peaks afloat on a sea of cloud. At the top of the pass we poured out of the bus like little children, to run across grass studded with gentian and admire the tremendous view, this last eastern edge of the Himalaya that swept across Asia as far as Afghanistan.

On the other side of the pass lay a famous scenic area, Huanglong or Yellow Dragon Valley, a broad, shallow gash in the mountains culminating in Baoding Peak which glittered ahead like a snowy pyramid. Limestone deposits here had formed three thousand karst pools, the frozen rock pouring over the edge of each pool like cake-mix over a bowl, linked by miniature waterfalls and streams tinted jade and turquoise by dissolved minerals: Guest Greeting Pool, Bright Moon-Mirroring Pool, Golden Dragon-Back Falls, Stone Pagoda Lake, Vying-for-Beauty Pool. The Chinese had with indefatigable imagination named many of them, but the place was marvellously remote and unspoiled: a meandering track through forest of juniper, Tibetan fir, Himalaya rhododendron, mountain oak and ash in a glorious blaze of autumn colour.

We spent the whole afternoon walking up the valley as the *waiban* staff trailed behind, splashing in the water and taking photos of each other. The Japanese students seemed to treat the walk as a personal challenge, forging ahead in their elegant new walking boots, puffed up like Michelin men in their brightly coloured down jackets. They had the correct equipment for every activity, I thought as I struggled in their wake in my battered shoes, remembering the Japanese boy on the bus to Xishuangbanna. In Chengdu they even had toasters and waffle irons and sausage-making machines and hair-dryers and video games, and received packages every week from Japan, full of Japanese food, even Japanese rice. I admired their refusal to accept half measures, their organisation.

As I walked on up the mountain, tiny white butterflies flitted drunkenly past like breeze-blown confetti, and I was treated to the sight of an eagle drifting above me in the sky, soaring like a drab Chinese kite. When I made it up to the abandoned Dragon King Temple, built in the Ming Dynasty, fortress-like in grey stone under the bulk of the snow peaks, the wind sighing through the pines seemed to speak of that lost time of eccentric monks and their incredible dreams, liberated by this remote fastness among the mountains. Now only the Japanese students were sitting on the rocks, drinking out of flasks and eating Japanese biscuits. I thought they looked at me pityingly as I collapsed, dishevelled, exhausted and empty-handed, beside them.

Even here it might almost have been Switzerland, but the mountains were wilder, more jagged—geologically far younger than the Alps—and there was a vastness, an emptiness and remoteness that was very un-European. Other foreigners were shouting and taking photos all around me, but I suddenly felt very alone. I had been in China well over a year now and had never regretted coming to this country, but sometimes it seemed like another planet, alien and hostile. Even the landscape was sharply warped and threatening in its immensity. I sat on the grass and thought of the trim little mountains of central Europe. I had often thought those little Swiss villages smug and self-satisfied, cloying in their ordered prettiness. These Swiss scenes were spiritually empty but to me full of cultural and personal references, soothing in their familiarity. I walked back down the valley on my own, feeling lost, and clambered back into the bus.

On the road back to Songpan, a Tibetan horseman materialised from nowhere, slowly riding along on his black pony, wrapped in a heavy tunic held close by a broad, coloured sash of red and green. His whole face lit up when he saw the bus; he lifted his arm high and waved vigorously before disappearing over a ridge and into the evening immensity. No doubt he was merely returning home to his farm after a day's work, but to me he was rendered mysterious by being unfamiliar. His appearance, his gesture, seemed like an omen, a signal, a question mark. Where had he come from? Where was he going in this wilderness? And why?

In the early morning the road out of Songpan, northwards through a broad valley, was already yellow with brilliant sunshine. Compact little villages with narrow, cobbled streets were surrounded by racks of drying hay. Women in native Tibetan dress and bright red headcloths, already at their back-breaking work, made a vivid splash against the brown fields rutted as coarse cardboard, and the white cloth tents of itinerant Tibetans, probably on pilgrimage, could be picked out along the river's edge. Little boys by the roadside casually watched the bus pass then ran to hitch a free ride, clinging with small hands to the ladder that ascended to the roof—no easy task on the pitted and winding mountain road. Their grinning faces peered at us through the grimy back windows in triumph.

Finally, when we stopped at Chuanzhu Monastery, the boys hopped off the back and scampered away. Their village consisted of little more than thirty wooden houses, some with shutters and eaves picked out in vivid colours (canary yellow, scarlet and sky blue), surrounded by high, rough stone walls. The entrance to each house, through a gateway with gabled roof, was flanked and guarded by pictures of fat, fierce-looking warriors with blue faces and multicoloured armour, pasted up to warn away evil spirits. In one sunny courtyard a man sat with his back against a sapling, singing prayers in a high, haunting tone, the open prayerbook on his lap inscribed with the hooks and slashes of the Tibetan alphabet. The village women wore long tunics, fringed with borders of pink, marigold and blue, with poppy-red headscarfs. Some had babies on their backs, held in place by patterned shawls.

The temple, the *raison d'être* of this little hamlet, was very large, with sweeping white roofs surging up at the corners into golden dragons and other mythical beasts, and decorated by prayers in huge bronze Tibetan letters glittering in the sunlight. Pillars and eaves were painted in vivid colours, and along the outside walls cylindrical bronze prayer wheels, or *manichokar*, could be spun on wooden stakes; as they turned, scrolls contained within them released prayers to the heavens, gaining merit for the pilgrim. An old woman prostrated herself full length on the floor, arms spreadeagled like a Catholic priest being ordained, while from somewhere overhead a drum beat and pulsed like a massive, throbbing heart, accompanying the chanting of monks in the darkened inner sanctum.

In contrast to the other Tibetans, the clothes of the monks were simple and unadorned—long, dull purple robes of heavy cloth. The monks we met at Chuanzhu were all young novices with shaved heads and wide, boyish grins, and they hugged each other as they spoke to us in excellent Mandarin. They appeared happy, content and trouble-free. (Maybe they were, but Tibetans have suffered more than any other minority nationality in China from religious and cultural persecution, and their life expectancy, literacy rates, infant mortality rates and income are still far below those of the Han Chinese. Only in recent years, after severe repression during the Cultural Revolution, have temples reopened and religious life begun to revive under strong government supervision.) The young monks peered through the camera lenses of the Japanese students, marvelling with a total lack of envy at this display of modern technology. They waved cheerfully in a flutter of trailing robes as we departed.

Jiuzhaigou, a national park on Sichuan's far northern limit with the border of Gansu Province, was approached through an arresting countryside of brown, barren hills eroded into gullies by frothing rivers. Further up into the mountains, isolated logging hamlets were the only signs of human life in this country of one billion people; the emptiness seemed strange, unacceptable. Jiuzhaigou, a forty-kilometre long valley in the mountains of the Minshan range, as well as being the haunt of some of the last remaining wild pandas and snow leopards, is famous for its lakes, stunningly indigo and cobalt blue in colour, piercingly clear, scattered through mountain valleys whose peaks rise up over four thousand metres. A book I had bought in Chengdu claimed that 'All this will arouse your enthusiasm to embrace the beauty of life. Besides, the bubbling brooks winding through grassland covered with bushes will give you the idea of being simple and unadorned.' But the colours of Jiuzhaigou, after the barrenness of the approach, did not seem simple or unadorned but brashly incongruous. The lakes sparkled like fake sapphires, and the hillsides were blanketed in green fir, sycamore, birch, hornbeam and wild peach in an extravagant autumn splash of russet and brown and copper and saffron.

Legend has it that these lakes were created when the goddess Worusemo dropped her magic mirror while struggling with a demon; the mirror broke and the pieces were transformed into lakes, connected by waterfalls and rapids. Certainly there was something other-worldly about the blueness. The skeletal remains of trees in the water gave the illusion of having been fossilised like flies in amber.

Our hotel—the only one inside the boundaries of the natural reserve, a series of low, barrack-like buildings in the inevitable concrete—advertised a place where one could indulge in tea and (a rarity in these parts) coffee. The coffee came with yak milk, strong and pungent and greasy, but creamy and not unpleasant. The café turned out to be a disco, too, though totally empty when a group of us arrived; nonetheless we made good use of the dance floor and soon attracted a gawping crowd of Chinese to the doorway. So many foreigners—Swedes, Japanese, French, Australian, British—were too good a show to miss, and soon the room began to fill up. Inevitably, for they were popular all over China, waltzes and foxtrots were soon blaring over the loudspeakers, to which the Chinese shuffled back and forwards in the same endlessly repeated basic chain steps. Men danced with men, holding each other stiffly apart, taking courteous turns leading and looking distantly over each other's shoulders. After each dance they returned to their chairs along the walls and sat smoking cigarettes. Eventually, with exceeding daring, some of them danced with women, though contact was equally remote, and both partners typically had slightly pained expressions. Physical friendliness with those of the same sex was acceptable—indeed enjoyed—in China, but any other contact was not: even lovers held hands surreptitiously, hidden behind bushes in parks. Now on the dance floor the women put their hands around the men's wrists, while the men held their fingers stiffly splayed like a secret signal; the less adventurous held each other by the elbows. Was I exaggerating, or did all the men wear imitation black leather jackets, all the women red shoes? It appeared that way.

'I like to approach beautiful girls,' confided one of the more adventurous dancers, plonking himself down in the sagging armchair beside mine. 'I am Mr Zhao. Sometimes I have become infatuated with some dreamy girls during a dance. Then I invite them for coffee, even dinner. In order to impose my impression on them, I eagerly show off my talent and humour.'

'You sound like rather a flirt, Mr Zhao,' I said. Mr Zhao had not heard of this word, and I explained it.

'Well, not really, you know. While in the face of unreturned love I get pessimistic and melancholy. Though I have suffered to varying degrees in the field of love, I have never given up seeking for my real love. I think that is not this flirt you mentioned. It seems a flirt does not seek for love, but only for entertainment.'

'What do you think love should be like?'

Mr Zhao stared off into the dancing crowd and thought for a few moments. 'Who can say? It is an image in my heart that I can never find in reality.'

'So you don't think you really will find love here, Mr Zhao?' I looked around the cramped dance floor, at the poorly dressed couples shuffling around this bar in a remote mountain valley.

'There is nowhere else to find it,' he replied, somewhat sadly, I thought. He looked about twenty-five, and many Chinese would have found him handsome, with his pale skin, wide eyes and mop of unruly black hair. 'Anyway, I like to come here. Music is a very indispensable companion in my daily life. I appreciate all sorts of music: pop songs, classical music, light music, dancing music and even American jazz, which most of my fellows find a terrible noise! It is not only the echo and rhythm of musical instruments, but also that of my mood and emotion. The lyrical music bestows me grace and profundity. Light music softens my daily vexations and exhaustions. With violent and exciting music, I cannot help moving, rocking and rolling.'

'What else do you like?' I asked, suddenly interested in this man. I squinted across at him through the cigarette smoke which writhed in blue tendrils in the air between us. Mr Zhao considered for a moment, head to one side.

'I like to be in a crowd of people. But sometimes I also like to meditate alone beside a window or before a lamp. I like to step into the white snow-plain and leave a string of footprints. And I like to drink Nescafé and tea bags.'

I grinned to myself. 'You speak very good English, Mr Zhao,' I responded. Mr Zhao, much to my surprise, did not refute this with deprecating modesty, as the Chinese normally did. He was silent for a few moments. He threw his cigarette butt onto the floor and ground it out under his heel.

'I love the colourful life so much, and the limited activities here are no good for my energy. I work in a hotel at the foot of the valley. I learned some English in middle school. I made up my mind to become a well-educated man, despite my poor family background and remote social environment. Now I have private English lessons and devote myself to study on my own. God helps me and answers me for all my efforts and hardships. I have learned much in English. It is a language that opens up many new horizons. I like to chat with foreigners who come to the hotel, and hope one day to become a tourist guide. To realise this I must recognise the mission of working and studying. I like to make all sorts of friends from whom I can get different pleasure and information about everything under the sun. I can get wholly absorbed in my books and papers without any absence of mind.'

'Is that why you come to this disco also? Not just to chat up the girls but to make friends?'

'Yes. And in a way, relaxing and enjoying myself here, dancing to my heart's content, can also lead to concentration and interest in my study tomorrow. This is why I can always get twice the result with half the effort! To my surprise, my way of study is always very beneficial and efficient. My favourite motto for life is "To work madly, to play madly". I play, and at the same time I work. I neglect neither cause in life. Without cause, I would become a worthless person, I would become a robot. Only the person who is concerned about cause and life, work and play, is a real man, a man with both soul and flesh. This is my theory of balance.'

It was my turn to be silent. Suddenly I had nothing to say. Mr Zhao got up and did another dance, waltzing distantly with an attractive girl in a blue woollen dress. Then he returned to the flabby embrace of the armchair.

'You look like a sad man, Mr Brian,' he said. 'I hope I have not said something wrong.'

'No. No . . . But I think I neither work very hard nor play very hard. I drift through life rather casually. A friend once told me I was a spectator in life; someone who sits back and watches, yet never participates. I am a dilettante—that is a good English word for you to remember.'

'Well, some people are dilettantes,' replied Mr Zhao, using the new word with ease. 'Some live like great heroes, some like dandies, some are political rascals, some pedantic bookworms. I live in my own way, and have my own theory of balance. I suppose the proper way of living is to answer to one's own wants. The whole world is a contradiction, so is every human being . . . Anyway, I think you cannot only be a spectator, or why would you have come all the way here, to China?'

I laughed. 'Ah, well, travel is the ultimate spectator sport, you know. The whole of China is the stage, and everywhere I look I am entertained but, because of my foreignness, not really involved. And there is a famous English writer who once said travel is a flight from the self, away from responsibility.'

'But you are not just travelling. You have told me you are living in Chengdu. Of course at first our China must have seemed very strange and entertaining, as you say. But after a while you got used to our habits, I think. Now you become more involved. Maybe you make close friends with some Chinese! Then you will know more about what it is like to be Chinese, to be of China, and perhaps you will become more involved than you wish!'

That was the last thing Mr Zhao said to me in his curious and remarkable English. He returned to his dancing, and he did not speak to me again. The floor was now jammed with waltzing couples. Less than ten years ago such decadence would have been anathema—in the early 1980s the Campaign Against Spiritual Pollution branded Western dancing, along with Western fashions, music, literature and hairstyles, as unproductive, individualistic and imperialist. Yet little more than a decade later, even in this remote spot in northern Sichuan, the Chinese now sipped Nescafé, listened to Hong Kong pop, 'New York, New York' and mixed tracks from *The Sound of Music* ('Edelweiss' was particularly popular in China), and shuffled formally around the dance floor. Old-fashioned as it seemed, it was a big step forward from the Cultural Revolution, when the politically correct 'Carrying Night-Soil Up Mount Yi' and 'Song of the Steel Worker' were the only permissible kinds of tunes.

Soon the waltzes faded away and more disco music appeared; today's Chinese, keen to be young and fashionable, immediately lined up in rows to perform follow-my-leader like a troupe of majorettes (one *two* to the left, and *back* to the right, and round in a circle, and *kick* the leg now . . .). This was obviously a familiar disco routine, for none of them faltered for a moment. Only the braver ones attempted to imitate the foreigners (all by now, including myself, exaggeratedly gyrating), wobbling uncertainly from leg to leg and looking sheepish to be caught out doing something original. Or was it original? Wasn't that girl imitating my every move?

'You're copying me!' I shouted across the din of the music. Her eyes opened in astonishment.

'Of course! I am learning the movements of the disco dance.'

'But you're not supposed to copy me. Just . . .' I did not know the Chinese for *ad lib*. I waved my arms in exasperation. She waved her arms too, in exactly the same way, giggling delightedly.

'Just do what you like!' I shouted again.

'Yes, yes, I like to do disco dancing!'

Our dancing earned us a great deal of attention and eventually a round of applause, but as we were leaving everyone went back to stamping up and down in long rows like soldiers on parade, one *two* to the left, and *up* with the arms, swing *round* to the right . . .

In traditional Chinese philosophy, an individual's value and identity could not be realised unless they devoted themselves to, or lost themselves in, society—that was the clear message of the Lei Feng Campaign. Such a thought had been taken up in a short story by the well-known writer Zhang Jie, called 'Love Must Not Be Forgotten', written in 1979, over which the author had been accused of undermining Chinese social morality. The story, referring to someone who has chosen to defy society and not marry, said:

> You will be called neurotic, accused of having guilty secrets or having made political mistakes. You may be regarded as an eccentric who looks down on ordinary people, not respecting age-old customs—a heretic.

I remembered a conversation I had had about this story, in which a Chinese had told me that a very individualistic person might be regarded with horror, as something incomplete, immature or simply immoral. The Chinese expressions 'To stick to one's way of doing things', 'A person in solitary splendour' and 'To cling obstinately to one's course' were derogatory, I had been told. I thought these were quite different from equivalent English expressions such as 'To stick to one's guns' or 'To stand out in a crowd', which if anything were complimentary. And yet, while this attitude seemed firmly entrenched and still manifested itself in disco dancing, I could not understand how a man like Mr Zhao, with his independent mind, reconciled his new spirit of personal autonomy with these old values. There was an enormous paradox, an immense strain on the foundations of society created by these young Chinese, but Mr Zhao was marching up and down, in happy accord with everyone else, waving his arms, one two to the left and back again.

As I was departing I looked around again for Mr Zhao. I felt I had something very important to say to him, something philosophical and meaningful, without being pompous. I wanted to say how much it meant to me, talking to him here in this place, how in a way I had come all the way to China for moments such as these. I could not think of anything that expressed my feelings. I went up to him and held out my hand.

'Goodbye, Mr Zhao,' I said.

When I was at the door I turned around. Mr Zhao was chatting with a friend, and had forgotten me already. I slipped out into the dark.

From my hotel room—more like a cell, with a hard wooden bed and bare, concrete floors—the noise of the disco could still be heard, or rather the dull thump, thump of the beat. It sounded like the prayer drums in the Tibetan temple, I thought as I drifted off into an uneasy sleep.

In the middle of the night I was awakened by a different kind of noise, a sinister rustling and scraping that made my flesh prickle in fear. It sounded as if someone were moving around the room. I strained my ears, hardly daring to breathe. There it was again, a scuttling sound, followed by a rustle. Then silence. I groped quietly through the dark, and flashed on my torch. Frozen into immobility for a moment by the sudden light, a large rat glared back at me from the top of my food bag, then scampered unhurriedly into the darkness. Cautiously I got out of bed, put my biscuits and chocolate into a plastic bag and suspended it from the bedpost that held up mosquito nets during summer.

Later the rat woke me again, and when I put on my torch it was sitting on the bedpost at the foot of my bed, whiskers twitching. My scalp crawled. I sat up until dawn with the light on, huddled in my blankets. I dozed fitfully, passing in and out of dreams where rats' feet pattered in the dry cellars of empty provincial towns, and crowds of Chinese stood staring at me, mouthing silent messages that I could not understand.

Breakfast in Jiuzhaigou was warm yak milk and fried cabbage with hard-boiled eggs. I did not want the fried cabbage, limp in a puddle of oil and soy sauce, and moodily cracked eggs, dropping splinters of shell across the table in changing patterns. I shook some powdered coffee from my supply into the yak milk, where it floated in slow-spreading particles, staining the liquid with rust. Beside me Hedvig stared into her own mixture as if thinking of drowning herself.

Up in the mountains there was a brushing of snow on the trees and it was very cold. Autumn had suddenly been edged away by crisp, uncompromising winter. The lakes were turquoise among the forests, their waters so clear that every pebble on the bottom was distinct. Chinese tourists took photos of each other and blew whistles among trees of brilliant orange, bronze and dull red, or dressed up in pseudo-Tibetan costumes, posing theatrically. They snapped branches of emperor-yellow leaves off the trees and threw rubbish under the bushes. I wandered off and tried a Tibetan drink, sold by a man in a makeshift tent—wheat powder, yak butter and sugar mixed with boiling water, a muddy brown liquid with an appalling smell like rancid milk. In contrast to its smell, its taste was almost acceptable to me.

There was an impressive waterfall in Jiuzhaigou, a wide horseshoe of sweeping water like a miniature Niagara. This was a tourist attraction too: more photos here. Chinese yodelled to each other among the rocks, trying to make themselves heard above the water, and heaved pieces of fallen pine branches into the river.

'This waterfall makes a beautiful sound,' said one of the *waiban* staff to me unexpectedly. I listened. It sounded like water running into a bath, a distant boom, boom of dull, incessant noise.

'Man-made music is artificial and disharmonious,' the man continued primly, enunciating every word with loud clarity, as if giving a lecture. 'Only nature, producing everything harmonious, is all harmony itself. If one goes back to nature, one will find that birds singing, harmonised with the winds whistling and roaring waterfall, echoed in the valleys, is so naturally melodious that these sounds consist of an excellent symphony. Unlike listening passively to a concert, one can enjoy this real harmony, happiness and fear. Confusedly mixed sounds such as pianos, violins, cellos, are not truly harmonious at all. It can be understood by nobody but the musicians themselves, and the concert audience just pretend to appreciate it.' He rubbed his cold hands together, then slapped the sides of his thighs, nodding sagely.

I thought the sound of waves upon a beach, with their constant ebb and flow, might be considered more harmonious and pleasing than a symphony. I did not think the dull roar of the waterfall was at all melodious, but I was too surprised to argue with his unusual comments and appreciation of nature. His

fellow Chinese had been treating this national park as they
treated the public parks in Chengdu or Canton. They stood in
the water downstream from the falls, wearing rented gum-
boots, having their photos taken in suitably studied poses, a
habit that had always bewildered and amused me. (On return
to Chengdu, Xiao Han showed me her photos of the trip,
which soon bored me—innumerable pictures of herself in
various stances, behind which splendid scenery could be only
dimly seen, like an artificial backdrop in a photographer's studio. She was equally unimpressed with mine, wanting to know
why I appeared in so few of them. The one she picked as the
best showed me draped coyly over a rock; it was my 'China
pose', deliberately tongue-in-cheek.) Later in the day the
Chinese rented rusty paddle-boats and surged about on one of
the lakes, shouting incoherently among the splendours of nature.

Near the boundary of Jiuzhaigou reserve (the name actually
meant Nine Village Valley), still within its borders, was a
Tibetan village called Shuzheng. It was a tight huddle of
wooden chalets with hay barns under the eaves, cabbage
patches, hideous black pigs with squashed Pekinese faces, and
racks of vivid orange corn.

'Beware of Tibetans on the road,' said Xiao Han anxiously
as we approached, with Chinese conviction that these minority people were semi-barbarian and quite likely to be dangerous. 'Beware of Tibetans,' she repeated like a soothsayer
warning of the Ides of March.

Women with long, braided hair and cloth boots with leg-
gings up their shins like bandages worked in the tiny fields,
forking hay into disciplined piles before transferring them to
racks. The Tibetan men wore *chuba*, heavy quilted cloaks of
woollen cloth, daggers stuck ominously through their sashes at
the front, symbols of virility. They looked romantic but not
dangerous. The village was very quiet, full of fluttering prayer
flags, their colours of astrological significance, giving the village and outlying farms an air of permanent festival.

Then I saw another rat. I was ambling slowly along a dirt
track between houses at the upper end of the village when it
suddenly ran out not far ahead of me, an ugly black creature
with a skinny tail. With a sudden flurry, an elderly Tibetan
woman who had been sitting on her doorstep leapt to her feet,
hitched up her skirts, and with amazing sprightliness ran up

the path after the beast. With an expression of absolute delight she caught up with it and stepped on its head. I stared, horrified and motionless in surprise, as the rat squirmed helplessly under her shoe. Finally she lifted her foot; the rat crawled disjointedly forwards, squeaking. Still hugely enjoying herself, the woman started stoning it with pebbles. I hurried past, turning only with ghoulish curiosity to see the woman finally dropping a large rock on top of the animal. This was survival; rats gnawed at her stored vegetables and poisoned the corn with their droppings. Two weeks later, in the *China Daily*, I read that rats were an increasing problem in this country—there were twice as many as there were people. Two and a half billion rats, I thought in horror.

And I wondered how I had seen so few.

On the day we set off again from Jiuzhaigou some of us were the worse for wear; the previous evening had been spent toasting each other's nations and singing songs in half a dozen different languages. The Japanese had known all the words to 'Jingle Bells' and the Beatles songs, and had roared them out in accented English, tossing back cups of *baijiu*, a fiery Chinese spirit. Now they sat slumped on the bus, nursing their heads. There had been a heavy frost, perhaps a light snow, during the night—a frozen white landscape of brittle trees as artificial as Christmas decorations. Soon we were down over the mountains and passing Tibetan farm land. Feeling queasy, some of us demanded that the bus stop for ten minutes for some fresh air.

'No,' said Xiao Han, flashing a hurried look of alarm out of the window. 'There are many Tibetans.'

But we felt rebellious and insisted, laughing in unconcern. Finally the bus drew to a cautious stop and we scampered out into the fields.

'Be careful,' said Xiao Han again weakly, patting at her hair nervously with her hand and looking genuinely troubled. 'There are Tibetans on the road.'

But we did not see any Tibetans, only yaks, important animals in traditional Tibetan life, munching their way across the hillsides. The yaks skittered with unpredictable nervousness across the narrow track in front of the bus, great shaggy black or piebald creatures with long, curving horns and vacant expressions. We were heading up into the high grasslands. In the words of a Chinese tourist office brochure, 'The road itself breaks through the belly of the mountain and the slopes of the hill and oh . . . down there is a ravine's mouth widely opens that it would raise a horrible feeling if you looked on it for some time . . .' At over three thousand metres above sea level we were suddenly onto high meadows of gentian and rock jasmine, cushion plants and lichen staining the windswept rocks under a blue sky that seemed very close, supported in the distance by barely visible snow caps. Against the skyline rose a huddle of white tents and a group of mounted Tibetans. We were apparently expected, for when we approached the bus was surrounded by a ragged jostle of knees and steaming horses' flanks as we were offered rides—for a price—on the Tibetans' ponies. These men were handsome, with hard high cheekbones, their proud, independent looks and stone-black eyes. Despite the extremely insistent sales pitch and the contrived atmosphere, it was exhilarating to be riding across the roof of the world, suspended between land and clouds in the pale, almost luminescent sky, with no sound but the high-pitched keening songs of the Tibetan men. I rode horses so seldom that it made me feel adventurous, like a character in an old Hollywood western, a time when I could feel like a hero, larger than life, carefree and bold.

The adventure ended in an ugly haggling over previously agreed prices that resulted in a good deal of bad feeling among the foreigners, ill-disguised jubilation among the horsemen, and unease among the Chinese. The Tibetans shouted and gesticulated, demanding fifty *yuan* a ride instead of the five *yuan* agreed upon, an extortionate amount that was half the monthly salary of many of the Chinese accompanying us. The *waiban*, intimidated, handed over more money from the tour funds; the foreigners grumbled and protested as they were herded back onto the bus. Xiao Han looked as if she were going to faint now that all her dark warnings had come true. She stared mesmerised through the window of the bus at the men on horseback with their wild, scruffy clothes and daggers, in the way an Edwardian spinster might have stared in fascinated horror at a naked man. I thought these Tibetans were greedy but harmless, making an empty show of fingering their daggers and throwing threatening looks, and their behaviour simply made me angry. But the hysteria of the Chinese seemed like guilty conscience; they had treated these proud people with disrespect and violence for decades. Xiao Han seemed prepared to pay them anything, to strip off her earrings and necklace and hand them over, if they would only go away.

'Tibetans,' she said, peering like a frightened hen through the window. 'Tibetans.'

She almost spat out the word, making it sound like a Chinese curse.

On the morning we set off from Songpan back to Chengdu, the *waiban* purchased a large quantity of cheap yak meat to bring back to our canteen. The large, red cuts of fresh meat were loaded unceremoniously onto the roof-rack of the bus and loosely covered with bits of cardboard, the whole process watched in appalled fascination by the assembled foreigners. We had not been long on the road when one of the great chunks of meat, such as one might throw to a lion, slid off the roof and fell into the dusty track behind us. There was some delay as it was bundled back onto the roof, and this time tied down with string.

The road home was fairly typical of those we had been travelling on throughout the week—an unsurfaced, narrow ribbon of potholes and bumps winding perilously around mountainsides. The only other mountains I had ever been through on a bus were in Switzerland. No Swiss postal coach, yellow as a trumpet fanfare and trimmed with red and black, would have ventured along such a road (had there even been one in Switzerland), but our own ramshackle coach survived the week miraculously. The dust was incredible, seeping through every gap and settling thickly on clothes and hair, at times almost asphyxiating us. Our engine overheated. The wheels stuck in a ditch and when we pushed them out the bus slid alarmingly across the road and nearly over the edge into the river. We were delayed by accidents barring the way, we were jolted and banged about and half-choked amid the magnificent scenery so jealously hidden in the wilderness.

The road back into the heart of Sichuan was indeed harder than the road to heaven.

a fleeting visitor

ten

Beside Sichuan University, adjoining the river, lay Wangjiang Park. It was the most beautiful park I visited in China. Because of its proximity to my flat I was a regular visitor, and I often passed through the ornate gateway with its massive, studded doors guarded by stone lions. (If I was with Wang Ming or other students wishing to avoid the two-*jiao* entrance fee, I climbed with them over the crumbling wall behind the bicycle sheds at the far end of the campus.) From the main entrance one walked through a tunnel of interlocking giant bamboo that filtered the sun into a dim, dappled gold light, and emerging from it one had a view of the park's renowned pavilion. Built in the Qing Dynasty, it was called the River-Viewing Pavilion, and its four storeys soared over the water, complete with layers of upturned eaves.

Near the pagoda and teahouse of Wangjiang Park stood a somnolent, snooty-looking and offensive-smelling camel with a red saddle, on which children could be photographed by a man normally occupying a makeshift photo booth bedecked with examples of his art. There were porcelain lions and pandas edging the park's paths, the gaping mouths of which were meant to encourage the correct disposal of litter. Further along the river there were bumper-cars and a children's playground, and a couple of goats harnessed to little carts in which one might take a short ride. But, for the most part, the sprawling park was the quintessential classical China of Wedgwood plates and mother-of-pearl inlay cabinets—elegant wooden pavilions and weeping willows draped gracefully over ponds afloat with waterlilies. There were humped stone bridges, a

160

teahouse with low, long-backed wooden chairs where men smoked pipes, and rustling clumps of bamboo. This casual juxtaposition of old and new, of bumper-cars and pavilions, seemed very Chinese.

Sometimes, arriving at the teahouse, I would meet one of my students, such as Xu Jing, attending a teachers' refresher course at the university for one year.

The spring day I saw him in Wangjiang Park, Xu Jing was full of indignation over his recent attempt to find a new teaching job at the University of Electronic Science and Engineering in Chengdu. No sooner had he entered the place than he had been irritated, he told me as we ordered two bowls of green tea.

'One of the secretaries received me with her two hands constantly knitting. She had a pair of beautiful eyes and an over-powdered face,' he recalled. 'After she looked through my resumé, she told me to wait a minute. She continued knitting for a quarter of an hour, then she went into the next room. Another ten minutes, and an old man came in, the director of the Foreign Languages Department.'

He paused, fumbling with the lid of his bowl of tea, slurping its contents inelegantly. He spat tea leaves onto the ground, where they lay as formlessly as swatted flies. The director had claimed the university needed a teacher, but had wanted him to do a month's teaching practice first, he explained between slurps.

'So I went there twice a week, although the extra hours were difficult for me as a student again, with a lot of homework. Still I stuck it for a month, and I was sure my teaching was appealing and my classes attractive, because I had put a great deal of work into them. On the last day I was called to the personnel office, where a long-faced fellow was waiting for me. He told me I had been a success in my teaching practice, but that they couldn't hire me because I had a family! They only wanted single teachers, for they couldn't afford to alter my wife's residence card to Chengdu. You know we have a joke in Chinese, based on two characters with different intonation but similar pronunciation—to transfer (*diao*) is harder than to commit suicide (*diao*)! My wife is working in Wanxian,' he added as an afterthought.

'So what happened?' I inquired.

'Well, I said to the man, "Why didn't you tell me this before?"

'"Why did you marry so young?" he shouted.

'"I'm thirty-three now, I've got a right to marry!"

'"So you lost your right to have a job here!"

'I don't know how I left the office and returned to my room. The only thing I remember now is that I didn't eat for two days!'

Xu Jing laughed. I knew that laugh; it was very Chinese, empty and hollow and despairing. I thought of his wife in Wanxian, far away on the Yangtze River, a town that has been called the Gateway to Eastern Sichuan, a name implying far more bustle and colour than that grey, indifferent city had possessed on the brief visit I had made to it. When Xu Jing left me I went on sitting at the low wooden table in the teahouse, a fleeting visitor in the harsh realities of China.

I had already been in Chengdu months before I realised that Wangjiang Park, on my own doorstep, was a popular place to practise *taiji*. Despite Mr Jing's continued expressions of despair I thought my own *taiji* had been improving, and Hedvig, full of unexpected ambitious energy, finally dragged me to the park at seven o'clock one spring morning. There, under the rustling bamboo, gathered rows of silent Chinese. Most were past retirement age, and they dressed in grey trousers and blue Mao tunics like the uniform of a religious sect. And it was like a religion here, under the dimness of the leaning bamboo fronds that touched to form a cathedral vault above our heads, filtering the sun into mellow circles like the splintered light of a stained-glass window. One could join any group here, and be absorbed into the congregation with friendly humour, as the instructor led the movements.

There was a hush as the Chinese moved in unison, broken only by the low counting of their teacher as he marked off the stages of each movement, one two, three four. It was the most spellbinding sight I saw in China, this synchronised harmony of silently sweeping arms and curved forms, supremely poetic in its repetition and lyric grace. One two, three four. I rippled my limbs, spreading my hands as if offering a libation, the movements flowing smoothly in timeless gestures. It was here that I suddenly experienced the energy of the earth, the being carried away into mythical realms of power and concentration that was supposed to result from shadow boxing, as I felt the strength flow up from the ground through my body and up through my outstretched hands, grasping at the glory of the sky through the simple beauty of the bamboo leaves.

If Mr Jing had seen me then he would have been pleased, for I shifted my weight gently from left to right, raising my toes and looking at my left hand. One two, three four. I moved in fluid movements with the assembled Chinese, passing with no thought of time from one slow motion to the next.

Slooowly, slooowly, Mr Jing, I thought happily. Slooowly, slooowly.

My favourite market street in Chengdu, which I still visited regularly, was the long, narrow road that led up from behind the modern Minshan Hotel in the centre of the city, northwards in the direction of the Chairman Mao statue, almost parallel to the People's South Road. This street was lined with traditional *siheyuan* residences, in which houses were centred on an inner courtyard, filled with flowers and washing. The houses in this part of the town were old, having been spared the fairly comprehensive rebuilding that had scarred most of Chengdu. They teetered grandly like declining dowager duchesses, leaning comfortably against each other, built of wood, each with an overhanging second storey. There were small teahouses in this street, where old men chatted in the sun, sucking placidly on small, gnarled pipes and discussing their songbirds which hung overhead in bamboo cages. The birds sang lustily, trilling and puffing up their breasts; mynah birds, throats streaked with yellow, croaked in disconsolate competition. Underneath one cage I often saw the same old man hunkering, his face cold and haunted, in a grey overcoat frayed at the edges and with a dirty yellow scarf knotted around his throat.

Shops along this road sold dusty potted palms and limp aspidistras, chunks of tortured rock for landscape gardens, bonsai trees, ceramic pots decorated with dragons, bags of birdseed and plastic watering-cans. Further up the street, plants gave way to pets, goldfish with bulbous eyes goggling at the mechanical plastic monstrosities (a boy peeing from a red boat, a treasure chest with a lid that opened to reveal plastic pearls and gold ingots) that had been intruded into their aquariums. Kittens as tiny and fragile as dandelion puffs mewed in their baskets. One stall sold rat poison, the efficacy of the product attested by the row of dead rodents neatly laid out on the ground. A flower seller, bicycle adorned with chrysanthemums and gladioli, spat mouthfuls of water over her wares to keep them fresh, binding them into bunches with lengths of damp straw.

The top end of the market street, although it sold only food, I still found fascinating. Fish glittered and gulped in shallow basins; frogs squirmed in nets, bundled up like brussels sprouts in a European supermarket; glutinous digestive tracts hung enticingly overhead. Trestle tables were piled high with gleaming scarlet tomatoes, watermelon cool and pink as blushing icebergs, mottled pears, lotus roots and domed wicker cages containing somnolent candy-pink piglets. Pigs' ears, trotters, snouts and tails (stuffed, straight and surprisingly long) sweated under naked light bulbs but nobody seemed to buy them, which I found slightly depressing, as there were so many to be bought. Eels contorted in their basins, as if aware of horrors to come, as they were picked out, pegged to a stave of wood and slit, squirming, neatly down the middle as the fishmonger wiped the spurting blood from her eyes. Sacks of herbs and spices, redolent with the smells of China, jostled for space with piles of root ginger gnarled as an old man's fingers, dried chillies, black pepper and crumbling blocks of yellowish salt. I spent long hours wandering through these markets. Window shopping, I might have called it, except that the pleasure lay in there being no windows.

Often in these crowded markets and alleyways, in the teahouses and restaurants, Chinese approached me for a chat in English. One day in December I was accosted by a young man who soon discovered I was a teacher. Waving a newspaper in my face—it was the *Sichuan Daily*, I noticed—he was soon deep in conversation as he told me about an article he had just read.

'It's an article about teachers, in fact. It says that in a remote county of Sichuan, many teachers live in dangerous homes.

When rainy days arrive, they must place some basins on the ground to hold water dripping through their roofs. When teachers fall ill, all they can do is lie in bed, for they haven't received their salaries for several months and cannot call the doctor. But the local leaders in charge of education lead an opulent life. They have three- or four-storey houses of their own and can take a taxi or car whenever they go out. Even the secretaries of the leaders lead a much better life than the teachers!

'After careful investigation, it was found that these leaders had accepted bribes and had even used funds set aside for education. This kind of phenomenon exists in many places in China. These leaders are the parasites of our country, and we must get rid of them! Indeed, this article says these people have now been punished.'

The young man threw the newspaper back into the basket on his bicycle. 'So many countries have put education in the first place. For example, after the Sino-Japanese War which broke out in 1894, Japan plundered billions of dollars worth of silver from China, and spent it all on education. Today Japan can be rated among the most developed countries. But things in China are quite different. During the Great Cultural Revolution teachers and other intellectuals suffered a lot. Plenty of professors and experts lost their jobs and their lives. Today, although things are much better, what a teacher earns every month cannot support him in the style enjoyed by a taxi driver, a merchant or even a worker. In other words, the standard of living of teachers cannot be compared. Because of this, many teachers have given up their jobs. What a sad fact! No wonder we lie far behind Japan and your Western countries.'

I laughed. 'Well, in my country taxi drivers also earn more than teachers, who are poorly paid. Many people complain, just like you, that not enough money is given to education.'

The young man looked shocked, as if he could not imagine such a thing; the West for him was an El Dorado of all that was wealthy and enviable. We fell to discussing the plight of teachers in Britain, but I could see such information did not fit comfortably into his idealised view of the West. Unconvinced, but satisfied with his English practice, the young man got on his bicycle and rode away. I watched him disappearing into the crowd.

In April casting directors came to the foreigners' compound at the university looking for suitably Western-appearing actors for a television commercial being made by Emei Film Studios. As I happened to be sitting on the wall beside the pond gazing at the carp when they arrived, I was engaged on the spot. I suggested Hedvig should also participate, given that her long blonde hair and Nordic good looks were sufficiently un-Chinese to satisfy even the most choosy talent scout.

'Well, yes. Why not?' said Hedvig when I asked her. 'At least I can be a cinema dream-girl in China. Nice for my ego.'

Hedvig had a knack for saying things other people were too embarrassed even to think—resident foreigners liked China because it *was* good for their egos. As foreigners we were—irritating as it sometimes was—the centre of attention. The stares that we frequently attracted were also a compliment; we were exotic and unusual. We had special privileges and nice flats and good salaries by Chinese standards. Resident foreigners sometimes felt resentful and embarrassed by these privileges, but we could not also help being flattered. At home we were nobodies, one in a crowd, but here we felt important, noticeable, like film stars. That was one of the big dangers of living in China. It was a constant ego trip, and sometimes China felt like an unreal world, divorced from life back home and divorced from the life of the Chinese in China. It was sometimes a disturbing feeling, this limbo-like life. One particularly observant student had noticed it too, and had suggested that quite a few foreigners came to China only because they couldn't succeed or fit into their own society. It was an observation that filled me with despondency.

'Anyway,' Hedvig was adding, 'I was thinking of skipping all my boring plans on writing a thesis on farming enterprises. It's such a yawn. I was wondering instead if I should concentrate on the comparatively thrilling subject of Chinese commercials on TV, so even better if I participate in the making of them! This topic will at least give me a golden opportunity to spend my time in front of the TV pretending to do epoch-making research . . .'

We were to advertise Tianfu Cola, a sticky drink made in Sichuan Province. The filming would take only a couple of

hours and we would be paid fifty *yuan* each. I was so used to
Chinese prices now that I thought it quite a large sum of
money. But I was more attracted by simply being able to participate in a film, no matter how short. The director would sit
in a canvas chair, I imagined, and shout 'Cut!' or 'Shoot!', and
cameras on cranes would swivel around overhead. Every time
there was a break the make-up girl would trot on and dust my
face with powder. I imagined having to dress in a tuxedo with
a white silk scarf and a red carnation in my lapel, looking
dashing and suave in a café decorated, say, in 1930s style. I
would greet Hedvig, who would be wearing a gold-coloured
slinky dress with a fringe around the bottom, lots of long neck-
laces, and ostrich feathers in her hair. We might drink a toast,
saying something in the exotic English language to add to the
atmosphere, and then quench our thirst, making appreciative
noises and giving smiles as powerful as lighthouse signals, just
like film stars. I would be very gracious to the little boy with
the clapper-board.

We were bundled into a minibus and told that the filming
would take place at the airport, where we sat on a wall outside
the departure hall for forty minutes waiting for the camera
crew to arrive. When at last they appeared we were hustled,
along with a group of Chinese actors, onto the edge of the runway beside a stationary CAAC plane. Tianfu Cola had just
won a prize at an international food festival (fact) and the representatives of this company were now arriving back from the
Netherlands (fiction). They would come down the aeroplane
steps and the rest of us, pretending to be a reception committee and assorted journalists, would rush up in a surge of enthusiastic congratulations and commentary. It didn't matter what
we said, the director told us, as it would mostly be a babel of
voices anyway. Just enough for foreign sounds to be heard. He
gave me a camera. That was my prop. I was a journalist.

'How do they think such a small plane could possibly have
flown all the way from Holland?' I whispered crossly to Hedvig.

'Maybe they transferred onto a domestic flight at Beijing,'
she answered sarcastically. She was part of the reception committee. She had a bunch of flowers which she would thrust into
the hands of the arriving Tianfu Cola representative.

The shooting started. Three figures came down the steps of the aircraft, two men in Western business suits and a woman with a convoluted hairstyle and high heels. Hedvig, ten Chinese and I trotted timidly across the tarmac and clustered around the bottom of the steps. I put my camera to my eye and halfheartedly pretended to press the shutter button. High Heels held up some kind of certificate and a gold medal.

'No, no, no!' shouted the director. 'Not enough enthusiasm, and you should all be smiling! We'll have to do it again.'

We shuffled back. The three figures came down the steps again, and our reception committee thundered towards them like a herd of buffalo, grins pasted on our faces. When those in the front stopped abruptly at the bottom of the steps, two people at the back ran into them and one fell over.

We tried again, and again. Finally the director glumly said we should have a little rest. I was relieved. It was hard to be enthusiastic about repeatedly running ten metres across concrete and pretending to take photos as if one were doing a *Time* magazine assignment on the Chinese soft drinks industry.

Three figures came down the steps of the aircraft once more, two men in Western business suits and a harassed woman with straggling hair and high heels. We sprang towards them across the tarmac. With sudden inspiration I held my camera above my head and clicked it, the way I had seen photographers on television taking pictures of actors coming out of courthouses.

'I can't see the foreigner properly! Stop! She got lost in the crowd. Come forward. Next time let the foreigner stay in front,' interrupted the director.

'My God,' said Hedvig in what I privately thought of as her Viking accent. 'I feel some progressing insanity appearing in me.'

Finally we seemed to have got it right. Our enthusiasm was perfect but not overwhelming, Hedvig was well to the front looking foreign, High Heels was presented with the by now rather droopy chrysanthemums, and the certificate and gold medal had been displayed for all to see.

'Cut! OK, that's it, filming is over.'

The television crew gathered their belongings, coats, camera cases and cables. The Tianfu Cola representatives got into a black car and were driven away. We were taken to the minibus to be driven back to the university.

'I would like to offer you an extra reward for all your help and kind efforts,' said the man in charge of filming.

I smiled at him out of the window of the minibus, puffed up with pleasure at being praised for my cinematographic efforts. Someone was bound to see me on television and offer me a real role in one of the great Chinese films produced in Shanghai.

The director presented me with two cans of Tianfu Cola.

I was eating lunch in a tiny noodle shop open onto the street, surrounded by a cloud of steam and smoke. Large woks bubbled over glowing fires as the cooks rushed back and forwards with slabs of scarlet pork and wilting vegetables, devilish workers in their Dantean landscape. I was relishing spicy dumplings when a young man pedalled furiously up to the noodle shop and, applying his brakes sharply, leapt off his bicycle, waving a textbook and two notebooks in the air and peering at me frantically through thick glasses.

'Excuse me! I need some help with a translation. Yes! My teacher has given me a very difficult passage to translate from English into Chinese.'

'I'm not sure my Chinese is quite good enough for academic translations,' I returned modestly.

'But you can explain the English words,' the young man replied with undiminished enthusiasm.

'Can't you look them up in a dictionary?'

'I can learn nothing from a dictionary! You are a native speaker of English, I'm sure it is my chance to improve my knowledge.'

The young man feverishly thumbed through his notebook, as if afraid I would run away, sweeping the hair out of his eyes and keeping up a constant stream of conversation, as if trying to fit years of English practice into these few moments.

'My teacher is very good . . . but strict . . . passages for translation . . . When I was in middle school I was eager to learn English . . . I see you are enjoying some Chinese food . . .' he gabbled. At last he found the appropriate page.

'There!' he said triumphantly, putting his finger on the open page. I took the book off him, and read the passage:

> They will smash all the trammels that bind them and rush forward along the road to liberation. They will sweep all the imperialists, warlords, and corrupt officials, local tyrants and evil gentry, into their graves . . .

I recognised the quotation; it was rather famous, and came from a revolutionary manifesto written by Mao Zedong during the 1920s. Quite certainly this man knew it well in its Chinese version. Suddenly, overcome by high spirits, I found the whole situation vastly amusing. I looked down at the words and started to laugh. The young man pushed his glasses up his nose and looked at me anxiously. Still I laughed helplessly. Suddenly the young man looked angry. He snatched the book from my hands, and before I had time to say anything he had leapt on his bicycle and had ridden away into the crowd. I felt guilty then. But still I laughed.

Unfortunately propaganda and communist rhetoric were not always a joke, as Chengdu's Mao statue frequently reminded me. Around it, during the student demonstrations in May and June 1989, protest marches had assembled. The statue stood at the top end of the People's South Road, the city's main thoroughfare, and was the largest remaining in the country, for many had been dismantled during the 1980s. Like all Mao statues, this one had an arm raised like the signal of a traffic policeman, which seemed appropriate, standing as he did on a main junction that was always a swirl of bicycles and impatient cars.

'At the Mao statue during the first major demonstration,' Wang Ming had once explained to me as we sat in the same spot, 'there were several rows of police with linked arms to prevent us approaching. We stopped just in front of them, many thousand students from several universities. Then we just surged forwards again. I was near the front, and could see the policemen with helpless looks on their faces. The police retreated to one corner of the steps but we shoved them all off. I think everything was recorded. We could see police with video cameras and binoculars up there'—he twisted around and pointed up at the roofs of the monstrously ugly buildings beside the Exhibition Hall—'looking down at us. But after that we occupied the steps around the statue permanently'.

'In fact, in the evenings, when we were sitting on the steps— you know at this time students were now staying there all day and all night—it was a little like a carnival! Many people were walking about, those drinks sellers had come with their carts, selling soda and sweets. Even students from the Music College were singing! How exciting it was, I think we students were all so happy and free at that moment.'

I stared down Chengdu's main street, watching the cars, buses and bicycles flowing around the ornamental flower beds and the empty fountain, trying to imagine those moments of seeming freedom before, in conjunction with the clampdown in Beijing, the Chengdu military police had moved in, killing and injuring all in their way to clear the area, their guns and bayonets flashing in the early morning sun.

On television politicians now flashed their teeth, though almost surreptitiously, like crooked bridge players giving secret signals. When in Chengdu during term I nearly always watched the evening news, preceded by its scenes of Tiananmen Square and pristine naval forces on the decks of warships to the strains of the national anthem. Ten minutes of international news came at the end in scenes of war, crime and pestilence, a shocking contrast to the soaring agricultural yields and quiet serenity of China. The first fifteen minutes were always devoted to ceremonies in the Great Hall of the People. Premier Li Peng, cheeks bulging like a chipmunk's, greeted visiting dignitaries and welcomed new foreign ambassadors from behind the fronds of potted palms. He sat overstuffed in an overstuffed armchair, conversing with visiting foreign ministers in other overstuffed armchairs, each twisted uncomfortably sideways across a table scattered with tea bowls. Interpreters hovered in the background like nurses over unpredictable mental patients, and teeth and cameras glinted. This was China, apparently—a daily coming and going and bowing and greeting, presided over by Li Peng, as in the past vassal princes had offered homage to the emperor. Sometimes Li Peng ventured outside and planted trees, congratulating workers on their vastly improved steel outputs. He wore a blue trenchcoat and walked around with his hands in its pockets like a French detective, but—misleadingly—he looked far more affable.

Television was a tool for unabashed propaganda, although it also showed a wide selection of Western television programs from re-runs of *Dallas* to BBC wildlife documentaries, as well as some high-quality Chinese dramas. But it was still difficult to switch on the television and avoid seeing Deng Xiaoping or Li Peng popping up like genies out of a bottle, congratulating the army on its various heroic actions and helpfulness. I had once wondered how anyone could be taken in by such crude methods, but in fact it was perfectly simple—one could accept anything if one heard it repeated often enough. Both these leaders looked very benign, and after a while I found that I had heard the same stories so often that I almost believed them myself.

Such propaganda represented the fundamental principles the government wished to inculcate into China's youth, principles repeated in the hours of regular Political Study classes taken each week by my students—classes that had doubled in number since the crackdown in 1989. Most of the students bore the discipline and Political Study classes with resigned gloom and, like Ping and Pong, took along their knitting or devised ways of missing these lectures. I admired their spirit, the small remaining spark of defiance—a defiance in which laughter maybe had its place after all. One student tied his head in a massive bandage, like a wounded soldier returning from the Crimean Wars, and opted out of socialist re-education for a week.

Time passed. I continued to teach in the classroom, and outside it there was still the city to ride through on my bicycle, further afield into new suburbs and hidden alleyways. There were *taiji* lessons and Chinese lessons on a rather haphazard basis, there was my regular ping-pong practice, and most of all there were those irregular and unexpected events, like the Tianfu Cola filming or Cui Jian's concert, that lent excitement and adventure to ordinary living.

And still time passed. In the winter months rumours had flown about suggesting that Cui Jian had been arrested, or that he had fled China and was now in Taiwan, but now that spring was here another of his albums appeared in the shops, putting paid to such speculation. Soon it was too warm for heavy blankets and the winter coldness had been left far behind, and then it was so humid I found it difficult to sleep. I did not travel very far afield any more, happy to avoid the hassles of journeying through Sichuan for weekends now that the initial excitement had worn off; China was not a country that made travelling on limited time easy or enjoyable. I stayed mostly in Chengdu, spending large amounts of time with my Chinese friends.

A Campaign to Establish a Sanitary City was launched, and the Women in the Red Armbands also donned yellow hats and even greater authority as guardians against litter dropping. In the city five new department stores had opened their doors, and there were more Western goods available than ever before. Timotei shampoo and Nivea Creme, among others, had made an overnight appearance in shops throughout the city, and in the Bamboo Bar one could now buy real ice-cream, hitherto unknown in Chengdu though common elsewhere. Like the figure in the Cui Jian song, I realised the world of China was changing fast, even here in a provincial backwater. I read books about China written by Western journalists during the 1970s, full of an atmosphere of suspicion and unease and disapproval of friendships between Chinese and foreigners. Sometimes I thought they were writing about another country, and I wondered if the China I knew would have changed so much, or maybe more, in twenty years.

It was to be my last term of teaching; I had decided to leave China at the end of the summer. I had come here for a year and stayed two and a half, far longer than any other foreign teacher at Sichuan University and longer than many of the students. Only Hedvig was still here and planning to stay yet another term; she was to marry a Chinese, and the bureaucratic arrangements would probably take her months. I knew I would miss her, but I was secretly pleased that I would still have a strong link with Chengdu, a reporter to tell me all the latest gossip and happenings.

It seemed a very long time since I had spent my first morning in this country, sitting in an empty flat feeling scared and somewhat intimidated. I knew a lot of Chinese now, and some of them were close friends; Wang Ming was possibly the closest friend I had ever had anywhere. As I packed my bags and gave away most of the belongings accumulated over more than two years, I knew I was still leaving Chengdu with much more than I came with. It seemed a long, long time since I had imagined the Chinese as cunning and amusing in turn, all alike and united in their homogeneity into a bland and impenetrable nation. Now I looked forward to seeing the east of the country, and then Beijing, that distant and almost mythical capital which loomed so vast in the imagination and lives of all Chinese.

'Since I first met you in the class, you gave me a very deep impression,' one of my friends wrote in a card with true Chinese sentimentality shortly before I left. 'We students felt very warm for you, even though it was cold in the classroom. And I'll never forget the day, a cool spring noon, when you came into our dormitory. We could not help stopping the tears from coming to our eyes. We felt that your sudden appearance in our bedroom not only expressed a deep feeling of love to China, but also a great love to the people of the world. In a way, it showed that the differences between Chinese and foreigners should not exist. You are the first person of a foreign country who comes to the dormitory of we students.'

That was what I had really come for—not for temples and museums and politics and philosophy, but to find out about the people. Those words were the best goodbye he could have given me. And before the student signed off in a flourish of Chinese characters, he wrote in engaging English, 'I wish you happy for ever.'

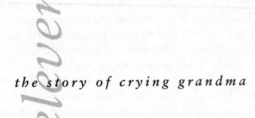

the story of crying grandma

In Shanghai one must swim through the oncoming crowds on the pavement, as slowly and laboriously as one first does the breaststroke. People are everywhere. There are hordes of people in the streets, tangles of people in the shops, people shoehorned into restaurants, vacuum-packed into buses and stacked mercilessly into vast apartment blocks as battery chickens are stacked in cramped cages. Babies yell, bicycle bells ring furiously, shop counters pullulate with customers, horns blare out of the chaotic traffic, and the Shanghainese shout and converse and roar and fight for breathing space and give living reality to the socialist concept of the masses. 'The people and the people alone are the creative force of world history,' Mao Zedong once said, and in Shanghai I found that this was close to the truth; the extras on this world stage crowded so thickly that they had become the focus of the play. Every day Nanjing Lu, the most famous shopping street in China and eight kilometres from end to end, was as crowded as Oxford Street on a Saturday afternoon before Christmas.

Shanghai has a population of over eleven million. It is the most populous city in a China of populous cities, and this single inescapable fact is impressed upon visitors more so than in any other place in the country. It buffets them on all sides as soon as they arrive at the train station, a gigantic echoing vault of immense size where trains disgorge thousands and a stream of people surges towards the exits like an inexhaustible human tidal wave, hauling suitcases, shoulderbags, sacks tied with twine, and crying children. I arrived here with Wang Ming, who had just graduated from Sichuan University. I trailed closely behind him, almost clutching his sleeve like a small child, overwhelmed. It was a scene from some epic film, but this Red Sea of people never parted. I was swirled about in its undertow, and could only hope to find momentary respite in some quiet eddy in a vain attempt to avoid getting sucked under.

As I left the train station in Shanghai a massive billboard displayed a happy family holding up a single healthy girl: *Birth Control is a Basic National Policy of China* it screamed in red and yellow. This 'One Couple, One Child' policy had been introduced at the end of the 1970s and had reduced the population growth rate substantially, but the law was often still flouted, especially in rural areas where peasants wanted to have children to work on the land and to ensure descendants. China's aim of limiting the number of people to 1.2 billion by the year 2000 was now admitted to be unrealistic. It was estimated that China's population would be 1.3 billion by 2000 and more than 1.5 billion by 2050.

These figures were large and impressive, but before coming to China I had little idea of what they really meant. In Shanghai one had to learn quickly or fail to survive. It meant undisciplined queues at the train station to buy tickets, and if one wanted a sleeper sometimes a three-day attempt before one was successful. It meant that the electricity, as in Chengdu and other Chinese cities, was turned off in different urban districts at different times of the day, because there simply was not enough to go around; even when on it emanated dimly from low-watt bulbs which saved energy for the more important industrial sector. It meant a sagging infrastructure designed for a fraction of the city's present population, that gave rise to immense problems in pollution, sewage disposal, housing and transport. And it meant, in a city crazy about football, that most people watched it on television and hardly ever played it—a football field was a luxury, wasteful of space. So was keeping livestock, and dairy products in China were hard to come by, milk rationed only to babies and young children. In the country as a whole the government struggled to feed four times the population of the United States on only forty percent of America's cultivable land area; put another way, a quarter of the earth's population on less than a tenth of its agricultural land. The fact that the Chinese now had enough to eat was a great success story. But population was still the single biggest problem facing the Chinese, and nowhere was this more evident than in Shanghai.

Taking a bus in Shanghai, as I soon discovered, was like completing a combat course. It was Darwin's survival of the fittest. The ones with the sharpest elbows, strongest shoves and ability to contort themselves eel-like into the most restricted spaces got on; all others were left, literally, by the wayside. Jammed inside as I travelled about the city, I hardly had space to expand my lungs, but had I fainted I could not have fallen over. The greatest challenge was not to get swept into the middle of the bus by passengers boarding at subsequent stops, for then I was doomed to the impossible task of making my way towards the door when it was time to get off. The heat was stifling. The passengers yelled and conversed and passed others' money to the conductor wedged in her box by the window. They pressed unabashedly against each other, knee against thigh, shoulder against shoulder, back against back, pushing firmly but not usually roughly. Shanghai was crowded and overpopulated, but the Shanghainese seemed to take this fact in good spirit, as a demonstration of life and vitality. I was always a little claustrophobic on these bus journeys, my tall foreign devil's head crushed against the roof and giving me a bird's eye view of a black-haired jostle of heads, and always a little anxious of being able to contort my way off. But always, as I finally erupted from the exit like a cork shot from a pressurised bottle, I had a great feeling of triumph and achievement, of having participated in the swirling humanity that is Shanghai.

Wang Ming's cousin had loaned us his flat in Shanghai, a small studio on the eleventh floor of an apartment block that offered spectacular views over the city towards the tower of the Hilton Hotel. It was the most comfortable and well-equipped flat I had seen in China, and a quiet eyrie to which I retired thankfully at the end of each day. We spent many evenings there admiring the view of sparkling lights over Shanghai and eating watermelon bought from the street below, discussing our futures. Wang Ming, having just graduated, was worried about his job assignment. The Foreign Languages Department at Sichuan University had told him he was to be assigned back to his native Jiangsu Province (which surrounded Shanghai) but he did not yet know exactly where he would be working or what he would be doing. Shortly, at the beginning of August, Wang Ming would have to present himself at the assignment office in Nanjing, his hometown. He talked often of his worries and his life.

In the evening we would walk over to Wang Ming's uncle and aunt's flat, along streets lined with old mansions and plane trees that still had the atmosphere of continental Europe; this area had in fact been part of the French Concession at the beginning of the century. Wang Ming's aunt would give us dinner every evening, lavish affairs of fried eels, crab, delicious fresh fish, chicken in soy sauce, marinated cabbage, and various other dishes of fried vegetables produced in honour of the foreign guest. With such luxury and attention, after several weeks of travelling around Jiangsu Province before coming here, it was even easier to enjoy Shanghai.

My friend's uncle had once been in the army and had then gone into business. He was short but well built, growing to fat somewhat around the waist and stooped over at the shoulders, an effect enhanced by the faded, baggy cardigan he often wore, hands thrust deep into its pockets. He kept three tortoises in the sink in his bathroom, which he said he was fattening up before eating.

Uncle Wang was a fussy man, straightening ornaments and fiddling repeatedly with the bamboo-chink curtains which blocked out the harsh sun, a mannerism which annoyed me immensely. On the first night we had gone to his house he had ordered us to take our shoes off before even greeting us, and thereafter he followed us around wherever we walked, sweeping behind us with a broom as if we left a trail of dirt in our wake. He was now retired, a knowledgeable man who had worked and made contacts all over China. He kept a pile of business cards—thousands of them, stacked in a cardboard box—and he would sit shuffling through them as if telling his own fortune, reminiscing about people and incidents they brought back to his memory. He had a melodious voice, one that made me think of Shakespearean actors, and I liked listening to him.

'Huh. Li Bing,' he would say, flicking a card up into his palm like a conjuror. 'I remember him, I met him in Qingdao when I lived there, the head of a college library. His slowness and forgetfulness were without compare!' He would look around to see if we were listening, and we would smile encouragingly.

'You could always see him prowling from room to room looking for his keys, his spectacles or something else. One day he locked the door as he went out for lunch. Upon returning he found some students pounding violently on the door. He had mistakenly locked them in, but alas he had forgotten where he had put the key. After a long search he discovered it was actually in his pocket!'

'That doesn't happen in real life!' Wang Ming protested.

'But it does!' said Uncle Wang, delighted rather than put out by his nephew's disbelief. 'I will tell you something worse about Mr Li.' He waggled his finger at us. 'People still tell the tale that in 1969, after he had been in northern Shanxi for over a year, he came back to Qingdao, his hometown. As soon as he got off the train, he saw a woman coming towards him.

'"Comrade, could you tell me where Mr Li's house is?" he asked, having forgotten his own address.

'The woman became very angry. She boxed his ears, crying, "Don't you remember me?" He thought very hard, and then his face brightened.

'"So it's you! My wife and mother of my children! No wonder you looked familiar!"'

Uncle Wang chuckled contemplatively to himself, shaking his head from side to side. After such an anecdote he would pluck another card from the pile in front of him.

'Mm. Teacher Qian. An insignificant man, timid as a rabbit . . . I sat beside him once at a banquet in Tianjin, I think it must have been in '78 or '79, anyway I can't remember much about *him*, he had nothing to say for himself . . .'

'The Chinese don't seem to talk much over meals,' I ventured, coming to Teacher Qian's defence. This was true; most

Chinese wolfed down their food as quickly as possible and hardly uttered a word, and as soon as the meal was finished they would leave the table.

Uncle Wang looked at me with a puzzled air, as if I had suggested something of enormous complexity.

'In Europe people might take two hours or more over their meal, especially in a restaurant,' I added, feeling the need to explain.

Uncle Wang said nothing. I realised he wasn't really listening. He dismissively shoved Teacher Qian's card back into the box.

He looked at me sharply. 'Do you have a business card?'

'No. I'm sorry.'

Uncle Wang gave a grunt. He put the lid on his box, and heaving himself to his feet pushed it into the back of the cupboard. The session was over for another night.

On my last evening I gave Uncle Wang a handmade card, on which I had laboriously written my name and address in small, regular black characters like a typewriter. He took it from me unsmilingly, and slipped it into his pile. I wondered what stories he would tell about me.

Shanghai—the name means 'on the sea'—is one of the world's great cities. I had always wanted to visit it, and now I was here. To me, it is one of those names, like Istanbul, Hong Kong or Rio de Janeiro, that conjure up visions of the exotic and adventurous. It was the only city I could think of that had given a word to the English language, which otherwise contains so few Chinese words. Shanghai was a special place, which had been called the Paris but also the Babylon of the East; it was exciting and violent and very much alive.

The Shanghai I imagined was in fact mostly a Shanghai of past history. The International Settlements set up here had been like displaced fragments of France or Britain (Edward VII Avenue, Quai de France, Oxford Street). Mansions stood graciously along French-looking streets lined with plane trees, and were modelled on Bavarian castles and Swiss chalets and English country homes. Many could still be seen, crumbling into suburban disrepair. There had once been more cars here than anywhere else in Asia, and more foreign capital, and the biggest port and the tallest buildings. The Bund, along the river, still lined with 1930s neoclassical buildings that included the former headquarters of the Hongkong and Shanghai Bank, was once the Wall Street of China, where foreigners lost and made millions behind New York facades.

But the Shanghai of the 1920s and 1930s was also an open sewer of opium addicts and peddlers, beggars, petty criminals and pickpockets. Much of the criminal activity was controlled by gangs who ran gambling syndicates and prostitution rings and controlled the flow of opium. In factories and sweatshops owned by foreigners child slaves and adults put in fourteen or fifteen hours a day to earn enough for a bowl of rice. Not surprisingly, Shanghai had also once been a city ripe with discontent. The First National Congress of the Chinese Communist Party met here, and armed uprisings by workers during the 1920s were brutally suppressed. The right of workers to assemble or strike was forbidden by the controlling Nationalist forces, with the help and support of the Westerners of the International Settlement. When the communists marched into the city in May 1949 they received an overwhelming welcome.

The American journalist Edgar Snow, in his famous book *Red Star Over China*, called pre-Liberation Shanghai a city of glitter and glamour, pompous wealth and naked starvation. The glitter had gone, and I found modern Shanghai unlike the Shanghai of my imagination. The communists had thrown out the foreigners and had rehabilitated the prostitutes and opium addicts, whom they estimated to comprise one-fifth of the city's population in 1949, and had made gambling and drug-dealing illegal. Rickshaw-pulling was also abolished, as degrading to human dignity. The government had pushed forward massive housing projects and closed the amusement and gambling dens that had thrived in Shanghai, replacing them with staid recreation centres for the proletariat. It had eliminated cholera, plague, smallpox and the nutritional and venereal diseases that had been rampant in the city, and in the rest of China.

If the pompous wealth and naked starvation had gone, something nevertheless remained of Shanghai's glamour. There was nothing of the brashness of Canton about this city, despite it being much newer. There was a refined beauty about it that grew not so much out of its buildings as out of its people. Shanghai, unlike all those other Chinese cities suspended in a purgatorial present, had a past and a future; one could feel the dynamism and the momentum as it hurtled through the twentieth century, factories belching and citizens buying. It retained what I imagined must have been the early optimism of great European cities during the Industrial Revolution, a Victorian aura of derring-do that supposed anything to be possible. It was the most cosmopolitan and energetic of Chinese cities, providing one-sixth of China's exports and nearly a quarter of its industrial output.

Since the mid 1980s, when 'Getting Rich is Glorious' was the slogan of the day, prosperity has been encouraged by the Beijing government. Shanghai, built on commercial foundations, wasted no time in taking the lesson to heart. The *China Daily* claimed that Shanghai's factories daily produced close to half a million bottles of beer, four and a half million items of clothing, thirty-seven thousand watches, thirteen thousand colour televisions and just over nineteen thousand bicycles. Colour televisions, tape recorders, washing machines, sewing machines and other durable consumer products were now the mainstay of the city's light industry, an indication of how far China had come in consumer-oriented business. The best bicycles came from Shanghai, as did the best refrigerators and washing machines, the best watches, and even the best chocolate. It had the most famous film studios and theatre companies in China. I soon discovered that it had by far the best ice-cream and the best Foreign Languages Bookstore. Shanghai had everything.

Nanjing Road, the city's famous shopping street, was permanently crowded. Factory workers in Shanghai, in fact, had different days off during the week, depending on the industrial sector in which they worked, in order to avoid overcrowding in the streets and shops. Innumerable huge department stores—one of them the largest in China—and smaller boutiques lined Nanjing Road, their escalators and stairs a cascade of shoppers. There were banks and camera shops, hairdressers (Shanghai had the most fashionable hairdressers, too), a Hong Kong fast-food restaurant, a Kentucky Fried Chicken.

Blue-and-white buses pressed slowly through the crush of bicycling humanity in the streets like exotic tropical fish through a swirl of insect larvae.

There were few special tourist spots in Shanghai; the real tourism lay in watching the people, for the people were Shanghai. Young women in tight miniskirts and sequinned blouses, scruffy Uighur minority men from the far north-west of China eager to do black market deals, frantic traffic police in shiny peaked caps, street vendors, harassed shop assistants, suited businessmen, mothers with screaming children, affluent youths in designer clothes . . . TV sets, sneakers, jackets, stereo equipment, traditional scroll paintings, art books, suitcases, sewing machines, perfumes and cosmetics, skateboards. Wang Ming was an avid shopper, and we spent days tramping Nanjing Road and pushing our way into every shop. While he looked at sports equipment I watched the people, the tumbling mass of humanity that enlivened the city.

I left Shanghai with reluctance; I had been happy here, although I did not usually enjoy big cities. Now I was staring at a totally changed scenery as the train passed westwards through Jiangsu Province, following the course of the Yangtze River inland. There had been flooding in China that summer, and the fields on either side of the raised track were covered in water, from which emerged soggy trees and the roofs of inundated houses, a sorry and depressing sight. We passed Suzhou, a Chinese city renowned for the beauty of its women and its ancient gardens which I had long wanted to see, but I had read in the newspapers that the gardens had been destroyed by flooding and we reluctantly passed through without stopping. I saw only the train station, where Wang Ming leaned out of the window and bought two ice-creams from a woman in a white coat with the air of a dentist's assistant.

Six hours westwards of Shanghai the train arrived in Nanjing. With a population of over three million, Nanjing is one of the major ports along the Yangtze, and also the capital of Jiangsu Province. It had been built as a stronghold for the storage and distribution of grain, in which this fertile region had always been so abundant; when its walls were completed they were over thirty kilometres in circumference—the longest city walls in the world. Nanjing played a central role in the overthrow of the Qing Dynasty that ushered in the republican era—delegates met in the city in 1911 to elect Sun Yatsen as president and to formulate a new constitution. His mausoleum lies in the hills outside the city, a splendid monument with a blue-tiled roof among green cedars and a centre of pilgrimage for many Chinese, both from the mainland and Taiwan. In 1928 Nanjing became the capital of the Nationalist forces under Chiang Kaishek until the Japanese took over in 1938, slaughtering more than a hundred thousand residents—three times that many, according to the Chinese—and completely destroying the city.

Nanjing, along with Chongqing and Wuhan (also ports on the Yangtze River), is one of the so-called Three Furnaces of China, renowned for its stifling summer heat. Away from the sea breezes of Shanghai it was indeed unbearably hot, and perspiration ran down my back in never-ending rivulets. Nanjing was an attractive city, but Wang Ming and I spent a large amount of time in our hotel room, taking advantage of the air-conditioning that was the only respite from the humidity and soaring temperatures. The famous Jinling Hotel, designed by a Japanese architect and boasting China's first revolving restaurant, perched at the top of its thirty-seven storeys, was another convenient retreat. Its swimming pool was a cool oasis in the middle of the city, where outside in the streets the heat shimmered in hazy waves from the pavements and the roofs of cars.

Neither Wang Ming nor I felt like doing much in Nanjing. I was preoccupied with thoughts of leaving China, Wang Ming was worried about his job. One early afternoon it was finally time to walk down to his assignment office. It was a bare, makeshift concrete room, along one side of which ran a trestle table at which worked three people. Wang Ming went inside and spoke to one of them. I did not know how he felt, but I rubbed the sides of my hands repeatedly down my trousers, nervous for him. I had a terrible hollow feeling in the pit of my stomach, aghast at the thought of one's life being determined over a ledger in a government office. Wang Ming sat down in a chair and spoke to the man opposite him. The clerk ruffled with a bored expression through the big book in front of him, and then it was over. It had taken two minutes. Wang Ming came out of the room and looked at me.

'I have been assigned to a factory in Nanjing, one that makes components for televisions,' he said with deceptive casualness. He was trembling slightly, and his face was ashen. 'It's a Sino-Taiwanese joint enterprise company. I will start work at the end of August.'

'And what are you supposed to do there?'

'They are getting a supply of new machinery from abroad, and I have to translate the operational instructions from English into Chinese.'

'And after that?'

'I think just general secretarial work. The company doesn't normally do any business with English-speaking countries.'

Later that evening Wang Ming said to me, 'You know, nowadays many people in China are making a fortune. They regard money as the most important thing. Intellectuals are always looked down upon in society. But I always admired skilful and well-educated people. When I was in high school, I was eager to become a college student. You know that my parents were poor peasants and struggled hard to give me an education. In order to pass the entrance exam, I often stayed up late to study. Sometimes, I also felt tired of study, but I had to get rid of this feeling. I must learn and learn. Finally my dream was realised and I went to Sichuan University. I'm sure to get a better job in the future if I have really good qualifications, I thought at that time. And I wanted to learn English because I thought it would be useful for me and my country.'

He lay on the bed, silent for a moment, tracing patterns with his finger on the sheet.

'I think I will hardly use my English in this job, soon I will forget it. The government doesn't seem to care so much about well-educated people, because they only waste them in assigning such work. Now I am bound to this factory and dominated by the manager. I don't want my fate to be conquered by other people.'

Wang Ming turned to look at me. 'My greatest dream is to travel around the world. Like you. Especially my dream is to see the Olympic Games. I wish it were not just a dream.

How can I be happy now in China, in this job? Surely I never regret meeting you, for you are one of my best friends. But since I have met you I think I cannot be happy any more.'

There was a great silence which hung heavy in the air like the sum of all human disappointment and regret. Suddenly I felt very tired and very sad, and I did not know why I had come to China.

We took an inter-city train, travelling for an hour back eastwards from Nanjing, then changed to a local train which crawled through the countryside for another forty minutes. We arrived at a small country town in the blazing heat of midday. From here it was over an hour's walk to Wang Ming's village, a hot and dusty tramp along an irrigation canal that wound through the fields. It was a long way from cosmopolitan Shanghai and busy Nanjing. This was another China, one that I had previously had little chance to experience first-hand.

Wang Ming's parents had died some years ago, and we stayed in the home of his elder sister, who seemed unsurprised to see her brother and a foreigner appearing unexpectedly in her doorway. The peasants of southern Jiangsu were relatively prosperous, and she had a large house, although it contained little furniture. She did not have a bathroom, running water or a refrigerator, but Wang Ming's sister did have electric fans and a large television as evidence of new prosperity.

'I didn't see a television until I went on a visit to Shanghai at the age of seventeen,' Wang Ming had commented in Chengdu, I remembered. 'It was at the same time that I saw my first foreigner! When I was growing up there was no electricity in my village, and water came from the duck pond in the centre of the village, or from the stream. Now there are quite a few wells, and the water is much fresher.'

Wang Ming's sister worked the land with the help of her younger son; her husband and her elder son were seasonal workers on construction sites in Shanghai, sending money back to their village every month. Wang Ming showed me his parents' old house, now derelict, in comparison to that of his sister—a tiny cottage of two rooms.

'In fact my parents were the poorest family in the village at that time. I grew up in that house, I slept in that room on the left with my brother.' He stared at the shabby building as if doubting his own story. 'We washed in the stream, and took our drinking water from it. It's quite polluted by factories. I think that's why both my parents died of cancer, from the poisoned water. Many villagers died at that time . . .

'Whatever happens, my life is at least better than my parents'. They had nothing—no education, no electricity, no water, no proper roads, no money, a poor diet. I could never return permanently to this village and work in the fields as I did as a child. But still, look at the children in the village today—they can read and write, they have the possibility of going to university as I did, they have bicycles to travel to the town where they can buy fresh fruits to supplement their diet.'

He turned away and gazed over the stream out into the rice fields which vanished away into the heat of summer on the horizon. I did not know what mirage he gazed at, except that I knew he realised, as I did, that these were only words and he did not have what he really wanted, which was freedom to choose his own life. There were tears in his eyes.

Isabella Bird, the Victorian adventurer and writer, said that the worst aspects of travelling are lack of privacy, mosquitoes and bad smells. There were certainly mosquitoes in the village (though I thought the clouds of flies worse), and plenty of bad smells. But it was the lack of privacy that most disturbed me. I had been travelling for weeks with Wang Ming now, staying in hotels and with Chinese families—friends and relatives of Wang Ming—all over Jiangsu Province. For the last weeks I had barely had a single minute alone. Staying with Chinese was mentally exhausting, not only with the effort of constantly trying to understand a difficult eastern dialect and being the centre of attention, but quite simply because there was no privacy. Few Chinese had bathrooms, and I used the communal toilets and communal showers belonging to the work unit or block of flats. In the village I stood in the courtyard and used a bucket, hoisted up from the well, for washing. Meals were taken

together and evenings were gregarious times, in which neighbours were likely to come in for a chat or a game of mahjong.
I slept in cramped rooms with other people, and suffered for
the first time from claustrophobia.

Wang Ming said he could not remember ever sleeping in a
room on his own. Few Chinese did, and most could scarcely
conceive of spending time without being in the company of
other people; although I recognised that this did not necessarily
mean they did not want to. An acquaintance in Chengdu had
once said to me, 'I like sitting on the grass closing my eyes to
hear the sound of bicycle bells and the noise of people's feet. At
that time I feel so quiet and happy as I can know.' It seemed
like the closest condition to solitude to which she had ever
come, a solitude surrounded by passing people.

I enjoyed staying with Chinese families, and I liked travelling
with my Chinese friend, whom I felt closer to than any other
friend I had known. But I nevertheless became dispirited and
bad-tempered, and longed to be alone for an hour, a day. When
I walked through the fields the villagers watched me, waving in
a friendly fashion. I was the first foreigner to visit the village
since the Japanese had come here during the war, they told me,
and I wondered whether it was a compliment. I was a novelty.
The only respite was at night, when Wang Ming and I climbed
up onto the flat roof of the house to sleep in the cool breeze. I
could sit up there in the darkness, looking at the stars which
clustered thickly in the sky, and think myself the only person in
the world.

One night I crept up on the roof by myself, early, and sat in
the darkness. Down below hens pecked around in the earth,
jerking their heads like factory robots and emitting metallic
clucking noises. Wang Ming was sitting out in the cool courtyard around a low table with his sister and cousin and several
neighbours. Seven of them, talking quietly to each other. I had
never seen them looking so relaxed before, at ease with themselves and with their surroundings. I seemed to be closer to the
moon, which hung improbably large and orange over my left
shoulder, than to these villagers. Had I been sitting among
them they would have been different, these Chinese peasants—
more stiff, their conversation more stilted and self-conscious.
They would have watched me without seeming to watch me,
and asked Wang Ming innumerable questions about me, all of

which he was tired of answering. I saw in that moment that my very presence changed the way the Chinese behaved, like Einstein's rule, in which the very act of observing something changes its nature. I felt incredibly lonely. I had been in this country more than two years, and yet I sometimes thought I knew nothing about these people. I had given a lot of my time to the Chinese, and I had grown to admire and respect them and be very proud of having this opportunity to know them, but I was still the *waiguoren*, the foreigner or outsider.

I knew their attitude was not particularly Chinese, but only human. I knew that only too well, for I had lived in Switzerland for twenty years and knew the Swiss even less than the Chinese. But in China one's sense of foreignness was more pronounced, because one was also more immediately obvious; wherever I went I was branded with my blue eyes, my blond hair and big nose. These people fascinated me, and I wanted to shed my skin and emerge with black hair and Chinese features, and understand this race. And I could not. Without a common culture or upbringing nothing could be taken for granted, and every meeting was like a leap into the void. Such a feeling was particularly pronounced in the countryside, and it made me realise that my views of China were very urban ones. It was easy to forget, living and travelling in cities, that eighty percent of the Chinese were still peasants.

I knew it was time to leave China; looking down from a roof on a group of peasants had shown me that. I was becoming immune to the foreignness of my surroundings without having become any closer to its people, I felt, just as one might be indifferent to a younger sister, making no effort to know her better. I thought it was time to leave China, to contemplate it at a distance that would enable me to understand it more. I was too close to it now, too involved. Later, one day in the future, I knew I would come back here.

That night I told Wang Ming it was time to leave. He did not seem very surprised. He asked little and appeared uninterested, but in fact he was quietly observant. He would have to start work soon himself anyway, he said. But he would miss me. We sat on the roof, under the stars, and talked for a long time into the night.

Those stars, Thomas Carlyle wrote, that glisten with tears over the insignificant lot of men.

'Don't look so miserable. Everything has two sides, good and bad. Sometimes people feel they are unhappy because they only see the bad side and ignore the good.'

'I'm not ignoring the good side. There isn't one.'

We were standing in Nanjing Railway Station. I was going to Beijing, then home.

'There was once a grandmother whose name was Crying Grandma,' Wang Ming continued. 'When it rained she cried, and when it was sunny she also cried. Someone asked her the reason for this. She said, "I have two daughters, one married to a shoemaker, and the other to an umbrella seller. When it rains I am worried about my elder daughter, for there will be few customers to buy shoes. When it is sunny I worry about my younger daughter, for few people are likely to buy umbrellas. So I cry all day."

'Then the other person said to her, "Why don't you think oppositely? When it rains, there will be more people to buy umbrellas, and when it's sunny sales of shoes will increase sharply!" The grandmother suddenly understood this and never cried again.'

'Is that your own story?'

'No. It is a traditional tale . . . what do you call it—a fable? It shows that happiness is up to you, and depends on what side you look at the thing itself,' Wang Ming replied in rather confused English.

I smiled. To me it summed up the resilience and optimism of an entire nation. I liked this Chinese fable.

In the station we sat on the platform waiting for my train. More and more people began turning up until there were literally hundreds of peasants and workers, all with enormous bundles, waiting with us. As the train drew in there was a mad rush to the doors as people shoved to get on first, pushing their baggage and their children through the windows. The length of the platform was a seething mass of yelling people, climbing over each other, pushing, shoving and doing battle.

I said goodbye to Wang Ming, shaking his hand. I looked at him and thought what a good friend he was. I was amazed sometimes that we were friends at all—a Chinese from a poor peasant family, from a village lost in the Chinese countryside, thousands of kilometres in distance and attitude from the wealthy, middle-class Swiss city where I had spent most of my life. It was a marvellous thing.

I looked at Wang Ming, and thought, 'There's so much more to say to each other, so many more good times to spend together, and now it's too late.' This was my real goodbye to China; I knew Beijing would be no more than an epilogue, an afterword that bore no connection to the friendships and humanity and happiness that I was leaving behind me here and in Chengdu.

The train pulled out of the station with a protesting shriek of wheels on hot metal. Beijing lay ahead, eighteen hours up the track. My last Chinese friend was already disappearing behind me, and I wondered if I would ever see him again.

in tiananmen square

Beijing was Shanghai through the looking glass, its opposite and its complement, a different reflection of the same country. It was the administrative centre of China, as Shanghai was the industrial one. Having emerged from the initial chaos of its train station I found it quiet, controlled and dutiful, where its southern cousin had been boisterous and undisciplined. Where in Shanghai the buildings had seemed to me a merely trivial extrusion compared to the overwhelming tide of humanity, in Beijing the people were rendered insignificant by the capital's colossal architectural creations, which bludgeoned the citizens into submission by their sheer size and symbolism. Behind its mask of potted plants and refurbished apartment blocks I thought it was a grey, indifferent place. Canton was more brashly commercial, Chengdu more intimate in scale, Nanjing more purposefully energetic. Shanghai was more naturally cosmopolitan, with an attraction that derived from the vibrant spirit of its people. In contrast, Beijing had the same fusty cosmopolitanism as one of those decayed seaside towns on the French Riviera which clung to its reputation as the resort of ex-kings. It was the only capital in the world that I had visited, with the exception of Canberra and Berne, that felt parochial. There wasn't even an ex-king in Beijing, only political cadres and bored diplomats' wives and office workers and bureaucrats speeding past in limousines or crowded buses.

Beijing, tucked away in one corner of the nation, was nevertheless the nerve centre of China. From the distant borders of Afghanistan to the Gulf of Bohai, from Mongolia to the islands of the South China Sea, the Chinese ran on Beijing time and attempted to learn Beijing dialect, the accepted standard Mandarin Chinese that the government promoted as the national language. The name 'Beijing', like 'Whitehall' or 'Washington', had become synonymous with government. Neither Sun Yatsen, Mao Zedong, Deng Xiaoping, Yang Shangkun nor a host of other leaders past and present were from Beijing. It was the political and administrative centre of the land, and most of the urban population worked in offices and government departments. They were unimaginative and obedient cadres, shuffling papers and poring over the latest instructions from their leaders who lived in the very centre of the city but came from other, more energetic, parts of China.

There were settlements here as long as three thousand years ago, and in the early thirteenth century Genghis Khan built his capital just north of the present city, calling it Dadu. In the early fifteenth century the city was renamed Beijing, or Northern Capital; it was at this time that the Forbidden City was built. Beijing continued to flourish through the ages, and by the Qing Dynasty it had become one of the largest cities in the world. But Beijing seemed to have sloughed off its turbulent history like a snake its skin. The roads of the capital, its long sweeping avenues and endless boulevards, stretched out from the heart of the city at Tiananmen Square like the arteries and limbs of a dismembered corpse laid out on a pathologist's slab for inspection—intricate and impressive, but with a spirit that was dead. In many ways the town seemed new, without history, perhaps because of the grid pattern of its streets, its modern architectural uniformity that dispensed with the random clutter of towns that had evolved over the centuries and made the city a showpiece, not a living entity. Here the Chinese had hauled themselves out of the feudal ages but had not yet designed a credible future. There was an end-of-the-world feeling about Beijing, and indeed most Chinese cities, floating as they did between a time past and another not yet truly born. The buildings of Beijing were symbols of this feeling, as stolidly unimaginative and megalomaniac as the pyramids in Egypt. There was no future suggested in their architecture; they were everlastingly set in a stultifying present, a colossal affirmation of changelessness. Briefly Beijing pleased me, as I too lingered in transit between China and my return home, between a past of journeys recorded in thick notebooks and a future as yet uncertain and undecided. But after a while it depressed me unbearably, for it seemed to represent all that was negative about this country and so little of what was positive, of what I had come to admire and appreciate.

In Tiananmen Square there were no casual, cheeky pigeons, poised to swoop with an ink-purple flurry of wings around the strolling citizens. There were no cafés, no seats, no trees, no fountains. This was a place inhibiting life, not a true town square at all, simply a space, a void. It was the largest square in the world, surrounded on all sides by the ugliest buildings in the world: the Museum of Chinese History and the Chinese Revolution, the Mausoleum of Mao Zedong, the Great Hall of the People gigantic in Soviet symbolism—many of these buildings, in fact, had been erected in the 1950s with the help of Soviet experts. The first time I entered the square I gazed at these colossi over a hundred-acre sea of paving slabs, and felt as small and insignificant as if I were in a canoe on the Pacific Ocean. The granite obelisk of the Monument to the People's Heroes, all thirty-five metres of it, seemed as small as a needle, and the Hall of the People was massive, concealing the paucity of the power wielded within it.

Mao Zedong said that, of all things in the world, people are the most important. And yet Tiananmen Square, his creation, was intimidating; it was the triumph of state over individual. Tiananmen Square negated human feeling; humanity here was only some kind of footnote to these titanic structures. Ten thousand people would scarcely have been noticed in Tiananmen Square; a million would have begun to make it crowded. There were indeed a million, at the beginning of the Cultural Revolution, swept away by revolutionary enthusiasm, weeping at the sight of Mao Zedong. As a teenager I had watched old television documentaries in which huge crowds of Chinese youngsters with slanted eyes and black hair waved red flags and red books in the air, as hysterical as teenagers at a rock concert, looking as if they were having a wonderful time.

Perhaps then the place had felt alive and full of purpose. Now the stage was empty but for photo booths and boys flying kites, and the vastness desolate.

I went to Tiananmen Square again and again, awed by its immensity. In the early morning, as the sun rose, soldiers marched through at over a hundred paces a minute, running up a Chinese flag the size of a double sheet; at the top of the flag pole it fluttered as small as a handkerchief. I had always found communism an intellectually pleasing idea, but standing in Tiananmen Square I realised that in reality it was a tough philosophy lacking in sentiment. Although aimed at the rights and dignity of all individuals, it required a practical and collective task to be carried out with objectivity, obedience and stoic acceptance, and did not take into account the emotion and concern for feeling that was the well-spring of human existence. Tiananmen Square was its symbol and reality.

There had been a million people in this square more recently than the Cultural Revolution—a million students, workers and citizens of Beijing had stood here in this wasteland during June 1989 to assert their human dignity. It was not the first time Tiananmen had seen such demonstrations, for student movements have a long history in China. There is even a public holiday in May in celebration of a student demonstration. The May the Fourth Movement of 1919, protesting against the Treaty of Versailles' allocation of Germany's possessions in China to Japan, began a wave of nationalist and anti-imperialist feeling which had resulted in China's refusal to sign the treaty; the Communist Party of China had been founded the following year. Significantly, this had been a student-led protest, and the student movement had become increasingly important in subsequent years. These demonstrations generally denounced imperialism, called for Chinese unity, and protested against the unpopular policies of the Chinese government. Many of these past demonstrations had also received the support of the public, and particularly of writers, journalists and intellectuals. In more recent times, during the 1970s and 1980s, student protests had surfaced again and again.

The parallel with the demonstrations of 1989 was obvious, especially to students who were generally sensitive to, and proud of, their cultural and historical background. Just as in the 1970s mourning parades for the deceased premier Zhou Enlai had escalated into demonstrations, in 1989 the death of another top leader, Hu Yaobang, acted as a catalyst. Greatly respected by students, Hu Yaobang's death initiated large mourning parades which soon developed into more wide-ranging, peaceful demonstrations in which students demanded educational reforms, greater recognition for intellectuals, a better standard of living for themselves, and greater freedom of speech, particularly in the media. By early June 1989 there had been more than a million people demonstrating in or around Tiananmen Square. Outside Beijing—unfortunately largely unreported abroad—turmoil spread through the rest of China as sit-ins and hunger-strikes took place in Shanghai, Xian, Guangzhou, Nanjing, Hangzhou, Chengdu, Tianjin, Lanzhou and Wuhan, where strikers blocked the bridge across the Yangtze River, disrupting rail and road transport services.

And then, early in the morning of the fourth of June, the Avenue of Eternal Peace and the Square of the Gate of Heavenly Peace, with their cruelly ironic names, had become a battleground as China's leaders fought to maintain their positions. A television newscaster, I had been told in Chengdu, had appeared in black on the same day, and after that most of the news items had been shown without pictures or readers, a sign that media personnel were being unco-operative. This was the real China, not the bowing and greeting of foreign dignitaries that I saw every night on television, but these newsreaders in black clothes and with white faces who avoided looking into the cameras as they gave news of their government's crackdown. Chen Xitong, the mayor of Beijing, claimed that two hundred civilians had been killed; the Chinese Red Cross told journalists that twenty-six hundred had died and ten thousand had been injured. Amnesty International and protest leaders put the dead at about one thousand. No one would ever know the truth.

I sat in Tiananmen Square and thought of all this. Even had the place been pleasant, it would still have been marred, and I could only view it through the blood that had been spilled on its flagstones, through the haunting television pictures of sanctioned violence. The tank tread marks had been scrubbed away, the bullet holes filled. But the spirit of the Chinese I did not think was so easily erased, and one day I thought they would get what they wanted and deserved. I sat and watched the Chinese tourists pass to and fro, talking excitedly, the people pedalling past on Changan Avenue, the packed buses and the limousines, the silk flags fluttering from the tops of the government buildings, the foreign tour groups with their cameras, the little boys pulling on their mothers' arms, the country folk on their first and probably only trip to the capital, the Beijing residents (the ones who walked quickly across the square, without gazing around), the young men taking photos of their girlfriends. The soldiers with their guns.

I met a Canadian in Tiananmen Square; he wanted me to take a photo of him standing with his back to the Gate of Heavenly Peace. He alarmed and depressed me. He was one of those energetic travellers I frequently met, hurtling across the length and breadth of China, making quick judgments and glib observations that simultaneously distressed and impressed me. They were often, I thought, woefully inaccurate, but I admired the way they could stand back and observe their surroundings as they might have watched a play. I was too involved in this country now to make quick judgments, and the more I thought about things the more confused I became; I envied these travellers their certainty and decisiveness. I wondered whether the best way to feel the spirit of a country was to spend as short a time in it as possible.

The Canadian said China was the most interesting place he had visited. He had been in the country a month, and had apparently been to more places than I had. (In fact, when I looked at my journeys on a map after having spent more than two years here, they seemed miserable snail-like trails left in the corners of a huge field.) I asked him what had struck him most about China.

'The lack of privacy, I guess. It's amazing. The Chinese just don't seem to have much idea of privacy at all. I mean, not just because they all live in the same room. But I met Chinese who read my letters, looked through my things, without the least shred of embarrassment.'

I said nothing. I looked over at Zhongnanhai, across the road to the north-west of the square, the present-day Forbidden City. Behind its high walls the highest members of China's Communist Party lived and worked in enviable seclusion, emerging from their screened houses in black cars with curtains on the windows, just as in the old days the emperor, on the rare occasions he left the Forbidden City, had sat in a closed-in sedan chair, while other sedan chairs proceeded along different routes so one might never guess which one contained the ruler. The old and new forbidden palaces seemed to me like massive statements of Chinese privacy.

I shrugged to myself and said nothing. The Chinese thought that Westerners' desire for privacy was peculiar, but surely only because it was outside their experience; I remembered Mr Zhao in northern Sichuan and how he had said he liked meditating alone, or walking through isolated fields of snow. I thought the apparent lack of sentiment about privacy among Chinese was a condition of their environment, not a condition of mind—any Chinese who could afford privacy soon acquired it. But I did not know. I was tired of thinking of China—at least, of a China of theories and abstracts.

The Canadian started talking about the terracotta army at Xian and his troubles finding a hotel room in Qingdao, about the Chinese spitting and the communist collective spirit.

I thought of Xiao Li, the factory worker in Xiamen, of the young woman on the bus to Xishuangbanna—I couldn't remember her name now—with her desire to be different, of the novice monk in Dali, of my friends from Chengdu. I became animated for a moment, talking to this Canadian, saying what I felt about China, saying that Tiananmen Square was built for a collective meaning and had seen people die in it for their independent spirits, telling him about my friends. But he was not concerned—these were anecdotes to him, not people. After the Canadian had gone on his way I continued to sit in the middle of Tiananmen Square and think of them all, and suddenly I felt very sad. I did not know if my sadness was nostalgia or loneliness or pity or admiration. I felt like weeping.

The Mausoleum of Chairman Mao Zedong, who died in September 1976, was completed in 1977 and has since been open to the public. It was the first tourist attraction in China for which I paid nothing. Some years ago I would have needed a special letter of introduction to visit the mausoleum, but Mao's appeal was obviously dwindling, and now anyone could join the queue at the entrance door. A brochure I picked up in the mausoleum said that it was built in unique national style. To me it looked like an oversized public convenience, square as a Tupperware box, tiled and clinical. I approached it up a flight of steps in frozen cascades of white marble; the walls loomed grim in purple and yellow granite quarried from the four corners of China. In the centre of the steps ramps were carved with evergreens and sunflowers, symbolising that 'the socialist country created by the older generation of proletarian revolutionaries is rock-firm and everlasting'. We shuffled through the huge doors and entered the outer hall, where we came face to face with a seated marble effigy of the Chairman, in the same pose as that of Lincoln in Washington; I did not know if the similarity was coincidental or deliberate. 'This is the place for commemorative activities,' my leaflet indicated, but I did not know what a commemorative activity was. But there was a hushed expectancy hanging over the devotees and the merely curious. I felt an unreasonable desire to giggle, which I restrained with difficulty. It was the first time I had been in a crowd of silent Chinese, and it was unnerving.

Finally I reached the inner sanctum, the Hall of Last Respects, where Mao lay beneath a crystal coffin lid on a raised dais covered with the Chinese Communist Party flag. His face was barely human, waxy as an artificial fruit, glowing slightly orange in the bright spotlights. His tunic was blue and taut over his chest, reminding me of the overfilled bolsters used as pillows in French hotels. He could have been any one of the cadres in their own blue tunics, filing past his crystal sarcophagus; he looked rather inconsequential and out of place. One could not stop; the line was hustled forward by attendants with walkie-talkies. Behind the coffin stood a guard, stiffly to attention. Like all Chinese soldiers, he looked deceptively harmless with his smooth cheeks and his baggy green trousers, like a schoolboy dressed up for the day. My first reaction was disappointment—this huge building, for this little man. The Chinese were whispering and shuffling their feet, the attendants looked bored and harassed; it was all kitsch.

In Moscow, two weeks later, passing by the similarly embalmed corpse of Lenin, I was to feel a frisson of excitement. The crypt was dark, the stonework blood-red, and officers stood forbiddingly in the shadows. Lenin lay, elegant and dapper as a businessman, in a pin-stripe suit and tie, hands fastidiously arranged. No one dared whisper there—it was awesome and eerie. There was an intimacy about the cramped chamber and gloomy shadows. In contrast, Chairman Mao's mausoleum was ostentatious and vulgar. He was made insignificant by the echoing hall, the bright lights and the six-deep crowd of onlookers. Like Tiananmen Square, there was something impersonal about this place. Neither it nor the mausoleum of Lenin had any humanity. I thought of the tomb of Suleyman the Magnificent, the great sultan of the Ottoman Empire, which I had visited, tucked discreetly behind his mosque in Istanbul. It had been small and rather understated, a great unadorned stone sarcophagus in a tiled chamber. Only the ceiling had been stunning, painted deep blue and studded with diamonds to resemble stars. There had been something deeply human about the place—the plain finality of death, and yet the aspiration of the once-living to beauty and inspiration.

Mao Zedong will always remain a controversial figure. Lying in his mausoleum in Tiananmen Square, he was likely to forever remain enigmatic; there was no hint here of human understanding. Nevertheless, he was a great revolutionary, military strategist and political theorist (as well as a not insignificant poet) whose achievements—and mistakes—should not be underestimated. I thought he deserved something better than this gigantic, meaningless mausoleum. Perhaps more significantly than anything else, he had forged the unity of a whole people, giving them a national voice and a national pride and a place on the world stage. The Chinese were still very proud of their country, and rightly so. Saint-Simon suggested that no man could rule guiltlessly and, whatever his faults,

Mao Zedong stands across his nation's history like a colossus, irrevocably altering the destiny of a quarter of the world's population.

Directly opposite the entrance to the mausoleum, north across the square, a huge portrait of Mao gazed down benignly from the Gate of Heavenly Peace. I looked up at it. It redeemed the great man after a visit to his tomb; he gazed out with a slight smile on his face, comforting as a happy father looking down at his new-born progeny. In a similar way the exquisite Gate of Heavenly Peace redeemed the whole of Tiananmen Square; more intimate, more human, more historical than any other of the buildings, it glowed red like a beacon among the surrounding sea of grey buildings. Five white marble, humpbacked bridges led over a moat towards it, arching elegantly like waves breaking on the seashore. The gate was built in the fifteenth century and was used in imperial times for proclamations to the people, and on the first of October 1949 Mao Zedong declared the founding of the People's Republic of China from its balcony.

In former times only the emperor could pass under the massive central arch of the Gate of Heavenly Peace; now the Chinese wandered back and forwards, in towards the Forbidden City or out towards Tiananmen Square, taking photos of each other with this symbol of China—which appears on the national emblem, stamps, government seals, policemen's caps, banknotes and on television just before the news—looming in the background. Behind it, encircled by a moat and a wall three kilometres in circumference, sprawled the best-preserved and most famous cluster of buildings in China—the Forbidden City. With nine thousand rooms and eight hundred buildings, it was so large that the last emperor, Pu Yi, had pedalled around it on a bicycle, and today tourists can get lost in its wonders for an entire day or more. In imperial times up to seventy thousand eunuchs served the court, carrying their severed organs in cloth bags, so as to enter heaven complete in body. Nowadays, hundreds of tour guides cater to package groups, waving yellow flags and calling to their recalcitrant flock through plastic megaphones.

It was the first time since coming to China that I had seen such a concentration of foreigners. I thought how ugly they looked, coarse and ungainly in appearance after the slender Chinese. There is a character in *The Strain of Meeting*, a story by modern novelist and one-time Minister of Culture Wang Meng, who reflects: 'And when she saw those yellow-haired, blue-eyed big-nosed thin-lipped foreign devils with blue veins showing through white skin, she always felt a shudder of revulsion. She felt more at ease watching the monkeys and birds in the zoo in the west suburbs.' I too was now staring like the Chinese; these foreigners seemed outlandish, unacceptable. Their casual confidence seemed more self-conscious and contrived than the retiring public modesty of the Chinese, more vulgar. I knew going home would be more alarming than coming to China had been. My sense of normality had been dislocated to another plane, another framework, and somewhere back in Europe there would be the painful process of reinstating it in its original place.

I entered the Forbidden City by the Meridian Gate, where the emperor once reviewed his troops, controlled the destiny of prisoners of war with a nod of his head, and proclaimed a new calendar each year. It was like stepping into a giant and elaborate film set that had served its purpose and was now left desolate, its crew packed up and gone. My attitude towards the Forbidden City was, I knew, influenced by Bernardo Bertolucci's film *The Last Emperor*, which I had seen while at university and again in Chengdu, and which added to its air of unreality. Here was the courtyard where the royal family had played tennis and the revolutionaries had come to take the emperor away, under the watchful gaze of Peter O'Toole. Here was the great space where thousands of extras, dressed in saffron robes, had kowtowed to the deputy of heaven on earth. I stood in it now, a courtyard in which a hundred thousand people could be assembled for an imperial audience. Sparrows fluttered through it like wind-blown scraps of paper.

'They're all fakes, of course,' said a Japanese man to me in English with a great deal of satisfaction, standing beside me in one of the Forbidden City's halls. He rapped the glass partition sharply, making me jump. 'Plastic. Glass. Perhaps crystal,' he added, waving his hand expansively.

I stared at the Aladdin's cave of show-cases: emerald daggers, jade seals, Ming Dynasty porcelain as fragile and blue as a bird's egg, ornamental landscapes encrusted with pearls and precious gems, music boxes in the shapes of elephants and pavilions, cabinets in mother-of-pearl and ivory, solid gold clocks from France and Switzerland. (The Chinese had invented the first mechanical clocks as long ago as the Tang Dynasty but had then forgotten all about them; they were re-introduced from Europe when things European were all the fashion at court.) I rather resented the speaker telling me this; I had been caught in a spell from Xanadu and was lost in labyrinths of imagination. How did he know they were fakes? I asked with hostility. And why were they behind thick glass, with attendants lurking in every corner, if they were indeed made of plastic? The man sighed, pointing out that they naturally didn't want the tourists to *know* they were fakes.

'And if they are,' I cut in spitefully, 'It's because many of these treasures were looted by the Japanese during their occupation of China.' This was true; much of what had been left behind was then hauled off to Taiwan by the fleeing Nationalists.

The Japanese looked crestfallen. He pretended to look closely at the imperial seals, and then inched crab-like away. I was glad to see him go.

I strolled outside, where there were less ambiguous marvels: gigantic tortoises and sundials and incense burners in bronze that rang dully under my knuckles, huge guardian lions glittering in the sun, slabs of stone carved with dragons and a constellation of other animals from a Chinese bestiary. I slouched along, knocking on everything, testing the rough surfaces of pillars with my fingers, poking and prying and tapping like a suspicious bank teller testing a consignment of coins.

Construction of the Forbidden City, now referred to as the Imperial Palace Museum, was begun in 1406 under Emperor Yong Le and completed fourteen years later, from which date, though burned to the ground, restored and extended at various times, it has retained its original design. Most of the buildings one can see today, however, date from the eighteenth century and later. The Forbidden City served twenty-four emperors of the Ming and Qing Dynasties and was their power base, the principal imperial residence, and the administrative and political centre of the empire for five centuries. The last imperial ceremony held here was the marriage of Pu Yi, the by-then deposed emperor, in 1922. Its extent and sumptuous richness were, I felt, the real Cathay that lived in the imagination of the West, redolent with inspiring names: the Hall of Concentrated Beauty, the Hall of Preserving Harmony where robed Confucian students once sat their examinations for the imperial civil service, the Pavilion of Heavenly Purity, the Hall of Literary Glory, the Palace of Eternal Spring, the Hall of Mental Cultivation.

In the Six East Palaces had lived the empress and imperial concubines in a myriad of enclosed rooms. According to Marco Polo, the emperors of the thirteenth century had sent emissaries every year to the Tartar Province of Kungurat, where the women were renowned for their beauty. Several hundred women were inspected minutely, and those who received the most marks for their beauty and modesty of character were sent to the capital. Here, the girls were again subjected to a number of tests, and the thirty or forty maidens who passed were then sent among the wives of the emperor's noblemen, who observed them closely at night, making sure that their breaths did not smell, that they did not snore, and that they were virgins. Finally, the pick of the bunch were presented to the emperor in groups of six; they administered to his every need and whim for three days and three nights, after which he had them replaced by a new batch. The discarded girls returned in triumph to their hometowns, where they could make advantageous marriages; the most gifted might become the minor concubines of important noblemen.

If one could forget their claustrophobic purpose, the monstrous patriarchal egoism they represented, these now empty palaces still retained a faint air of mystery and intrigue, closed away from the world, where princesses, noblemen, concubines and eunuchs fought and lived and struggled over the reins of power. I sat in the sun, dozing. It was very quiet; few of the tour groups penetrated this far into the Forbidden City. A

Chinese man was sitting beside me in a blue Mao tunic, in his fifties, perhaps, with the tired face of a disillusioned journalist. He had deep gouges running down the sides of his mouth and he looked old, but his eyes were the eyes of a younger man.

After a while I expressed to him my surprise that this palace had escaped the wrecking of the Cultural Revolution, which had sacked so much of China's architectural heritage ('that comprehensive, long-drawn-out and grave blunder,' a government resolution on Chinese history had called it with almost British understatement).

'You worry about these buildings,' he replied, gazing about him at the weathered wood and tiled roofs. 'Yes, and I suppose you should. And yet, there were millions of human beings, too, broken in the wreckage of the Cultural Revolution.'

I did not reply. To say 'I know' seemed trite, and besides, I did not really know, not like this man who was old enough to have lived through it. To me, the Cultural Revolution was a story of accidental judgments and casual slaughters, and I did not understand it.

'I do remember it. I never knew my mother, but was brought up by my father. One cold morning a mob of hooligans, who called themselves rebels or Red Guards, stormed into our house, turning everything upside down and taking my father away, charging him with being a bourgeois academic authority. It was not until two months had passed that I was granted the chance to see him. After having a piece of steamed bread for breakfast, I went out. I remember that, I don't know why— having steamed bread for breakfast. Outside it was bitterly cold, the wind blowing hard from the north, cutting at my hands and face. But I hardly noticed; I hurried down to the administration building, which was serving as an improvised prison. At the gate, a young man with a red armband stopped me.

'"Who are you looking for?" he demanded, his eyes flashing with malice. I told him whom I had come to see. At my father's name he frowned a bit and then, peering suspiciously at me, said, "And you are . . .?" I told him I was his son.

'"Ah, but," he stole a glance at me and paused a little. Then with a mysterious air he said, "But I'm afraid he can't see you now, I mean, he can't see a damned thing now!"

'"What?"'

'"I tell you, comrade, your damned father's blind now. He'll never see anything again. He refused to confess his crimes. We gave him a bit of a scratch, and from now on the old bookworm needn't bother with his books."'

There was a silence. Two Chinese schoolgirls with yellow bows in their hair came noisily into the courtyard in which we were sitting. The man had spoken with a detached indifference, as if he were relating a story he had read in a book. He did not invite sympathy, but I guessed he was a man for whom history was a nightmare from which he was struggling to awaken. He waited until the schoolgirls had gone.

'Not long after that I was exiled to a distant farm to receive re-education. I was a teacher of classical Chinese, and physical labour would do good in transforming me from a bourgeois intellectual to a proletarian intellectual, I was told. One day, in the village to which I had been sent, I was washing my clothes at the well when my superior came by. He commented that I was always washing.

'"You see, my clothes are dirty, especially at the collar and sleeve," I answered. "I must wash my clothes carefully and keep myself clean."

'Soon after that I was sent for by the Party Secretary, an ominous sign of punishment to come. I was puzzled. Soon I was told of my fault. You see, one of our terms for leader is *lin xiu*, the former character meaning "collar" and the latter "sleeve", as you maybe know. This referred to the great leader, Mao Zedong, almost exclusively. I had committed the offence of saying my collar and sleeve were dirty and needed washing!

'It was a terrible time, you see, and yet absurd too. I do not talk about it much. I am a teacher of classical Chinese once more, and my father is still alive. He seldom leaves the house, but sits in his armchair listening to the radio. As for myself, I like to come here and sit in this beautiful place, and think of ancient times. They were not less cruel, I think; surely more. But they are far away.'

The Cultural Revolution had been a decade of violence and family disruption and mental horrors and incredible perversity. To me it seemed, like a Shakespearean tragedy, to go beyond the simplicities of human good and evil to a realm touching on the extremes of the human soul, that could not be judged. I could not comprehend it but nor, I suspected, did the Chinese. Yet I sympathised and felt a shared guilt; I thought such horrors human, not Chinese.

I walked out through the Forbidden City, into the emptiness of Tiananmen Square.

I did it all in Beijing: the Summer Palace with its three thousand buildings, the magnificent blue-tiled Temple of Heaven where the emperor used to pray for a good harvest and, outside the city in the surrounding hills, the Ming tombs of thirteen emperors and their empresses and the Great Wall. Never since coming to China had I indulged in such hectic sightseeing—I did not like guidebook tourism—but now I feverishly tramped around the city, guidebook in hand, glutting myself on historical trivia. I was lonely, perhaps, for the first time, isolated from all my friends, not wanting to think, finding solace in the printed, assured words of my Lonely Planet. I hardly spoke to anyone; I did not want to speak. I was living on borrowed time, waiting for my train to Europe, feeling the days before I was to leave China slip away. As I had suspected, Beijing was an epilogue, an afterword. This was a museum city, and I visited museums, a city of tourists passing through, a city in which human endeavour was embodied in cold buildings and guidebooks.

Secretly, though I hardly would admit it to myself, Beijing bored me. Even looking at a list of the sights of Beijing was enough to make one die of boredom, I thought: the Agricultural Exhibition Hall, Beijing Exhibition Centre, Military Museum, Beijing National Library, the China and National Art Galleries, Lu Xun Museum, Beijing Planetarium, the Museum of Natural History. There were in fact eleven museums, six exhibition centres, a score of libraries, nearly a hundred cultural centres and fifty-odd universities and colleges, according to tourist pamphlets. But life had been battered out of Beijing's universities, and students attended Political Studies classes and were watched by plainclothes police. In the diplomatic areas of the city soldiers guarded the embassies to protect the foreigners—really to dissuade any Chinese who might approach. True, markets and old houses could be found down side alleys, but they had to be sought out, and anything that had to be sought out was atypical. Everything in Beijing was classified in a library, behind a show-case or a fence, and all the temples, spiritually dead, had been carefully restored for the tourists. Somehow soulless, it was as if the life-blood had been sucked out of Beijing like the juice from an orange, leaving only an empty skin.

On my last night in Beijing I abandoned my solitude and went to the cinema with Shu Ling, an acquaintance from Chengdu, a university student now at home for her holidays. After seeing a rather mediocre Chinese love story we went to a restaurant and ate steamed dumplings. I asked Shu Ling what she thought of the film.

'Actually I didn't like it much. Even I don't like watching any film. It is both useless and deceiving, just like drama or television also.' She manipulated a dumpling with her chopsticks, lifting it from the metal dish and taking a bite out of it. I asked her what she meant.

'Life is complicated and mysterious, and film should reflect its complexity and enigmas. One has to solve a lot of worldly troubles every day, and one's endeavours never come to an end. No one can fully understand life, and many a problem has no rational answer. There is joy and ambition, hate and love, frustration and despair. However, in films everything becomes clear and easy to cope with! The most dangerous thing is that the audience are always taken in by its falsehood, which is often mistaken for the reflection of actual life. Therefore film, the twisted copy, is misleading. It suggests that we can triumph over all the happenings that are really beyond our control.'

'If that's what you think then it's not just films, is it? It's books as well, and paintings and music and all art,' I asked. I thought of all the notes I had written about China, of the book I wanted to write, and how Shu Ling would despise it as something that aimed at reflecting Chinese life but that was a falsehood, contrived, written by an outsider.

'Yes. All in all, art is destructive, misleading and deceiving,' said Shu Ling. 'Even think of this small detail: have you ever seen anyone spitting in a Chinese film? No! How false! Art is of no use, and life itself is all nothingness.'

Suddenly it occurred to me that Shu Ling was not only talking about films but about Beijing. Even in Beijing the Chinese had been trained not to spit, and few did. Shu Ling had unconsciously given me the perfect metaphor for this city. I remembered how I had thought the Forbidden City a film set, but now it was all Beijing that was the film set, not deserted, but with actors playing the wrong roles. Beijing too was a falsehood, suggesting rational answers and duping the audience by its orderly facade. It was a city built in the early communist innocence and revolutionary spirit that was lost in the blood-dimmed tide of the Cultural Revolution, of the Tiananmen crackdown. In it lived only ordinary people who survived hostile and uncertain circumstances that concluded not with contrived happy endings, where a sun rose in a red eastern sky, but with compromise and disillusionment. They were the real Chinese. Beijing was not typical of China, and that was why I disliked it; it was a twisted copy of what China's leaders wanted the nation to be. But the people on the set were not character actors; they were real humans with real emotions, who wanted to move beyond contrived endings.

As I crossed Tiananmen Square towards my hotel soldiers stood in the shadows, watchful in its great emptiness, and my footsteps rang hollowly on the flagstones.

epilogue: passenger on a train

The Trans-Mongolian train, gleaming dull-green in the early morning light, groaned and creaked, sending up wraith-like puffs of steam from the undersides of the carriages. It seemed incredibly long, winding far down the platform like a somnolent dragon. Doors banged, passengers climbed aboard with their baggage and off again to wander up and down, guards in grey-blue uniforms checked tickets. Each carriage was embossed with the seal of the Chinese Railways (inevitably showing the Gate of Heavenly Peace) and carried a metal plaque that said *Beijing–Ulan Bator–Moscow* in English, Chinese and Russian. The Cyrillic alphabet—and even the Chinese characters, which I still found fascinating—seemed impossibly exciting and romantic, an offer of adventure that was about to become reality. I touched one of the plaques surreptitiously, as if for good luck, running my fingertips slowly over its surface as if reading Braille. I was going on the world's greatest train journey, nearly eight thousand kilometres, skirting the Gobi Desert across the vastness of Mongolia, passing on into Siberia, travelling through the Ural Mountains and over the Volga River and all the way to Europe. I felt excited, an excitement shot through by a strange, melancholy regret. I was leaving China.

I hung out the window of my compartment, watching the people and the station clock. Finally, with a lurch, the train departed at 7:40 a.m., the uniformed guard scrambling onto the accelerating carriage and banging the door closed with a heavy metal clang. I would arrive in Moscow five days, ten hours and twenty-five minutes later, according to the timetable

I consulted as the train crawled out through the suburbs of Beijing; I had five days to metamorphose back into my original self, to replace my visions of China with my life's past normality. But at the moment it was just like being on a local train anywhere in the world; we went slowly through the city outskirts, past back yards hung with washing, seedy apartment blocks, industrial estates. A woman on her doorstep, scrubbing the stone, paused to look up at the train, pushing back straggling hair from her forehead. I strained my eyes back in her direction, wondering about her life as she faded away into the creamy blue freshness of early morning.

Soon we were passing the Great Wall at Badaling, winding like a crumbling snake's spine across the crest of the hills not far north of Beijing, marking the turbulent border of ancient China. The Great Wall swept across the country for sixty-seven hundred kilometres, in a long arc said to be the result of a dragon which fell asleep against it, pushing it out of alignment, unnoticed by workmen on their lunch break. Its construction was begun under the first Qin *Emperor* and unifier of China, Shi Huangdi, one of the most significant figures in Chinese history; in his tomb was assembled the famous terracotta army. His reign saw an end to political chaos and to feudalism; warlords were replaced with civil servants of nine different grades, all attaining their position through examination, irrespective of their background. The emperor asserted the authority of the state, unified the administration, built a road and canal system, extended his army and his frontiers, and created standards for laws, the written language and weights and measures. (He has often, for these reasons, been compared to Peter the Great of Russia.) But the Qin Emperor was also fiercely opposed to traditions, especially Confucian teachings, and ordered all books to be destroyed. During his cultural revolution music, poetry and history were condemned as worthless and dangerous subjects. Anyone quoting Confucian classics or keeping books was executed, and the emperor formed a secret police force to ensure his decrees were carried out. The Qin Emperor's administrative reforms were not the only way in which he seemed like a remarkably modern man.

The emperor's most famous and lasting achievement, however, was undoubtedly the Great Wall of China. Three hundred thousand men under General Meng Tian were ordered to join and lengthen the smaller walls already existing along the borders of various northern states into a single unit. When completed, the wall began some distance east of Beijing and ended far away at the foot of Qilian Mountains in present-day Gansu, the province north of Sichuan. During the Han Dynasty a further thousand kilometres was added along the Yellow River, and in the Ming Dynasty the last major renovation was completed, when earthen parts of the wall were faced with brick and stone in an exercise that took over a century.

The Great Wall was such a special construction in the minds of the Chinese that it even got a mention in the national anthem:

> Arise, ye who refuse to be slaves
> With our very flesh and blood
> Let us build our new Great Wall!
> The peoples of China are in the most critical time,
> Everybody must roar his defiance.
> Arise! Arise! Arise!
> Millions of hearts with one mind,
> Brave the enemy's gunfire,
> March on!
> Brave the enemy's gunfire,
> March on! March on! March on!

went the lines of this rousing martial song. I never quite knew what this new Great Wall of the anthem was meant to signify, except perhaps that China had been first united behind the original wall, and was unified once more under the communists after long years of civil war and foreign incursion. It was interesting to note that the communists, like the Qin Emperor, had centralised their administration, standardised everything that could possibly have a standard, reformed the written language, and (at least until recently) condemned Confucius. The comparison was one of the many echoes between past and present that tantalised every view of Chinese history.

At Badaling, a tourist spot not far north of Beijing which I had visited a few days previously, the average height of the wall was about seven metres and its width five metres. It was built of brick on a foundation of granite blocks each weighing more than a ton, and filled with stone, earth and—according to legend—the bodies of workmen killed during construction. We were passing Badaling now in the train, too early for the mass of tourists who flocked here during the day. The wall was pristine and empty, a spectacular rippling monument that surged over the mountains and out of view. We were out of classical China now, I thought. Before us lay the lands of the barbarian tribes the wall was designed to keep out.

In the early afternoon the Trans-Mongolian reached Datong, once the capital of the ancient Northern Wei Kingdom and now one of the most important coal production centres in the country. In Datong was the only factory in the world that still manufactured steam engines. Steam trains puffed and groaned across the landscape, movable parts turning as awkwardly as a child's clockwork toy, dinosaur relics of an earlier age brought to life in a corner of China.

The train, sending up clouds of dust, progressed across the dryness of Inner Mongolia, a scenery of coal heaps, houses made of mud brick with enclosed courtyards, and broad, lazy rivers in meandering loops which barely seemed to move, sluggish as brown treacle. The sky was vast and fresh, puffed with great whirls of creamy clouds above rolling, deeply eroded hills grazed by flocks of sheep and yellow with rapeseed flowers, and dry valley bottoms scalloped into waves and hillocks by the wind. Such sights were rare in the parts of China I had been in; I had not seen such immensity, such emptiness, for a long time, and I gazed out, awed and subdued, feeling exposed. By dinner time, outside the windows of the dining car the land had become totally flat, completely bare of trees, stretching away towards a finely ruled horizon. Only telegraph poles, strung across the view like oversized washing lines in a neighbour's back yard, interrupted the immensity with stubborn human defiance. Inner Mongolia was more than a million square kilometres in extent, with a sparse population. I felt tricked, once more, by China. After more than two years in the country I was only now, on my last day, experiencing what half of it was really like—this emptiness, this vastness that encompassed not only Inner Mongolia but the whole of western China. I looked out of the window and saw no people, only a sea of grass.

The Mongols of this hot and arid region were united by Genghis Khan in 1206 and went on to conquer most of their known world, from the steppes of Russia to the Burmese jungles, showing that the Great Wall, constructed to keep them out, had served little purpose. Kublai Khan of Xanadu fame, grandson of Genghis, establishing his capital at Beijing, subdued all China by 1279 and became—at least in the West— China's most famous emperor, thanks largely to the popular success in Europe of Marco Polo's *Travels*, which recounted the life and times of the great Mongol conqueror. But by the 1360s the Chinese had regained power and established the splendid Ming Dynasty, and by the end of that century the entire Mongol empire had fallen apart, lapsing into feuding tribes and petty states that were conquered in their turn by the Qing emperors. Governed by China until the downfall of the Qing Dynasty in 1911, Mongolia became an independent state for eleven brief years until the Chinese reasserted their authority. In 1924 the Russians took over much of the area, and made China recognise Outer Mongolia as an independent territory.

Now Inner Mongolia, still part of the People's Republic of China, had a population of just nineteen million, of whom only two million were Mongols. The economy was based on the breeding of cattle, sheep, horses and camels, and it was China's main source of hide, wool and dairy products. The land was also rich in mineral deposits, as yet underexploited. It was another of China's new border regions, like Yunnan Province, that seemed to hold enormous potential.

I sat gazing at the scenery and eating my last Chinese meal; at the border the Chinese dining car would be uncoupled and replaced by a Mongolian and then a Soviet one. Later, the Chinese would view the food most suspiciously, picking their way through lumps of beef and mashed potatoes, scooping the latter up with their knives. They would hold their cutlery clumsily, almost vertically, at awkward angles. One young man would finally give up and, bending down with his lips at the edge of the plate, suck the potato in, flicking it with his knife the way one does with chopsticks and a bowl of rice. Two years ago I might have found this disgusting but, already homesick for China, now I would only find it rather endearing. Seen from the Chinese point of view, Western food (especially on a train) must seem bland and unappetising, and Western eating methods clumsy and confusing. But that was later; now we bent over our bowls, flashing our chopsticks. To me it had become the most natural movement in the world, and eating with a knife and fork seemed ridiculous. I felt the train was dragging me back into a world with which I was no longer familiar.

Out of the dining car windows the landscape could almost have been European in everything but its daunting size. Hour after hour it was the same slightly rolling flatness, huge meadows and tiny villages dwarfed by the steppes, thousands of kilometres of grass and flower-studded fields under a huge sky. The atmosphere of Shanghai, where people dominated in their sheer numbers, had been pulled inside out. Here, habitation seemed merely incidental, a human postscript to the vast text of earth and sky: minute haystacks, peasants cutting the grass with scythes, cabbage and cauliflower patches that were mere flecks on this carpet of grass. I sat mesmerised, staring with small European incomprehension at these vast dimensions of time and space, glad of the enclosing reassurance of the railway carriage. I knew this was only a small corner of a flatness of silent trees and grasses that swept thousands of kilometres through Mongolia and Siberia as far as the Ural Mountains. It was easy to believe, in such a landscape, in an indifferent god, paring his fingernails, while below humans toiled and suffered and eked out their painful existence. This was a place to be passing through; I felt sure that if I stopped here the immensity would drive me mad.

By early evening we had arrived at the Chinese border town of Erenhot. The train entered a shed with high raftered ceilings and dim lighting, through which grimy-faced workers, with the wide, flat cheekbones that characterised the people of central Asia, wandered with lanterns held aloft. Here the wheels had to be changed to a narrower gauge suitable for Mongolian and Soviet railway tracks. The carriages were separated and hoisted on enormous mechanical jacks, while the passengers wandered about, spending their remaining Chinese money on tins of pineapples and peaches for the journey across Siberia. Poorly lit with yellow, sulphurous lights, the tracks and isolated carriages, patrolled by border guards, looked strangely familiar—

this was a scene experienced in countless war films, in which prisoners passed by in cattle trucks and soldiers' boots crunched on the gravel. There were no prisoners here, but I waited with a feeling of dread. In an hour now I would have left China.

In Dickens' *Hard Times* the passengers on a train look out at the cruel factories and regimented houses of Victorian Britain and see them illuminated at night, so that they look, as the passengers speed comfortably by, like fairy palaces. It seemed my whole stay in China had been infused with this misleading vision. I knew that my Western perceptions and opinions of China were foisted upon the country from the outside, and that it was still difficult for me to judge from the inside and see China as the Chinese saw it. I knew, despite everything, that I was a mere onlooker, and realised little of the realities of living in this country. At times I thought I had penetrated into the heart and soul of a nation, but now I knew I had only hesitantly scratched the surface, an archeologist who had removed a few layers to reveal gold leaf and taken it for solid ore.

Even that analogy was misleading, for China was not a dead civilisation. I could only feel humble and confused against the vastness and intricacy of this nation, and yet it was not a feeling of which I was ashamed. The further one travels, it says in the *Tao Te Ching*, the less one knows. It was indeed easy to know much about China at home in Europe; to live in China made one realise that one's understanding grew less the more one learned. No country deserved to be casually summed up and categorised, especially by a foreigner. Books on the People's Republic often invoked adjectives with the glibness of a conjuror producing doves from a top hat; China was bleak, violent, magnificent, exotic, turbulent, depressing, regimented and of course inscrutable. These writings boxed the Chinese into neat little classifications and generalisations, disposing of them with the easy assurance of a clever politician parrying a complicated question.

I knew this was insulting; the Chinese were human and complex. Indeed, the Chinese seemed sometimes to be as impenetrable and confusing as their proverbs ('A tiger that has wounded too many men is bound to fall into a mountain ravine'), in which meanings lingered enticingly but unattainably below the surface of Western understanding. That too was the eternal myth of the inscrutable Chinese. But I knew the Chinese were no more nor less inscrutable than other people. What I learned, if anything, was that they were simply human. Many of them broke through the stereotypes of Confucian and communist conformity that clouded Western attitudes to China, and they broke through the disillusionment and restraints of their limited lives to assert their essential human struggles and proclaim their individuality and aspirations. 'People say: You are a strange girl! Yes I am a strange girl,' a young Chinese said to me soon after my arrival in the country. 'I like to be different from others. I like strange clothes; I like jazz music; I like to play with the boys; I like to cut my hair very short. Another always said: How strange you look! You don't look like a young lady. I will say: I don't want to be a young lady. I want to be what I am.'

The young Chinese had left their revolution far behind, but in them was a sadness that their education had brought them up to be the wrong kinds of people, no longer adapted to the new society in which they found themselves. Everything was in a state of flux, of readjustment and realignment. I had found there were not yet any conclusions, any patterns. The kaleidoscope was still twisting. There were still plenty of possibilities in the future for Chinese to be what they wanted to be, but the Chinese of the present had been lost, confused and abandoned between a world that was dying and one yet to be born.

There are no conclusions, I thought as I sat among my tins of fruit on the dark platform waiting for the train, for conclusions distort human reality. The Chinese were not living between two worlds, any more than they and Westerners lived in two separate worlds. The world was one and nothing was simple; everywhere there were echoes of other societies and other histories, ebbing and flowing like the endless interchange between *yin* and *yang*. As I sat in the border stations at the limits of China I abandoned conclusions, for all that I had experienced negated such trite endings.

We all boarded the train again and moved off into the dark night of Mongolia. I had invested much emotion in this country—without false sentimentality, for I knew it to be a land of trouble and pain and harshness as well as one of glory and *afterword*

I am happy to record that Wang Ming did not remain long in the Sino-Taiwanese work unit to which he was assigned on his graduation from Sichuan University. With considerable courage he gave up his 'iron rice-bowl' and, without references or any official support or recognition, left Nanjing and went south. He is currently living and working in Shenzhen between Canton and Hong Kong, and is at least somewhat more in charge of his own destiny. We have not met since the day we said goodbye in Nanjing train station, although we keep in touch.

After many months of bureaucratic procrastination, Hedvig was finally able to marry her Chinese boyfriend and returned with him to Sweden. She was soon drawn back to China, however, obtaining a job with a Swedish trade company in Canton and then in Hong Kong. She has seen Wang Ming several times, and in many other ways keeps me up to date with life in the People's Republic.

Sichuan University is no more. After my departure it merged with the neighbouring Chengdu University of Science and Technology and is now known as Sichuan United University. The foreign residents have been transferred from the Panda Park, with its pond, to a new building.

China's economy continues to progress rapidly and some superficial social changes have been implemented—more flexibility rather than more freedoms. However, politically China has seen further entrenchment of the hard-liners who have been in power since the Tiananmen crackdown in 1989, and the Chinese continue to live under a harsh and unforgiving totalitarian regime. Their dictatorship is treated almost benignly by Western governments, who turn an extraordinarily blind eye to activities they would have roundly condemned in the former Soviet Union and elsewhere. I would therefore like to record that the great admiration and affection I hold for the Chinese, and my gratitude for the exceptional two-and-a-half years I spent in their country, do not extend to the Chinese government in Beijing.

I have not been back to China since the events related in this book—afraid, perhaps, of the changes in it and in myself. But it is always in the back of my mind and has become a part of my life and my passions.

One day I will return.

chronology of chinese history

Date	Dynasty or Period
c. 5000 BC	First Neolithic settlements
2200–1700 BC	Xia Dynasty
1700–1100 BC	Shang Dynasty
1100–221 BC	Zhou Dynasty (including Spring and Autumn Period and Warring States Period)
221–206 BC	Qin Dynasty
206 BC–220 AD	Han Dynasty (including Eastern and Western Han Dynasties)
220–280	Three Kingdoms Period (States of Wei, Shu and Wu)
265–420	East and West Jin Dynasties
304–439	Sixteen States
386–589	Southern and Northern Dynasties
581–618	Sui Dynasty
618–907	Tang Dynasty (including Five Dynasties and Ten Kingdoms Period)
960–1279	Song Dynasty (including Northern and Southern Song Dynasties)
947–1125	Liao (or Khitan) Dynasty
1038–1227	Western Xia Dynasty
1115–1234	Jin Dynasty
1279–1368	Yuan (or Mongol) Dynasty

1368–1644	Ming Dynasty
1644–1911	Qing (or Manchu) Dynasty
1912–1949	Republic of China
1949–present	People's Republic of China
1958–1959	Great Leap Forward
1966–1970	Cultural Revolution
1989	Tiananmen crackdown

acknowledgements

Translations

Tao Te Ching: Arthur Waley, *The Power and its Way*, George Allen & Unwin, London, 1934.

The poems of Li Bai and Du Fu: Yang Xianyi and Gladys Yang, *Poetry and Prose of the Tang and Song*, Panda Books, Beijing, 1984.

The Travels of Marco Polo: Ronald Latham, Penguin Books, Harmondsworth, 1958.

Love Must Not Be Forgotten by Zhang Jie: Gladys Yang, Panda Books, Beijing, 1987.

The Strain of Meeting by Wang Meng: Denis C. Mair, Foreign Languages Press, Beijing, 1989.